PRAISE FOR *In Her Wake*

"*In Her Wake* is as engaging as a well written novel, with truths and insights that are meaningful to every family."

"This inspiring book reaffirms the strength and resiliency of the human spirit."

"*In Her Wake* is a moving story of mother and daughter, and the intimate echoes of family complications across the generations; as Nancy learns more about the mother she never knew, she also tells the story of her own journey and the story of a troubled but fascinating family, and helps the reader understand the twists and turns that love and loss can take."

"*In Her Wake* speaks to all of us who have lost a loved one to suicide and offers new and healing insights to a survivor's journey. She helps us better navigate the maze that suicide leaves as its legacy and comforts us with the knowledge that we are not alone in our confusion and grief."

In Her Wake

In Her Wake

A Child Psychiatrist Explores the
Mystery of Her Mother's Suicide

NANCY RAPPAPORT

A MEMBER OF THE PERSEUS BOOKS GROUP

New York

Published by
Basic Books, A Member of the Perseus Books Group
387 Park Avenue South
New York, NY 10016

Books published by Basic Books are available at special discounts for bulk
purchases in the United States by corporations, institutions, and other
organizations. For more information, please contact the Special Markets
Department at the Perseus Books Group, 2300 Chestnut Street, Suite 200,
Philadelphia, PA 19103, or call (800) 810-4145, extension 5000, or e-mail
special.markets@perseusbooks.com.

A CIP catalog record for this book is available from the Library of Congress.
LCCN: 2009024475
ISBN: 978-0-465-01450-7
10 9 8 7 6 5 4 3 2 1

FOR MAMA AND MY FAMILY

ACKNOWLEDGMENTS

To Colin Flavin, who gives me endless comfort.

Many a late night as my family was sleeping, I wrote this story trying to understand my mother. For my children, I wanted them to know their grandmother. For me, I feel she comes alive across time. She missed out on being with my three children who taught me how to be a mother. My vital love for them helped me to grasp the enormity of what it must have felt like when my mother thought she had lost what was most precious to her during a protracted custody battle.

To Mama.

To Dad, I will be forever grateful for your love and encouragement. To Phyllis, who has always been supportive of my family and me.

To find out about my mother, I interviewed many people who kindly tolerated my insatiable curiosity and questions. Peggy Melgard, I am so grateful that you kept my mother's trunk of belongings and her novel for over forty years. To Elaine Werby, Charlotte and Mike Alexander, Ed English, Robert Lamere, Barbara Whitehill, Clotilde Larsen, Ted Raniszewski, Sydell and Ed Masterman, Judge Weinstein, Dr. Weinberg, Dorothy Newell, and Dick Sears, who helped provide details of this story. To Barbara Rappaport, who provided great attention to my manuscript and was generous with her time and sharp copyediting. To my brothers and sisters, who understood that I was out on a limb and gave me countless memories. To Andrew, you made me laugh when all I thought I had left were tears. I remember when you consoled me: "Hang in there, people get through it, otherwise libraries would be full of empty shelves." To Jim, who fact-checked my work with caring precision. To Martha, who gave me the written logs from the 1965 and 1966 family trips, and gave me courage. To my big sis Amy.

I write this also as a child psychiatrist who has come to appreciate over the years how fiercely loyal children are to their parents. When we are able to build a coherent narrative, this capacity for reflection provides a source of strength. Often we are asked to endure more heartbreak than seems fair. To my patients who inspire me with their humor, wisdom, and courage.

My friends made this possible. To Melanie Boulet, who always made me feel that I had something important to say. To Jean Rhodes, who had the proper dose of irreverence, and with her compassion helped me to mobilize when I felt bereft in the woods. She was my first morning reader. To Kelly Woyewodzic, who always encouraged my progress and kept me laughing. To Maggie Alegria, Bobbie D'Alessandro, Ann Parker, and Carola Suarez Orozco. To Ceci Lopez and Ele Cruz, buscando el burro andando en él. To Damaris Lopez.

To my running buddies, Penny and John Lynch, I would hire you as body-guards any day. To my power yoga groupies, recharging my battery has been key on a journey like this. To Dr. Wolfberg, who encouraged me to explore and who stayed by my side.

To Elaine Markson and Gary Johnson. Elaine is my guardian angel, shepherding this book. She is warm and wise. To Amanda Moon, an amazing editor who identified when I needed to sharpen my narrative. To Whitney Casser for her attention to detail. To copyeditor Christine Arden and Basic Books production editor Michelle Welsh-Horst. To graphic designers Nicole Caputo and Jennifer Carrow, as their cover design captures the essence of my book. To Sarah Train for her ability to organize and find necessary references. She reread and proofed the manuscript more than anybody else. To Alexa Geovanos, who typed my original "Dear Mama" letters and the court depositions when it was too hard for me. To Mari Badger for giving me confidence in my own voice. To Alison Harris, a gifted friend.

To my readers Perri Klass, Connie Biewald, Anne Green, Jill Harkaway, Andy Clark, Wendy Gordon, Paula Rauch, Deb Kulick, Sam Hynes, Misha Stojanovic, Rachel Nardin, Jim Gilligan, and Jean Frazier. To my Harvard Freshman Seminar Students (2006–2008).

To Dr. Jay Burke, the Cambridge Health Alliance, my professional home-base Teen Health Center, and the Cambridge public schools.

And to you as my reader, this is my offering.

A NOTE TO THE READER

In order to protect the identity of several people in this publication, I have made symbolically equivalent substitutes for aspects of people's life circumstances and characteristics.

In Her Wake

Chapter One

We shall not cease from exploration
And the end of all our exploring
Will be to arrive where we started
And know the place for the first time.

　　　　　　　—T. S. ELIOT, *"Little Gidding"*

The day my mother killed herself, she had just finished preparing her house on Marlborough Street for the anticipated return of her children after a fierce custody battle with my father. There were six of us and much to do. My sister Amy, who was 9 at the time, remembers that my mother asked us how we wanted our rooms to be decorated. Amy wanted her room to feel like a ship, and so my mother arranged for recessed shelves and curtains that billowed like sails. My grandmother was coming to live with us too, in a stylish third-floor suite. I do not know where my room was; it might have been the smallest room closest to my mother's. I was her youngest child, barely 4 years old.

It was a house expecting people—fourteen rooms and five-and-a half baths in a turn-of-the-century townhouse on a tree-lined street near the Boston Public Garden where my mother lived with her new husband, Alex.

In her notes on the renovation, she recorded ideas for tastefully designed purposeful rooms—an octagonal dining room for dinner parties of roast suckling pig; ample bedrooms with fireplaces; a dumbwaiter that might have figured in the escapades of six mischievous children; a butler's pantry; a spacious kitchen with a sleek Roper gas stove and a space-age intercom system between floors. Every convenience was state-of-the-art in 1963. There were capacious closets, perfect for hide-and-seek, and a graceful stairway winding down to a secluded backyard garden.

On this high-stakes day in September of 1963, Massachusetts Supreme Court Justice Arthur E. Whittemore[1] considered my father's appeal to keep custody of his children, and stayed our anticipated return until the appeal could be heard. We would not be coming home to my mother after all.

My mother and the new husband she had married a few months before would be the only people to fill these rooms. I imagine that when my mother heard Judge Whittemore's decision, cold dread must have overcome her. In my mind, she was white as powder, her body slack and weighted down, stumbling from one room to the next, overwhelmed by the vacancy.

It is family lore that I am the last person my mother saw before she killed herself. She drove to my father's house pleading to see the children, but I was the only child at home. My father demanded that she leave. Bee, our housekeeper, hustled me out the door and down the driveway toward my mother who waited desolate on the street. She bent down and caressed my hair—I *remember*—as she whispered instructions to Bee to watch over us, especially me. And then she left.

She left a suicide note as well as a grocery list—a list in preparation for our arrival that would never happen: Six tangerines. Two boxes of Kleenex (*pink* is crossed out and replaced by *blue*). Sugar-free root beer. Blue toilet paper. Four pounds rump roast. Lettuce. Tomatoes. Food for a family....

∞

I am often asked if I remember my mother. I appreciate that the question is a way to express the hope that my loss has been tempered, at least, by a photograph, a necklace, or her words—anything I might call on to evoke her presence. But I have few mementos and even fewer memories. My mother is defined by her absence.

Yes, some treasures can kindle her presence: a dainty birth announcement on elegant paper stamped with the date of my birth; a tarnished silver baby cup, dented at the rim and inscribed with my name; my worn woolen baby blanket; a pamphlet from my mother's campaign for the Boston School Committee. I have a few photographs, including a formal portrait of my mother taken by a professional photographer when she was about 30 years old. In it, she looks self-assured, hair cropped fashionably short, a woman in control of her life, secure. She is wearing a dark wool suit with oversized buttons. The jacket is generous at the neck, revealing a strand of large pearls around her throat. She gazes somewhere just above the lens. Perhaps she is bothered by a racing thought. Her distant look gives the portrait a regal quality. When I look at photographs of myself at age 30, I notice a striking resemblance that is at times unnerving.

The pictures, a tatty blanket, a baby's cup—these objects are all that I have after my mother's death. When I was young, I thought a fire had destroyed all her belongings. But my father tells me now that "Alex would not turn over anything for the kids."[2]

I have our shared name, Nancy. I have one vague memory of traveling by plane with my mother, of coming down the stairs onto the tarmac, sick to my stomach: It is hot, and I am wearing a blue and white sailor dress with a long red ribbon. I have tight braids. Mama is holding my hand and cleaning my face.

I have copies of old newspaper articles, which my older sister Judy retrieved from microfilm in the Boston Public Library when we were teenagers. Our curiosity about our mother was clandestine, sisters playing family telephone. The articles give details of my mother's life, my parents' marriage, divorce, and custody fights. In the vacuum created by my father's hesitancy to talk about our mother, the articles allowed us to piece together an incomprehensible, soap-opera version of our history.

The most haunting article in Judy's collection was on the front page of a local paper from September 17, 1963. It carried an elegant photo of my mother with a headline so large that four short words took up two lines:

SOCIETY WIFE A SUICIDE

And underneath,

LEFT 2 NOTES: FEARED LOSS OF CHILDREN
Ends Tangled Life

And in detail:

Rappaport Custody Row Ends in Wife's Pill Death

The bitter two-year custody fight involving the six children of Atty. Jerome Rappaport and Mrs. Nancy Vahey Rappaport Stanley took a shocking and tragic turn last night when the brilliant young mother died of a massive dose of sleeping pills.

Suicide Notes

A family spokesman said the attractive 34-year-old socialite was found by her husband Alexander O. Stanley, a lecturer at the Harvard Business School, in their apartment at 285 Marlborough St., Back Bay, last Tuesday afternoon.

In sealing her doom she dramatically and desperately tried to place the plight of her six children before the public.

Her death act climaxed a day of reversals for her. A custody award made in her favor in Suffolk Probate Court by Judge Edmund V. Keville was in danger of being reversed when the case was ushered into the state's Supreme Judicial Court.

Appeals to the Judge

She had gone to the Quail St., West Roxbury, home of her former lawyer husband early in the day, had made an appeal to see her children and had been refused.

Rejected, she returned to her plush Marlborough St. apartment.

The note to Judge Whittemore was highly critical. In it she made a dying appeal to the judge to put the children in the custody of her present husband, Alexander Stanley, and her mother Mrs. Edith Vahey. This note was signed "Nancy Vahey Stanley."

The second missive was addressed to Alexander Stanley. It read: "Dearest Alex, This is too much to keep putting you through. You have been more help than I could ever hope to have. Please take care of the children and don't ask any more of me. I love you. Nancy."

Under the court decree in July 1963, Mrs. Stanley was to have taken custody of the children Martha, 11, Amelia, 9, Judith Ann, 8, James W., 7, Jerome Jr., 6, and Nancy, 4, last Friday.

Earlier in the week, however, Justice Whittemore took under advisement a petition by Jerome Rappaport for a stay of the order of Probate Court Judge Keville that the children be turned over to their mother.

Children with Dad

The "stay" would maintain the status quo and leave the children with their father at least temporarily, until the full bench of the high court could hear arguments on the law involved.

Of his former wife's death, Atty. Rappaport said, "I am sorry for her. I hope she finds the peace of mind she was seeking. I am very sorry for her husband and mother." . . . [3]

I was in high school around the time I discovered the articles with my sister Judy, and it was around this time that I read and reread *Go Ask Alice*— the bleak diary of a drug-addicted teenage girl who dies of an overdose.[4] I was fascinated and horrified by her self-destruction. I had trouble envisioning a future. I had a premonition that I wouldn't make it past age 34, my mother's age when she died. I worried that I too would be struck with depression.

My father eventually told me, when I was about 14, that my mother had attempted suicide two years before her death.[5] My sister and I discovered the facts ourselves in our trusted library's microfilm collection. We found a picture of my mother in the *Record American*[6] looking much younger than she does in her formal portrait. She wears a sporty silk scarf tied casually around her neck. She is spunky with her upturned nose. *Takes Three Handfuls of Sleeping Tablets*, the caption reads.

The article includes a picture of my father, too, thick hair pressed to the side, conservative horn-rimmed glasses, an immaculate white shirt, and a dark suit. *Took Wife to Hospital*, it says beneath his grim expression.

My mother sought treatment from a psychoanalyst after her suicide attempt. At that time, psychiatrists and their patients talked about neurosis, a term psychiatrists rarely use today. Popular movies such as *The Three Faces of Eve* and *Splendor in the Grass* romanticized the work of analysis, especially the analyst's ability to interpret childhood conflicts and relieve existential angst. In her diary, my mother reveals that the hard work of therapy was "not helpful at all.... The doctor takes me round and round, and I come out more confused and frightened than when I went into the office." She is cautious about sharing "the avalanche of unfamiliar feelings ... the most gruesome secret of my soul"—her secret desire for someone other than my father. In her words, therapy was merely "talking deeply to someone who must be paid." My mother's therapist might have softened her self-recriminations and explored the meaning of her desire, but hindsight is 20/20. With support, she might even have made a strategic exit from her marriage to my father without being "robbed of [her] children."

I wonder, had she lived, how my mother might have understood my choices. I wonder how it would have been for her to watch me come into my own mothering of my three children, holding them close while making way for the inevitable separations. As a child and adolescent psychiatrist—one of those "listeners who must be paid"—I, too, "take people round and round," trying to navigate together the agony of unbearable loss, and to fortify their determination to forge ahead, anchored with the comfort that may come from knowing that they are not alone in their sorrow.

Why did my mother kill herself? My memories don't provide an answer, and I am wary of my father's account because it's not my own. But as a psychiatrist, I'm prepared, I hope, to understand. In "The Anatomy of a Suicide," the clinical researcher Leston Havens writes that suicide is "the final common pathway of diverse circumstances, of an interdependent network, rather than an isolated cause, a knot of circumstances tightening around a single time and place."[7] Suicide demands to be explained by the living as a way to absolve or condemn the survivors. I have tried to create a meaningful narrative to understand what happened, recognizing that the truth is buried with the victim and that questions will always linger.

Chapter Two

*No one ever told me that grief felt so
like fear. I am not afraid, but the
sensation is like being afraid. The
same fluttering in the stomach,
the same restlessness, the yawning.
I keep on swallowing.*

—C. S. LEWIS, *A Grief Observed*

My son Cory asked me as a practical 5-year-old whether only my mother's bones were buried or if her head was buried as well. My daughter Lila, a first-grader then, wanted to know whether my mother was still wearing clothes. I told them somewhat irreverently that she was dirt in a box. I was uncomfortable saying that my mother had gone to heaven and mumbled something about love lasting longer than death. I was not sure how to explain her death to myself, let alone to them.

When Lila was 13, she asked me, clearly scared of what my answer might be: "Would *you* ever kill yourself?" I assured her that I would never commit suicide and besides, I told her, giving her a hug, I wanted to stick around to see who she would become. I didn't want her to hesitate to rely on me whenever she needed to. I didn't want her to fear that I would leave her. Yet her intuitive worry was not unfounded; the child of a parent who has committed suicide is five times more likely to kill herself than a child who is not exposed to this loss.[1]

Psychiatrists have studied what can seem like the Russian roulette of familial suicide, an ominous pattern of suicide occurring from one generation to the next called "intergenerational transmission." So far, researchers have demonstrated that children who have lost a parent to suicide are at greater risk of killing themselves if they have a mood disorder, engage in substance abuse, are "impulsively aggressive," or are exposed to intense conflict in the family.[2] Still unclear is the mechanism by which a parent's suicide increases the risk for these children. But losing a parent this way is also not a prophetic death sentence; it takes a lot of damage to lose the will to live.[3]

When I met people as I was growing up, all the way to medical school interviews, if I told them that my mother died when I was 4, they were curious about how she died—the question was irresistible. Most people seemed relieved when I said barbiturates, as if death and sleep are siblings. People wanted to know *why* and what was the *cause*. Such questions are usually edged with the fear that premature death, especially a self-inflicted death, might somehow be contagious: *Why would she kill herself?* becomes *What does this mean about you?* Somehow, confessing that my mother committed suicide felt incriminating: proof that my mother's life was out of control. I worried that they would mistakenly assume I somehow played a part in that.

Over the years my father and I have had only brief, difficult conversations about my mother's death. Reluctantly, he offered the occasional explanation. When I was younger, he would imply that my mother became depressed after my birth. "She lost all interest in the children after you were born," he would say with resignation. I was, after all, their sixth child in eight years.

I was mystified how that might have played out in our family, and I asked my father whether he thought she had post-partum depression (PPD). He replied that he would not have known what PPD was, and he just noted that she was lethargic after I was born. In his words, "I can't describe to you what I didn't understand."[4] PPD, which occurs in 10 percent of new mothers, is not just the "baby blues," the exhaustion that comes from sleepless nights and a crying baby; rather, this black mood is incapacitating, derailing a mother's ability to care for her baby or even herself. Some women seem agitated and anxious, while others can barely move. The causes of this debilitating but treatable condition are multiple—changes in brain chemistry and hormones, and emotional upheaval.

My father's suggestion that my mother was suffering is understandable. Seeing her as depressed and lethargic would justify his efforts to seek and maintain custody. By keeping her away from us, he might even be regarded by his children as the protector. "What if she decided to kill herself and you were all there?" he has asked me. My father's observation about her comment felt aggressive and hurtful. It left me feeling guilty, as if he were saying that had I not been born, she would not have died.

Yet after my birth, my mother was active in many volunteer projects. She was attentive about my siblings' education. She bathed and fed us. She threw parties and juggled social engagements. Though it's possible that she was quite skilled at hiding her depression, my mother's friends talk about her as someone who was genuinely enthusiastic about her many activities planned right after my birth. Mothers with post-partum depression are often withdrawn.

A secure mother-child bond is created when a mother provides her baby with the comforting rhythms of feeding, sleep, and an organized home.[5] Without that gentle sense of order, children may have difficulty managing their emotions, lack self-control, and lose confidence in their likeability.[6] Either I have a very active imagination, or my mother must have been able to keep her sadness at bay long enough to nurture me as a baby.

My father has also suggested that my mother took on too many responsibilities, and I suspected as a child that it was this overwhelming combination that somehow killed her. She was, he has said, a woman ahead of her time, balancing children, a public career, and political aspirations. The year before I was born, a local paper reported on my mother's lead role in community organizations. The reporter depicted a high-energy, focused woman eager to embrace many challenges. As chairman of the United Fund she "supervise[d] 7,000 people and organize[d] an educational program of shows, demonstrative one-act plays about soliciting, training plus making speeches and outlining a routine for the administrative aides within my scope." My mother revealed that the "secret of her success" was her ability to organize "right to the last minute" and that she took care of a "big, old house, eight big appetites (hers included)," attended five children "with the children born about every year," the oldest being 6, fulfilled various civic and collegiate organizational jobs, and followed a "demanding but fun" social schedule of "two nights out a week and parties once a month." She acknowledged her mother's help and admitted that she was willing to delegate the jobs that she didn't like ("Mother is a big help, of course, as mothers always are. And I will admit that I have a woman to do housework, which I abhor. However, no one takes over the kitchen. I do the cooking and I administrate all the work, even when it comes to a party for two hundred at holiday time.")[7]

In the photograph accompanying this article, my mother is kneeling on the floor, wearing a tweed suit, and knitting on circular needles. She has a telephone cradled on her shoulder and papers organized in neat stacks on the floor—she is an idealized portrait of the changing status of women. The article, I realized when I first found it, could have been an early publicity effort in advance of her campaign for the Boston School Committee. Even though this picture captures the outward appearance of a productive multi-tasking woman, I am still left wondering if she also had an underlying vulnerability to sadness.

During the 1950s, my mother was unusual—an upper-class woman who had six children and worked outside of the home.[8] The prevailing cultural expectation was for women to tend to the home, not orchestrate campaigns. My mother had enough resources to hire support to care for her brood so that she could conduct a career also. Because she had grown up as the daughter and granddaughter of Massachusetts politicians, she was enamored with politics. In the decade after the end of World War II, twenty-one women were elected to Congress, nineteen of them on their own merit (only two were political widows). Many pundits of that time, however, were disparaging about women in public life.[9] In 1956, *Life* magazine published interviews with five prominent male psychiatrists who blamed the rising divorce rate on the "fatal error that feminism propagated."[10] They warned that women were neglecting their "maternal instincts, competing with their husbands, and causing psychological damage to their children."

My father never shared the views of those who discouraged female ambition although he continues to believe that my mother was overextended, exhausted from her monumental juggling effort. And yet, there is something puzzling about this explanation from a man who is himself an accomplished lawyer, philanthropist, real estate developer, gentleman farmer, and father or stepfather to thirteen. He, in fact, has always been able to do it all. And even if my mother had been hanging on by a thread amid all that frantic activity, depressed and managing to hold it all in, what, as doctors like *me* want to know, was the "precipitating event"? What pushed her over the edge: Was it really the custody battle?

∞

I had no knowledge about my mother's relationship with her parents until my brother told me four years ago that he had met a man who was a confidante of my grandmother. This man, Ed English, was about to retire as a justice of the peace from a local city hall and I decided to contact him. I called him at 4 P.M. on my forty-fifth birthday and when I introduced myself, he said warmly, "I have been waiting for this phone call for forty years." He was eager to tell me details about my past. I listened in the fall light as he drew me back in time.

In 1916, my grandmother, Edith Fern Wyant, packed her bags and loaded them into the Jordan roadster of Captain Franklyn Floete and drove east to Boston from a cattle ranch in South Dakota. Edith was the oldest daughter of a rancher and the great-granddaughter of a Sioux woman. Franklyn Floete was from a wealthy family from Presho, South Dakota. He was coming east to pursue his studies at the Harvard Business School. Edith, his fiancée, was to accompany him and attend a finishing school. They married a year later. Edith had a dominating spirit beneath her fine clothes, high cheekbones, and catlike eyes. She was not afraid to make her own way in the world. She was dainty with tiny dancing legs. Small but regal. Her sister wrote in a diary that Edith used to send her sexy, stylish dresses and silk underwear. Edith had a taste for lovely things, but she could have a caustic bite. Especially when she was drinking. By some accounts, Edith could drink with the best of them. Born in the gay '90s, in the era of "bathtub gin," she traveled on drinking cruises.

When her marriage to Floete failed, Edith Wyant defied prevailing social convention and got herself a divorce. She started seeing "Young Jim" (James) Vahey, a Boston politician who loved steak and Italian food. She adored her Jimmy.

Young Jim was born into a large "two-toilet" Irish family, distinct from Boston's Irish working class. He was the oldest son of James H. Vahey Jr. and his wife, Margaret White. A distinguished trial lawyer and two-time candidate for governor, James was the youngest graduate from Boston Law School in his time—an attorney who loved a crusade. In a riveting 1904 court drama, he made one of the most "brilliant attempts in criminal history"[11] to prevent Charles Tucker from being sentenced to death for the bizarre and brutal murder of 40-year-old Mabel Page. In another high-profile criminal case—the famous Sacco and Vanzetti trial—James unsuccessfully defended Bartolomi Vanzetti, an Italian immigrant, fish peddler, and self-proclaimed anarchist.[12]

Young Jim joined his father's law firm and became a well-respected labor lawyer in his own right. When Young Jim fell for Edith Wyant, his family frowned on his choice of a woman who was a divorcée and a non-Catholic. But he courted the rancher's daughter, and they married in 1928. My mother was born soon after.

In 1949, when my mother was 20, Jim became chair of the Democratic State Committee. A news story offers a profile of my mother's father as "an omnivorous reader of pretty nearly everything from the Congressional

Record to reports from local committees or from heavy historical works to the latest and most spine-twisting detective yarn." He had a "gift for uniting feuding party factions behind a common cause." He was a movie fan who "liked to go to the movies with his daughter, Nancy," and the reporter notes that they were "great pals, perhaps more than the average father and daughter."[13] I like to picture my mother and her father going to the movies, affectionate and close. Maybe he was more protective of my mother because his other daughter Judy—with ringlets in her hair and bright eyes and an adventurous spirit—had drowned when she was only 4.

The newspaper report in 1936 of the accidental death noted that a 4-year-old girl fell through an open spring hole and that the young girl's family had moved only two weeks before the drowning. The child "disappeared while both parents were away from the home." The "tracks first went around the pond, then crossed it in the direction of the home and stopped near the open hole in the ice, through which a long hooked pole was placed to locate the body. The body was found three hours after the hunt started when the girl was reported missing."[14]

The police reports note that Edith left home sometime after lunch—although it doesn't say where she went. When she came back after dark, at around 5:30, Judy was gone. Jim was in upstate Maine on a hunting trip and didn't get back until the next day.

Over the years, I have investigated the life history of my mother, looking for any clue to figure out more about who she was. I found a report card that my mother saved from first grade, in which the teacher's comments portray a boisterous, bright, popular, and sometimes exasperating child:

> Nancy knows a good many words and has a good accent, but is sometimes too sure of herself and does not listen carefully. . . . She has a marvelous fund of general information, a real interest, and an insatiable desire to find out more about the subject she is interested in. . . . Nancy's idea of a grand time is to start some

kind of an argument with her friends. I have tried every method I can think of to give her another point of view. The most successful has been to give her responsibility. She is then very polite and thoughtful. . . . She is an unusually gifted child and intellectually she will be able to do very fine work.[15]

I found a picture of her at about 7 years of age with her arm hung casually around little Judy's shoulder. The sisters are standing on brick steps in front of a large house. My mother is a good foot taller than Judy and looks protective and self-assured. They are pressed against each other with a casual intimacy and smiling in a conspiratorial way, as if they are used to getting into mischief together. It is the only photograph I have that shows them together and I stare at it with morbid fascination, knowing something they were unaware of when this picture was snapped: that they will be abruptly, brutally separated.

A year later, over the winter, her sister drowned. There are no other school reports to reveal how this might have dampened my mother's spirit.

∞

I can only imagine how my mother reacted to her sister's death. Indeed, we often wish we could uncover the deep feelings of a family member who cannot share the memories. At the time of my aunt's drowning, Edith was reported to be in town socializing or, more likely, drinking. My mother may have been the only witness to her sister's drowning—although no one has told me where she was at the time. I wonder if my mother was taking a nap while her sister wandered outside to explore her new home. Once my mother realized that a police search was under way, I can only imagine how much she hoped they would find Judy somewhere safe and how terrified she felt when they did not. I hope that she had her eyes covered when the police recovered her dead sister's limp body. I wonder who comforted her. When a child dies accidentally, usually someone feels blamed. Did my mother feel terrible that she did not hear her sister's cry for help?

When I learned about Judy's death, I began to wonder how this may have influenced my grandmother as well. Ed English, the justice of the peace, told me that my grandmother's best friend Sylvia Fox Finn—who played Scrabble with her every night until two in the morning for fifteen years—was still alive. I tracked her down. Eighty-nine years old at the time we met, Sylvia told me that Edith never said anything about Judy's drowning during all those long nights of Scrabble. Her mourning had no words and Sylvia didn't pry. Yet my grandmother's dying wish was to be buried next to her dead baby rather than with her other daughter, my mother, who had killed herself. Sylvia noted that Edith and my mother never socialized together in my mother's adult years, and that they did not share any "mother-daughter warmth." Sylvia thought that Judy's death "colored Nancy's life," that "Nancy always felt that she herself was to blame," and that Jim and Edith "ignored Nancy and wallowed in their own grief." I believe that when my mother lost her sister, she was forced to grieve the absence of a distracted mother as well, and never learned how to cope with overwhelming sadness. She absorbed her mother's grief.

Did my mother and I both grow up with the same pervasive sense of guilt that we should have saved someone close to us? My mother's friend Patsy Goldfine told me that my grandmother blamed my mother for Judy's death and would lament, "Why couldn't it have been you?"

"What kind of a mother would say this to her daughter?" Patsy asked indignantly. But I know from the families I have seen in my work that there is no escape from the torment brought on by the death of a child. Many parents are not able to return to normal life, and they become clinically depressed regardless of whether there is a reasonable connection between a child's death and parental care.[16] Parents feel responsible; they will distort facts to punish themselves and, sometimes, those around them as well.

My mother left only a cryptic adult journal entry about growing up with her mother. Her reticence is curious to me:

> I hadn't tried to talk to my mother since I asked her to point out the road to school the day I went to the first grade. We had always lived together as intimate strangers. We knew all about

each other's activities and food and entertainment preferences
but never talked to one another about anything [that] either considered important. We had never trusted each other, we did not
even particularly like each other. Now when I was in trouble,
she could not try for a new solace in a relationship that existed
only by habit. No one could explain my mother's antagonism.

My mother sounds resigned, accustomed to not expecting much comfort
from an "intimate stranger." Perhaps her precocious cocky reassurance was
a cover for feeling so forlorn. She would need to find her own way.

Edith drank throughout my mother's childhood and early adulthood. She
was a surreptitious alcoholic—sneaking drinks whenever possible. And as
soon as my mother walked into Edith's house, she could tell that her mother
had been drinking, as children of alcoholics can always tell. According to my
father, my mother would fly into a rage, digging behind couches to find hidden vodka bottles.

In Edith's later years, my father demanded that she quit if she ever
wanted to see her grandchildren again and he paid for her hospitalization.
After she stopped drinking, she sold her house and moved in with my parents and her grandchildren. My father says she was helpful with all of us and
the Quail Street house was big enough to absorb a helpful mother-in-law.[17]
According to one of Edith's close companions, she reformed at age 55. Her
drink of choice became dark coffee with two ice cubes.[18]

My grandfather's drinking and response to Judy's death are less clear.
Early in his life, Young Jim was a heavy drinker. A family friend tells me
that Jim and Edith would lock my mother in their car while they made the
rounds of local bars. My sister Amy remembers that my mother told her
Jim quit drinking the day Judy drowned. My father says otherwise.

My mother was left to fend for herself when her parents were drinking.
In his memoir *Dead Reckoning*, psychologist David Treadway describes the
devastating impact of his alcoholic mother's suicide and the parallels with
the families whom he treats.[19] He describes how children learn to steer clear
of their intoxicated parents, as they can be explosive and unpredictable.

Children of alcoholics often assume they are the ones responsible for a parent's drinking and become scared, angry, and confused. He warns that "children survive growing up in an alcoholic family by learning to distrust others, becoming self-sufficient, blocking out their feelings and becoming rigidly attached to roles that give them a sense of their place and identity within the family."[20] Too often, children learn to minimize the damage, a temporary survival skill that can allow them to conceal their anxiety and look disarmingly precocious and self-sufficient. In actuality, however, they may be on constant alert, bracing themselves for their parents' unexpected oscillations between ephemeral euphoria and brittle temper outbursts. As adaptive heroes, they may fiercely guard their terrible secret and stubbornly learn how to get by on very little support from their parents, resigned to the false idea that they are not entitled to anything better. They may console themselves that when they grow up it will be different because they will escape the chaos, but they may secretly harbor the fear that things will never change.[21] Once her sister died, my mother had no one who might keep her company in the car when her parents went drinking; she no longer had another witness or someone for whom she stayed looking invincible even when she was afraid inside.

As addiction research has shown, children of alcoholics are more likely than those of nondrinkers to be addicted themselves and often have underlying illnesses, especially mood disorders. They drink at an early age and quickly escalate how much they drink.[22] My mother may not have been an alcoholic, but I have learned that she was addicted to sleeping pills. Addiction ups the ante, increasing people's susceptibility to suicide because they are more likely to act impulsively.

∞

Sisters and brothers provide scaffolding for our emerging sense of who we are. Roughhousing, teasing, playing dress-up, feelings of jealousy and affection, and countless negotiations all yield a sense of mastery and confidence. When a sibling dies, brothers and sisters miss sharing their lives and the security this brings. Many bereaved siblings believe that the death of a brother or sister has irrevocably changed their lives.[23] They often feel more vulnerable to illness and experience survivor's guilt. They are uneasy—unsettled by the disconcerting belief that they should have been the one to die. Surviving brothers and sisters are often melancholy during family celebrations and sometimes have difficulty concentrating. Healing occurs when family members comfort each other, when children are allowed to grieve in their own ways and share memories with their loved ones. Lacking comfort in her parents' house, my mother as a young girl was alone with her thoughts, her possible guilt, her questions.

I do not want the same kind of distance with my children, the shadow of unexplored grief. Rather than burdening my children with my bereavement, I want to let them see how I deal with the painful longing for lost family without depriving them of my presence. I don't want to be overly nostalgic about my mother. I don't want the upheaval from my loss to undermine how I connect with my children; rather, I want to find strength in understanding.

My children have watched me as I have tried to understand who my mother was, knowing that I write "letters to Mama" that are my way of telling my mother who I am and who my children are becoming. I try to penetrate the incomprehensible mystery of her death and to somehow show them our enduring connection to those we love. Cory, ever the concrete thinker, once asked me where I was sending the letters. Lila said that maybe in my dreams my mother would write back.

Sometimes, I peer into an apparent void, a one-way dialogue with too much room for projection. My family history gives me a fragmented and sanitized view of my mother. I often feel as if I am figuratively tugging on her apron strings pleading for something more, starved for a tasty morsel that will satiate my desire to know her in a way that is intimate and familiar.

Chapter Three

*We are time-bound creatures. We ex-
perience life along a time contin-
uum; things happen sequentially in
our lives, and we need to understand
the causation. But we never really do
understand it until we sit down and
try to tell the story.*

—JILL KER CONWAY,
Points of Departure

Weekends, for my family, offer a freedom from the routine of rushing off to school and to work. One day, a few springs ago, we settled down to eat our favorite breakfast, a sticky treat of popovers and honey. Cory tried to persuade his father and me why we should increase his allowance and Zoe, the youngest, was eager to invite two friends over and wanted us to make a decision immediately. Children come with their competing needs, and as a parent I am often impressed with the constant negotiations. How could my mother have organized six kids? I sometimes wonder if she had stopped to write each of her six children a suicide note whether she would have been daunted by the task and changed her mind.

The phone rang, disturbing our breakfast. I assumed it was a telemarketer with that annoying timing for interruption at the least opportune moment. But the voice belonged to Phyllis, my father's third wife. In her, my father finally feels, after more than thirty years of marriage, as though he found someone who can help him to be a better parent, grandparent, and person. She is not easily intimidated, and soon after she divorced her first husband and was changing careers, she had approached my father for business advice. She probably got more than she bargained for. Even though she is feisty and sturdy enough to hold her own with my formidable father, by marrying into our complicated blended family that was composed of Dad and Mama's six children—plus three sons from my first stepmother's (Barbara's) first marriage, two children from Barbara and Dad's ten-year marriage, and adding two children of her own—she has industriously balanced multiple roles.

I was 19 when my father (at 53) and Phyllis (twenty years his junior) were married. I resented her, as she was a force of nature and I thought of her as an intrusion in my life. Despite my suspicions of her hierarchy of affection, she has been supportive, making a spirited effort to connect, even when confused and frustrated by my ambivalent response. When Phyllis calls, she can speak with an urgency that I find alarming and on this day I braced myself for a calamity.

I couldn't help but worry that she was calling with bad news about my father. As he settles into his eighties, my father has ceded some territory to aging, or, as he wryly says, "acquired some sophistication," by allowing his formerly dyed dark hair to transition to its natural silver. Though he is humble now, and more considerate as he recognizes his own vulnerability after a few health scares, he is still strong and intensely curious. As I watch him occasionally pause to dredge up a word or remember names, I know that he is downshifting, and that his power and intellect—forces that I have both admired and feared—are ephemeral. He relies on Phyllis, who is sharp and sure-footed, and he has passed some of his decision-making power to her.

That spring morning, however, Phyllis was not so much urgent as she was careful. She told me that she was taking on a difficult initiative of her own making, which was to do the right thing, and she wanted to distribute some of my mother's things to me and my siblings. She suggested that I might be too busy to come over on such short notice. But I had never even seen my mother's handwriting before. I recruited Lila as my 11-year-old escort and went to meet Phyllis.

When I arrived, Phyllis had a blue trunk with brass hinges open and was meticulously organizing its contents into different boxes for each of my siblings—photographs, drawings, letters, all kinds of materials that my mother had saved. Seeing these objects stunned me. I stood there staring. I was nervous and intrigued about what I would discover, and irritated that Phyllis had taken charge of deciding what would be distributed to each of my brothers and sisters. But I couldn't help but be relieved that she had called me.

"Where did the trunk come from?" I asked. Phyllis could see how momentous this was for me, but she focused on the task at hand. She explained that my mother's friend Peggy Melgard had dropped it off at my father's office several years ago when she moved from Boston to Florida. I learned later from Peggy that for almost forty years Peggy herself had guarded the trunk. Alex, my mother's new husband at the time of her death, had asked Peggy to keep some of their possessions. But Peggy never heard from Alex again, and she began to have the nagging feeling that my mother's children would want the trunk. Peggy had known my parents before they were married and they saw each other socially as a couple for many years. After my father and mother divorced, she became an even closer friend of my mother.

Phyllis said that she was disturbed that it had taken so long for Dad to give his children the contents of the trunk and that she had stumbled across the box recently when she was cleaning out a closet at his office and brought it home. She was now, at least in her mind, doing exactly what needed to be done—"honoring" my mother's memory so as to "spare my father the painful reminders." Dad later told me he "had enough integrity not to destroy it. I kept it for a couple years and didn't know what the hell to do with it. I didn't want to be involved dividing things; God forbid something was missing. I never opened the trunk—and I didn't know what was in it."[1]

At that moment, apprehension outweighed any sense of appreciation for Phyllis's act; but looking back on it, I realize that there were lots of other things she could have done with that trunk, and in the end, I am grateful that she made sure she passed on tangible belongings of my mother.

Here was evidence of a life I did not know—small calendars with hand-scrawled appointments, a high-school yearbook, report cards, school awards, newspaper clippings, and chatty letters from her friends. A photo of my mother cradling me as a baby in her arms. A photo of my mother and father, their eyes filled with laughter. Her handwriting—big and full. I sat down on the floor and picked up a letter that Phyllis had placed to the side of the trunk. It was from Peggy.[2]

> *To the Rappaport Children:*
>
> *Your mother cherished these photos, cards, notes, and drawings. I thought you would like to have them. Also, in the trunk, is a novel Nancy was in the process of writing at the time of her death.*
>
> *The notes from those of you old enough to write at the time of her death show how much you loved her. I hope you still hold happy memories of her in your hearts as I certainly do.*
>
> *Fondly,*
> *Peggy*

I looked up at Phyllis. "Where is the novel?" I asked, worried. She burst into tears and confided that she was reading the novel. She wasn't exactly sure what to do with it, but she thought she would give it to my sister Judy, whom she considered the family historian. Finally, she sighed heavily and trudged up the staircase. I could hear Lila watching reality TV in the other room and let her know we would be leaving soon. A few minutes later, Phyllis came down not only with the novel, which she explained was over 400 typewritten pages on legal paper with my mother's handwritten corrections in the margins, but also with a few of my mother's thin journals.

As she handed me four bulky black folders stuffed with legal-sized paper, I sensed that she was relieved. She told me that she had a deep and abiding relationship with my father, and she wanted me never to use the material in any way that would hurt Dad. Not knowing what I was promising, quietly resenting that I was being asked to be honorable, and worried that the novel might be destroyed, I quickly agreed. It was an irresistible chance to know my mother's mind. At that moment, I would have agreed to almost anything.

∞

Outside in my garden the daffodils are weighed down by the rain. Armed with a strong cup of coffee, I look warily at the novel that my mother was working on so urgently before she died. Her mammoth tome holds both promise and disappointment as I try to understand her. For several years I had speculated and incessantly asked why she would have left her children. I had confided to an apparent void who I was as a mother, doctor, and wife. And now here I was with her novel. I was reminded of Beckett's lament: "I don't know, I'll never know, in the silence you don't know, you must go on. I can't go on. I'll go on."[3]

Many authors have borrowed liberally from their lives as a source of inspiration for their novels (Charles Dickens in *Oliver Twist*, Jane Austen in *Pride and Prejudice*, and Virginia Woolf in *The Waves*, to name just a few). Some critics would argue that writers—whether of poetry, fiction, drama, or literary criticism—inevitably impose some aspect of autobiography. Writers cannot escape that the person in charge of organizing a story reveals who she is just by the nature of how she fabricates the narrator's voice.[4]

My mother wrote in her notes about her novel, "Is this sheer purgative autobiography or do I want others to see it?" I can understand her trepidation. It is hard to be exposed and feel judged. As a psychiatrist I live in the land of thoughts, and at the risk of over-interpreting I hoped that this unexpected access to my mother's mind would reveal how she constructed a narrative of meaning, her personal truth. Perhaps it would illuminate how my mother came to see suicide as an option, or how she came to accept the apparent futility of life. As a daughter who has longed for a connection to my mother, I want to know her inner thoughts, to discover her secret messages to me. I want a good story so I can be proud of her. I want to read as a detective and discern what is autobiographical and what is fiction.

"The End of Freedom" is my mother's title, and this sounds ominous with the knowledge that the author killed herself. In her preface, my mother outlines how the novel's plot unfolds; she employs the third-person narrator, providing a panoramic view ("the omniscient narrator"). She explains that Diane, her main character, is "a woman of forty-two, who, for twenty years, has been active in Boston politics, first as a worker, then as a successful candidate for School Committee and the State Senate. She has four growing children and is at the peak of her career." She goes on: "In fact, the story opens with the first of a series of meetings to prepare her for the nomination (Democratic) for Governor.... She has a tremendous following which she has served well during her ten years in office. However, during this campaign she sees, for the first time, what politics is really all about: the degradation, the cheating, the lying (to oneself and others), the prevalent dishonesty, intellectual and otherwise. Finally, in despair, she turns from her husband, whom she comes to see as the incarnation of all the evils of the political world, to a love affair with a younger man."

In creating a protagonist who closely resembled herself, my mother wrote what the French refer to as a "roman à clef." She might have chosen this literary form because she wanted the freedom to explore the scandal of an affair by using the power of a narrator to examine her motivations from a distance. She was writing the novel while engaged in a vitriolic divorce. My father was questioning her competency to take care of us because of her suicide attempt at the time she separated from him. Without the safety of her novel, it might have seemed too dangerous to examine what drove her to such a desperate act. From that vantage point she could rearrange the mess that she felt her life had become.

The third-person narrator places the main character, Diane, in the center of a long grueling campaign while Diane's husband orchestrates bribes and strongholds votes so as to win at any cost. She is devastated to realize that he does not believe she can win on her own merits and that his underhanded tactics make her an illegitimate winner. Diane becomes increasingly despondent about the unrelenting demands of public life and a political machine that is not in her control. As her disillusionment grows, she has a "fatal attraction" to her obsequious campaign manager, driven by the desire for reassurance that she is capable and attractive. On the night that Diane makes a sweeping victory for Democratic nomination for governor, she realizes that she is losing her husband to her campaign manager's wife, and she wants to withdraw from the race. Her husband, Peter, hits her for the first time in their marriage and then, in a fairly unbelievable move, kidnaps her—along with the campaign manager and his wife—and takes all three of them to Bermuda.

Often when I read a novel or a memoir I fantasize what it would be like to meet the main character. My gold standard is whether I would want to go for a cup of coffee with the narrator and have a tête-à-tête. Not so with Diane: Diane annoys me. She is constantly reveling in "her personal magnetism," enjoying the adrenaline rush that comes from being seen by her adoring constituents, and then soaking for hours in the tub. My mother created a scene in which Diane is confiding to a priest, and he speaks in idealized platitudes that Diane does not challenge. ("I know the tenor of your intellect, and of your selfless struggle for perfection. I have always thought your devotion to the public welfare, with an almost cavalier disregard of your own satisfactions, was almost saintly.") Who talks like this? I wonder. I get impatient with this long-winded description of campaign politics and corruption and doting fans. But there is something else that draws my interest—a flash of connection and recognition.

I read voyeuristically as I learn intimate details about Diane's life. I read about how Diane carefully selected her outfits and I wonder if my mother's description is fashioned after her own sense of style. "She chose her favorite set of underwear, purple and luxurious with a soft lace appliqué slip, panties, bra, and garter-belt. Diane often chose her outfit for the day this way, deciding first on her lingerie, and then matching her street costume to it, rather than the customary reverse. Drinking her orange juice, she stood in front of her open closet, deciding at last upon her most expensive purple suit, a soft pink cashmere sweater, and purple accessories. Easy elegance. Her long pearls, a brief swish at her short, wavy, graying hair with a brush, a dash of lipstick, and Diane was ready to sweep downstairs."[5]

I have the warmth of familiarity as my mother describes a house that is essentially the house where I grew up. It is eerie to see it through her eyes: "There rose an almost perpendicular gray rock, through whose primitive beauty a small rutty road had been cut. Beyond the rock the road rose through woods of scraggly maples to the house, perched like the manor house it was, far above the rooftops. It was filled with children, hand-me-down furniture mixed with contemporary, simple in line and extremely comfortable furniture, modern paintings, books, musical instruments, servants. There were three cars in the garage and a dozen acres of woodland surrounding. At this time of the year the lights of the city could be seen clearly from the upper windows and Diane had been staring out at them."

I read intimate family scenes with Peter Castleman, who seems a lot like my father—a big man playing with his big dog, or seated at the head of the dinner table, or relaxing in pajamas. Peter is a character of contradictions—aggressive, manipulative, and often indifferent when he is with his wife, Diane. Yet, in a tender scene in the book, I see Peter saying goodnight to his children (two of whom my mother had named Jane and Tippy):

> The house was busy in its quiet. A faucet in the tub dripped. The branch of a tree brushed against the window. . . . Peter heard a noise from one of the children's rooms, and went down

the hall, opening each door, looking in. He hesitated at Jane's room, the first door. There seemed to be a barrier growing between them—what would be her reaction if she woke to find her father checking on her, as if she were still a child? But he went in, quietly covered her, leaned over and pecked her cheek, and quietly slipped out and closed her door.

The boys still shared bunk beds, arguing every night over whose turn it was to sleep on the top bunk. On the floor beside the bunk was Tippy's favorite truck, the probable cause of the noise that had begun Peter's nocturnal ramble. He rearranged the covers over his two sons, kissed them, and removed several more likely disasters from Tippy's bunk, which tonight was the upper. A train, two more trucks, and a teddy bear had, in the dark, helped confuse Peter enough so that he had first kissed the teddy bear, before finding Tippy under the pile of toys.[6]

My mother was writing the novel at a time when she would have been permitted to come to our house only as a visitor. Her family life had imploded, and the novel seems to be preserving a memory of what could have been. Diane "wants everything to be just right" for the "gay Christmas preparations," the "stairs festooned with ropes of fir" and "[the] enormous pile of presents already wrapped and waiting to go under the tree.... [She] wrapped and decorated into Christmas all the hopes and now avoided disappointments of her own lonely childhood. She radiated warmth always, but for the two weeks surrounding Christmas she seemed to be the eternal mother, a mother happy in her fulfillment, content."

While I read through the pages of her novel, I sip my coffee and try to imagine what it would be like to have my mother prepare a Christmas like the one she so clearly enjoyed. And then I pause, rereading and scrutinizing a passage describing Diane's effort to stay on an even keel:

Diane agreed with the majority of her friends who pictured her as never happier than when she was too busy, juggling tasks that would ordinarily have overwhelmed three people. Diane's propaganda worked on those other people and usually upon herself. Cyclically, however, she was overcome by a deep depression, all-pervading though of short duration. The depressions normally occurred when her workload was impossible of completion. Just such a crisis was now approaching. . . . This phenomenon usually woke in Diane a superstitious awe of her good life and all the good luck she had endured and could foresee. When, rarely, she was, as now, smothered by a sense of doom, of impending disaster, because life had been too good to her, she knew that she was in for a bad day. As she lay in bed and reviewed the projects for the day, she decided she could not indulge her desire to remain in this soft, warm, safe harbor, and ride out the storm of her depression as she sometimes did, but that she must get on with the business of the day.

The narrator describes how hard it is for Diane to feel dismissed by her children, although it sounds as if the panic and sense of abandonment have less to do with the children than with the crisis in her marriage.

Diane was always hurt when one of her children began to decentralize from his concern with her, but to have two children doing it at the same time became unbearable. She wanted to get dressed and run back into the campaign, or to grab her two sons, and force them to remain her babies, just a little longer, just until she was strong enough to let them go. As she had with the girls, she kept this panic of abandonment completely within herself, and smiled, and pretended, soon even to herself, that she really preferred to have the children so self-sufficient, so independent. It made her free. Sometimes it was hard to keep herself from noticing the loneliness and the panic, especially when the break was so fresh, as now. But later, she always told herself, they would all be much happier for being separate.[7]

When someone is depressed and begins to see herself as expendable in the lives of her family, when she starts talking about young children as self-sufficient, these are very troubling signs. Diane's determination to stay strong is worn down by the hypocrisy of it all, and the hypocrisy kills her. When she finally succumbs to her young campaign manager, she takes an overdose of sleeping pills and drowns herself.

So it is a suicide story after all. Perhaps it is one long suicide note, and my heart is heavy. If this was my mother's way of trying to understand her suicide attempt two years before her actual death, I realize I am not any closer to knowing why she thought she needed to die. I worry that her suicide wasn't as impulsive as I had imagined—not just a tragic momentary urge but, rather, a sustained deliberate choice.

Following Diane's suicide the narrator describes Diane's "highly successful wake": This phrase stops me cold—the suicide as a chance for a good party. I know that people planning their suicide need to minimize the effect that their death will have on others. Still, when I read my mother's description of Diane's death as a celebration, I am indignant.

My mother's novel ends not with Diane's suicide but with her eldest daughter Jane discovering her mother's papers, which she shows to her mother's trusted longtime friend, Angelo. It is unnerving for me to read this section, as if it foreshadows that as my mother's youngest daughter I will retrieve her novel and not always "know what to do" as I try to decipher this "piece of her soul." I know that she was seeing a psychiatrist after her first suicide attempt, and I can only hope that she talked about this novel as a vehicle to understand her turmoil.

I glance outside. There is a familiar softness in the air that comes with the cleansing after a rain, but I know that my kids are returning from school soon. What is my mother trying to tell me? And do I have a responsibility, an obligation to understand?

A few days later, I come across some notes that my mother had tucked in with her novel about her process of writing. Having worked on my own book, I identify with her trepidation as a writer:

> How do you go about writing a book? For years I've thought about it—often when I've been in the midst of an exciting story, or at the clever beginning of a long novel—but usually late at night, in bed, on my way to sleep, I've begun the open-ing chapter in my mind, or I've started to sketch the plot or a juicy love scene—all the love scenes are juicy. But the cold light of noon, the urgencies of living have always successfully submerged my embryonic muse, and here I am, unsung and unrewarded, looking back down a dark alley of tortured half-fulfillment and over-promise—and the alley has been much too difficult to travel and much too poorly lit by faulty self-knowledge and the time is right here and right now that I have to start writing of the journey. Because I don't see much up ahead that's going to change or improve the way and there are a lot of debits and credits that I'd like to tote up before I turn that last corner up there, the one with no street light at all.
>
> . . . I want to get at the truth. It's the search for truth, the thirst for truth, the agonizing, gut-screwing, soul-searching urge for self-destructive truth that has roused me at last, again at midnight, to begin setting down the who and the why and the how of what I am. The inner me—what a joke. There is no "inner me," just a jumbled writhing shocking mess of memo-ries, elusive and eluding, making out of life what I want—or, more accurately, what I don't want—an indictment, an indict-

ment of the people against me, Mass. vs. whom; that really puts me up against it, doesn't it?

(Just for the fun of it here I'll call myself Penny, because that's what I'd rather be called, and I know there are people who don't think I'm worth two cents anymore.) So let's go down that alley I mentioned and let's try to brighten up some of these street lamps. Let's go way back to the beginning—don't panic, we'll hop an express just stopping where the lights are brightest, or dimmest, none of that middle of the road stuff for us— the peaks and the valleys, the frosting on the cake or maybe the burned bottom but none of that sugary goo in between.[8]

Here is the mother I long to know.

Chapter Four

Dawn and doom
was in the branches.

—ZORA NEALE HURSTON,
Their Eyes Were Watching God

My mother was a student at an all-girls high school in Boston when her father took a job working in the Truman administration. He relocated the family to Washington, DC, where my mother, uprooted from her friends, graduated in 1946 from Roosevelt High School and started making plans for college. My mother might have decided to return to the Northeast to go to college but, instead, chose to head south to attend Duke. At Duke she studied mathematics and German and was active in The Duke Players drama society. She graduated in three years with honors. By that time, her parents had moved back to Boston, where her father was serving as the Massachusetts Democratic Party chair.

Prior to graduating from Duke, my mother announced to her parents that she wanted to go to Paris before taking a job in New York. Paris appealed to my mother's sense of adventure, romance, and optimism. My grandfather, who had often indulged her, offered to pay her airfare and to use his political connections to secure a job for her. It amuses me that he was already worried that "the parade" might pass her by at such a young age; he had high expectations for her. He cautioned her to make prudent decisions about whom she married and the type of work she chose, and was honest and candid in his approach.[1]

March 11, 1949
Dear Nancy:

Enclosed is a check for $75 for flying expenses. I trust you realize what a well-rounded man your pop is. No pun intended. On Paris, you may have guessed that I am not in favor of the plans you have outlined. If you intend a career in New York as you have indicated, you had better start a reasonable time after school closes or you will find that the parade has passed you. You can gain nothing in Paris, which will not be helpful to you in your chosen work. If you intend not to work as an actuary, but want to fritter around until you get a fish in the net that is all right with me except that for the purpose of husband-catching, Paris is a poor place. I have no desire to see you and I stuck with a five-foot-two Frenchman. If you or your gal friend just want to spend some time in Europe, I can probably get you hung on to the E.C.A. [European Control Administration] so that you may play at Uncle Sam's expense. This would mean that you would leave next September or October and you would have to sign up for a year. Sorry that I am unable to agree with your desires, but as you know I never could say yes as an expediency when I am convinced that you are on the wrong track. I await your reaction.

Love,
Pop

When fall came, she yielded to her father's advice and did not go to Paris. Instead, she took a job at John Hancock in the actuary department and lived with her parents. She put the brake on her fantasies.

∞

Choosing a partner is one of the more defining acts we do. Yet serendipity, intuition, and expectations shape this gamble for happiness and fulfillment. My mother and father found each other with a flash of intoxicating love, joined together by a determined idealism to change Boston politics and to invent a promising future.

Bostonians love to predict politics, weather, and sports, and in 1949 the mayor's race was shaping up to be one of the closest political contests in the city's history. A career public servant, city clerk John Hynes, was challenging the notorious, charismatic, and powerful incumbent, James Curley, for mayor.[2]

Almost everyone agreed that Curley was unbeatable. He had served at various times—for three terms as Boston mayor, as governor for two years, and as a member of Congress, running for office a total of thirty-two times. Indicted for mail fraud in 1947 while he was mayor, Curley was banished to a federal penitentiary while John Hynes dutifully filled in. President Truman pardoned Curley and he returned to Boston unrepentant to complete his term.

As mayor, Curley took pride in serving the poor and in being "Boston's master builder," widening streets, expanding the public transportation system, and building key tunnels.[3] He also handsomely rewarded his cronies with excessive patronage. Under his imperious reign, Boston, with its exorbitant tax rates, became one of the least efficient cities in the United States. But Curley had fierce pride: He sniped dismissively that he accomplished more in one day than Hynes did in five months. Infuriated, Hynes entered the mayoral race. Curley could be a vicious political fighter with undermining tactics.[4] To win, Hynes needed idealists who shared his progressive agenda of cleaning up corruption. Hynes recruited my father, a recent graduate from Harvard Law School and chair of the Harvard forum to organize young voters. Hynes's timing was perfect, as my father could not take the Massachusetts bar examination until he turned 21 the following year. He accepted the offer to start a group called Students for Hynes. As a young reformer, my father mounted an effort to support Hynes's candidacy: preparing radio addresses, organizing lectures, canvassing voters, and putting out a newspaper. In the adrenaline rush of a crusade, my father mobilized the students from the surrounding colleges to get out the vote and Hynes defeated Curley in a surprising upset.[5]

In late November, just weeks after the mayoral election, my grandfather died suddenly. Dad likes to tell us that my grandfather was a drunk and never beat alcohol.... He choked on a chicken bone that got caught in his throat and he died. The truth is more tragic, as detailed in my grandfather's obituary: "Too busy to interrupt a hectic political calendar of arranging a Democratic sail down the harbor and a Democratic ball in the Boston Garden and arranging President Truman's campaign tour of Massachusetts, for more than a month he ignored a severe cough that wracked the Democratic leader, a giant of a man." When he finally was persuaded by concerned friends to go to the hospital, it was too late, and he died of "internal hemorrhaging."[6]

Mayor Curley came to offer condolences to my mother and grandmother at the wake and while he was visiting, he mentioned a young pain-in-the-neck named Jerry Rappaport, who had worked against him in the election. My father says that my mother told him it was the first time she had heard his name and learned who he was.

Dad tells me he recruited my mother's aunt, Rosamond "Pinky" Vahey, to be on a diversified advisory board to bring about reform in the city: "Pinky was a business leader and on the chamber of commerce and a world-class amateur golfer, an early professional business woman and from a good respected Irish family." After Pinky met my father, she told Mama that "I met the man that you ought to marry" and Mama then went to an organizational meeting at the mayor's office at Pinky's suggestion. My mother's novel offers a fictionalized account of the circumstances leading up to that encounter, and I believe the exuberance of the main character, Diane, is a thinly veiled description of my mother's excitement over having won the lottery in finding this "vitally alive" man:

> [H]e was all that was good and true, he was tall and darkly handsome, and brilliant, and amusing, and free with his money, and smoked a pipe, and he wore tweeds, and he had graduated from Harvard and the Law School very high in his class, and he was interested in politics, and he was a comer. To be a comer . . . was the ultimate compliment, and her effusion, coming, as it did, from a spare, usually taciturn, sour old maid, had sparked Diane's curiosity.[7]

My father *was* a "comer," if by that my mother meant he was on a fast track to success. Admitted to Harvard at the age of 15, he graduated from Harvard College in 1947 and, at 20, from Harvard Law School in 1949, near the top of his class. After the election, Hynes put him in charge of creating a plan to restructure local government. It frustrated my father that there was no long-range master plan for the city to guide him—and, worse, no mechanism for developing one. He began pressuring Hynes, who quickly agreed with him, to make appointments that would include individuals with planning and development experience, and Hynes obliged.[8] Eventually, planning and development were to become my father's life.

In March of 1950, about the time she met him, my mother completed a psychological profile to help her determine what career paths would be a good fit for her. Similar to the Myers-Briggs tests widely used today, this profile purported to quantify personality in order to determine potential for management leadership. My mother's scores were varied, placing her in the ninety-ninth percentile for general intelligence but in the sixteenth percentile when it came to common sense. She was judged to have exceptional mathematical reasoning skills and an impressive vocabulary but poor impulse control and little maturity. The written portion of the report highlights a vivid analysis of my mother's character. Like her first-grade report card, this account of my mother's personality adds another dimension of her life for me:

> Even though she feels uncertain of herself, she gets into things with great vigor, but she will not find it easy to apply herself consistently. While she is excitable and her feelings are easily stirred, she makes effort to give good social expression to them. However, when her feelings are subjected to the impact of high stimulation, she tends to hold her feelings under restraint but feels a pressure of excitability active below the threshold of open expression that makes it difficult to exercise discriminating judgment.
>
> She is endowed with an exceptionally brilliant mind and has fine powers of concentration. She has also developed the potential for thinking in both a theoretical and creative manner exceptionally well. She does her best quality of thinking when dealing with problems where the facts are given to her and she is limited by the conditions and rules. Under these conditions she uses the procedures of logic effectively and usually exercises good critical judgment. . . . However, when dealing with everyday problems that involve basic attitudes and sentiments, she generally does not size up a situation in a realistic way and her judgment is not sound and in accord with common experiences. Her mind becomes very active in the presence of high stimulation, but she becomes excited and tense and goes ahead in a hit-or-miss sort of way. . . . She is also quite a dreamer, but we are not sure how productive and creative her dreaming is at present. . . . Sudden changes in her social relationships make her tense, may cause her to act without the influence of good observation and judgment. . . . There are many social situations that put her on edge, stir up conflicts in her mind and she may be critical of others. . . . [9]

The report discouraged my mother from pursuing careers in fields such as politics and public relations because these would "excite" her too much. The evaluators encouraged, instead, quieter occupations such as marketing or economic research. But she forged ahead with her political interests, perhaps as a way to carry on her family legacy as well.

Shortly after Hynes's election, my father formed a political reform group called the New Boston Committee (NBC). His plan was to bring together "men and women from all walks of life—from all religious and racial groups in the city, all neighborhoods, and all spheres of Boston life."[10] For my father to lead a reform group at the same time he was assistant to the mayor was a potential conflict of interest, but Hynes did not intervene to stop it.[11] The NBC was my parents' first collaboration. In this arena, their romance flourished.

In her novel, written in the year after their marriage had dissolved, my mother's initial enthusiasm for my father still resonates in the depiction of her fictional characters and their infatuation with each other. Even as late as 1962, she seems to be relishing the early mutual admiration of their relationship.[12]

> Peter gloried in her easy elegance, considering it a mark of his own good taste and good breeding, and though he kept up a steady stream of conversation, he secretly copied some of the more important refinements in Diane's table manners. Until tonight, he had been able happily to eat peas with a knife, and all the other horrors of the untrained eater, but for the first time it seemed important to him that he master this social world, as he had mastered the political. . . . Though Peter was astute, he had no idea that he could have asked any act short of patricide of Diane and she would have complied at that moment, so mesmerized was she by him.[13]

I struggle when I read this passage, wondering if I am substituting Diane and Peter's relationship for insight about my parents' relationship, but to me it offers some proof that my mother adored my father, his intellect, his dreams for the future. It is easy to see only my parents' bitter endpoint as defining who they were together, but it was not always that way. So who was this "wunderkind" my mother was planning to marry?

My father was born in a Jewish neighborhood in the Bronx. His father, Arthur Rappaport, was a second-generation, American-born Romanian Jew and oldest son. Arthur's father was a piano tuner who then started a children's clothing store. Arthur joined the family business after high school. He proved to be an astute businessman, and his store was a success.

My father was born in 1927, followed six years later by my aunt Sandy. But before Sandy came into the world, Arthur and Cora had a stillborn baby boy. Later in life, Cora, lost in the fog of Alzheimer's disease, would unravel her long silver hair and cry out for this baby. In her youth, she had been a sharp woman, a powerful thinker, capable of rigorous argument, interested in literature and her children's education.

My father and his sister attended public schools. Both he and Sandy were excellent students. When my father was about 11 years old, he briefly participated in a knock-off of the popular radio show called *The Quiz Kids*, which featured true child prodigies such as the young James Watson, who would later win the Nobel Prize for discovering the structure of DNA.[14]

As Hitler came to power, Arthur anticipated the coming crisis and financed the escape of a dozen of Cora's German relatives, saving them from the Nazis. He helped to pay for their housing and found them jobs when they came to the United States.

My grandfather, who had a raucous laugh and a distinctive mole on his prominent nose, smoked good cigars and relished their comforting cloud of smoke. He indulged in cashmere V-neck sweaters and when he felt he could afford it he would buy a Cadillac. Yet, he resoled his loafers whenever they wore out. He worked six days a week, long hours, fifty weeks a year. He felt proud that he could help his brother Morty when he needed to join the family store because he couldn't make a decent living as a lawyer. My father, always good with numbers, worked in my grandfather's stores from an early age and bragged that Arthur could tally the receipt faster than the cash register.

With gritty pride, Dad tells my kids that he belonged to a school gang. He tells them that these were fourth-grade kids—not bad kids, just bigger than him so he avoided the fights. Instead, because he was a clever strategist, he orchestrated the fights.

My father struggled with a stutter and set for himself the goal of defeating it. Franklin Roosevelt was his secret weapon. For years, he listened to Roosevelt's weekly radio address and to recordings of his speeches and deliberately repeated the words of the president with the same inflection and pace. He eventually achieved a high-class suburban New York/Philadelphia accent.

Often on Friday nights, my grandfather would close the store early and take my dad to the St. Nicholas Arena on 66th Street. My grandfather knew a boxing commissioner who gave him ringside tickets. Dad says that what he liked about boxing was learning the "art of self-defense," a combination of self-protection and fighting back. There was also the impressive fact that, in my father's words, "just one punch could take down an opponent." Even now, when my father describes seeing these fights, he lights up with delight. I can imagine my father coming to know through boxing the glory of winning, and of taking the punch but coming back stronger. He would later appreciate the value of having a strategy for winning and the courage to stick it out. My father doesn't like to lose and, when cornered, he can be belligerent. But more often than not, he's on the side of the underdog: He likes an upset and wants to see a king dethroned.

In fact, my father often likes to remind me that he saw one of the greatest fights of the decade—the June 22, 1938, rematch of the son of an Alabama sharecropper and the son of a Hamburg sailor. In just over two minutes, mighty Joe Louis quickly knocked out Max Schmeling, a German boxer championed by the Nazis. Those two minutes in the ring came to symbolize America's impending war against Germany, and reporters wrote about the contest as if America had defeated the Germans then and there.[15]

My father believes reading into the fight this way was foolish. "You never know how things will turn out," Dad said to me recently, alluding to his usual strategy of never burning a bridge you may need to cross some day. He told me that Joe Louis's managers squandered his winnings with bad investments and that when Louis died penniless, Schmeling offered to pay the cost of the funeral. "Things aren't always what they seem," he said cautiously. "Even Schmeling, rough and pugnacious as he was, *might* be—deep down—an honorable and compassionate man."

In 1939, Arthur opened a second clothing store. He moved his family downtown, too, into a larger apartment in Manhattan where my father and Sandy could each have their own room. Arthur lived until the age of 89. They butted heads frequently, especially over politics and labor issues when Dad was younger, but Dad always knew that his father respected and supported him. A staunch conservative, Arthur could be domineering. And when there was a vote for an employee strike at my grandfather's store, my dad sided with the employees, assuming that his father would not discover his liberal tendencies at the time because there would be someone who stood by Arthur. But the vote was 16–0 to strike and Dad was exposed.

As father and son they were close, and my father relied on his father for guidance through difficult periods. My grandfather had high expectations, but I also imagine it must have been hard for my father to be the man Arthur believed him to be, or to feel that he had Arthur's full approval, especially after the break-up of his marriage with my mother.

At 15, my father announced to his parents that he was going to Harvard. Arthur was not pleased by this development, as he'd hoped that his son would stay closer to home and work in the clothing store. But he quickly found that he liked the prestige associated with having a son at Harvard. My aunt Sandy says that the sun rose and set on my father, and Harvard only increased Arthur's feelings of pride. "Jerry was the golden boy," she tells me. "Dad was always talking about him, telling everyone how he was going to Harvard and Harvard Law School, Harvard, Harvard, Harvard, oh, what a genius he was. Well, I wasn't a moron," she says sharply. "I went to Hunter College. But for Dad, there was no one in the world but Jerry."[16]

My parents' courtship was intense and brief. Among her papers I found a letter from my mother to my father that was written within months of their meeting.[17]

July 10, 1950
Dear Jerome,

It is not often, I am sure, that such as I would dare to write such as YOU. However, in this instance, I am encouraged by such fortuitous signs in your bearing, and attitude toward me, as to make me think that perhaps, even little old i would have a chance to well be welcomed by you at least from the mail box point of view, which mail box, by the way, I found most dusty and even cramped, which, now that we are on the subject of cramps, I am most doubledupuncomfortable with. And you, my pet, were so tired, bedraggled, and, I must insist, shaky, this morning, and how do I find you now . . . besides absent . . . wwwwwoe.

I don't write letters to people, first, because people annoy me, and, second, I hate to think that posterity might benefit by my immortal prose besides by my remembered gems of incontrovertible logic, symmetry, beauty, rhythm, rhetoric, grammar, harmony, and luciouslucidluridlangorouslaconicloquaciousifitisimpossible language.

And I don't write to you because I fear that this might be seemingly soulfully
solidly soiled (and I nearly didn't get that work-ridden word soiled squeezed
out of the typewriter ... which you know is how I compose this stuff. What was
I saying when I was so interrupting myself? I guess it wasn't as important as
usual, and the first as was NOT A MISTAKE,,,,,,,,,,,,,,,,,,,,,PRETTY aren't
they, the commas, I mean.

I could write to you about the reading I did this weekend about which you
haven't heard, but the only reason that you haven't heard, is that I didn't do any
reading this weekend, iwas so busythinkingthinkingthinkingthinking about you..

Jim Gardner, the azz, haz beenannoying me all day, but his uzefulnezz in life
has been ascertained. He can now run down and get my sandwiches, and we
will have no more of the great questioning of the soul from you—and this let-
ter, I might fear would start up such questioning angrily again, but I know that
you are going to be lenient with mmmmeeee because of our common bond of
having noone else to looove us. Amirightorwrong? Andthetelephonemanworks-
and works and talksand talkswithoutpauseforbreathorrelaxation and I also
never stop

E
X
C
E
P
T
NOW

Illoooovvveeee Nancy

Her playfulness in this letter strikes me as intimate and affectionate. Her reluctance to write something such as this and have it become "immortal

prose" is consistent with her self-deprecating comments such as "even little old i." Sydell Masterman, my parents' friend from this short time period
when my parents were courting, told me about my parents' engagement:
"One night Ed [Sydell's husband] and I went out with your parents on a double date. I thought they had broken up because they were going back and
forth—they were so angry at each other, breaking up and then back together
again every few minutes. We had gone out for the evening to some little
restaurant. It was Valentine's Day, and it was bitterly cold. Your Dad said he
would see Nancy to the door, so Ed and I waited for him at the bottom of the
hill in the car. It was like a ski slope climbing up to that house—we could
see them zig-zagging up the hill yelling at each other. I think we sat in the
car for over an hour freezing ourselves to death wondering where the heck
your dad was. And then, what do you know, your dad shows up and bangs
on the windshield and tells us he proposed and your mother accepted."[18]

Dad called home to tell his mother that he was getting married the next
week. His mother hung up. His father called back and said, "If you are getting married, we will be there," and Dad told me with satisfaction, "They
were." My parents were married about a week later in a candlelit ceremony
at my great-grandmother's home on Boston's T-Wharf. A justice of the peace
performed the ceremony, and only close relatives and a few friends were
present.[19] Accompanying the wedding announcement was a picture of my
mother in a modest white wedding dress and Dad in a dark suit. They are
cutting the cake and Mama looks as if she is just where she wants to be,
close to my father. Off to the side, her mother Edith lurks, grim in a fur-
collared black tweed coat. My father says that Edith wore black to the wedding because she disapproved of the fact that Dad and Mama had been
living together at her house before getting married. My father likes to joke
that marrying my mother was the best decision he never made. My mother
had given him an ultimatum: "Marry or move on."

At the time, my parents were in the midst of organizing a campaign so
they celebrated the wedding by getting a big suite at the Copley Plaza and
then went back to work. They took a delayed honeymoon in the Bahamas

after my older sister Martha was born and then returned to Boston to live on Beacon Hill. Sydell's husband, Ed, recalls the intensity of my parents' relationship: "When I first met her, I remember thinking, wow, she's a very powerful personality, highly intelligent and very well-informed. They worked together a lot during campaigns. Nancy was very involved—she had strong opinions and she knew everyone. Jerry had strong opinions, too, and he liked that Nancy's family had connections at the highest level of politics. Their personalities clashed, but that never stood in the way of their being attracted to each other. *In the beginning* they loved each other. Like crazy."[20]

Ed fondly remembers the political gatherings at my parents' apartment on Beacon Hill in the early years of their marriage: "Your mother, she was his equal intellectually—no question. She wanted to be out front—no one was going to leave her in the dust. And your father was so full of promise—he could be anything he wanted to be. If he wanted to be a member of the Supreme Court, he was certainly smart enough. Or he could make a lot of money. He chose to make money. And both of them were knee-deep in politics."[21]

How we define change depends on where we sit. My father gained a certain notoriety as an outsider and Mayor Curley liked to insinuate that my father's education "across the waters" was not Cambridge but possibly "Moscow influenced." Others suspected that my father was upsetting the status quo because he was motivated as either an atheist or a paid agent of Wall Street or a Zionist revolutionary.[22]

Sometimes, though, my father was praised for his youthful idealism—for striving to make a working government. The *Coronet* noted that he was "merely a citizen who had decided to do something about winning better government for Boston, a city which was strangled by taxes, chronically insolvent, [with] much of its government in the hands of demagogues, bigots, and machine politicians."[23]

Elaine Werby, who worked and socialized with my parents, says it's hard to describe his influence on the city. He "captured the political imagination of the city and became a public figure himself. . . . But he was a very *young* man—the way he handled success, well, he's very human and not even a mature person could have handled it. I don't think he was mature enough at the time to put it in perspective." According to Elaine, "he enjoyed being a big shot. Why not?" She laughs when she tells me.

After the 1951 elections, my father and Ed Masterman opened a law firm and, at first, business was slow. "In the early days," Ed says, "we spent as much time playing gin as preparing cases—probably more, since we didn't have much work. We would play for pennies and Jerry would win most of the time. Winning was important to your father. He was always taking my money. We did some work for a real estate entrepreneur."[24]

Although the New Boston Committee had high aspirations of streamlining government, they became embattled in disagreements about viable solutions and competing interests. By 1954 this potent group had dissolved. Hynes advised Dad to leave city government as Hynes felt he was a talented civil servant imprisoned in the government. He encouraged Dad to transition to private life and spend more time "honing his skills" as an attorney.[25]

In the first ten years of their marriage, my father had accomplished quite a lot, and began planning what was at the time the largest urban renewal project in Boston's history, the West End Development of an area controversially seen as a "declining neighborhood."[26] My mother was eager to share the limelight and was somewhat envious. Though she'd launched our family and had six children to care for, she was still quite active in many local elections and Democratic politics and on the board of half a dozen varied organizations such as the Girl Scouts, the Museum of Fine Arts, and the Greater Boston United Fund.

Dad says warmly, with memories of their strong camaraderie, that in those early days they would often pull out a backgammon board from under their bed—they loved competition. When he is feeling magnanimous, my father describes my mother as a version of himself—smart, intense, and savvy. It is true that they made a strong team, but it was probably more about complementing each other than mirroring. Dad explains to me, "There was a lot of give and take, not all war and battle."

"You can't read anyone else's marriage," their friend Elaine warns me. "But they were so intense with each other, neither of them would give an inch and ultimately that became a problem. Plus, both of them had a quick temper."

Sydell Masterman recalls that when my father won the 1953 Jaycees' award as Outstanding Young Man of the Year for his contribution to the city of Boston, she and Ed went with him to the banquet while my mother stayed home with the children. "When we arrived back at the house, your dad gave the award to your mother and she said, 'What the heck am I going to do with this? Hang it in the bathroom?'" She sighs. "Your mother was often highly critical of Jerry, especially when he was more deserving of her praise."

Sydell goes on: "[Your mother] was difficult, argumentative, and she said whatever she was thinking, never with a second thought. . . . Most of the time, they were really wonderful for each other's egos. But after a while, you could see that it was awfully tough on your dad."[27]

I remind myself that they were young people only in their twenties at the time—not yet wise or confident enough to be kind and forgiving with one another.

My sister Martha recently sent me some home movies recorded during this time period; in them I discern my mother, father, my grandmothers Edith and Cora, and the old patriarch Arthur with his piercing blue eyes. There is no sound, only grainy images, unfocused. Sometimes you can only see a kaleidoscope of movement. The movies are like any family film, with fleeting views of one birthday party after another. We crowd around the dining room table, children parading paper hats and blowing streamers, smiling into the camera. My mother carries in the birthday cake piled with flower decorations. A pony trudges around with a sled of kids in front of our house; then, more cake and candles. My father in blue shorts and brown loafers deposits hundreds of Easter eggs on the lawn. The camera lingers on him. My sisters are splashing each other in the pool. Dad holds my brother Jim tightly in the water as he kicks hard to learn to stay afloat on his own.

I recognize myself. I'm being passed around from one lap to another. My older sister proudly feeds me a bottle of milk. Now my other sister gives me a kiss. My mother in a purple bathrobe leans close with a gently exhausted smile. I am in the high chair, and the sun is breaking through the curtains. More Christmas trees with presents, blue lights and silver tinsel.

My father and mother produced a family grown from an intoxicating promise of love. Each of us carries the patterns of our family, malleable in some ways. But there is also a constellation of forces, of unwritten rules and rituals, that makes it distinct. A scaffolding that may create unbearable pain or offer a retreat to comfort. A family is not only what you say it is. This family is caught for a moment in the ordinary magic of ephemeral living.

Chapter Five

Your absence has gone through me
Like thread through a needle.
Everything I do is stitched with its color.

—WILLIAM S. MERWIN, *"Separation"*

When you are working with teenagers, therapy is like chess.[1] The opening gambits are well known and follow a predictable order. Possible directions multiply quickly as the players seek to respond to each other's moves. Therapy with teenagers calls for ingenuity, spontaneity, devotion, and the ability to recognize those moments when they abandon their defense and reveal something important. My job is to try to achieve a careful balance, staying curious and remaining patient. And I don't always succeed. One of my former supervisors used to knit while she was seeing patients because the activity was soothing and allowed for intentional but not awkward silences, the feeling of being together without any demands. As I become more seasoned as a therapist, it is easier to appreciate that often people avoid talking about what hurts the most and to respect the patients' pace of self-disclosure. We all need the time to choose whether we want to share our heartache and to reveal what matters deeply to us.

It is easier for me as a therapist to wait for a child or teenager to come around than it is for me to do the same thing as a parent. As a parent I know I am too quick to offer what I can mistakenly see as parental wisdom. When I offered friendly piano advice to my daughter Zoe, her legs barely reaching the floor as she sat on the bench, she was infuriated. Six-year-old Zoe played valiantly, but did not yet understand how the notes related to her fingers. When I offered help as a former piano player, she dismissed me with "Mama, you don't know anything about the piano." She was defiant, proud to demonstrate her competence. I need to accept her mistakes and relish her independent spirit, but it's not easy for me. I can be impatient, wanting her to get it right. She isn't deterred; she'll make her own music and assign me the role of spectator.

My mother had her own strong opinions about how to prepare her children for possible disappointments. She wrote about these opinions in her diary, showing an unusual confidence for her time that children were capable of understanding emotions with a certain level of sophistication. In a vignette about preparing my sister Martha for camp, she was upset that Edith was not reinforcing her style of parenting:

> Typical of the major difference in mother's and my attitude toward handling a situation (preparing Martha for camp). Drawing on my own experience, I told Martha that she would feel strange perhaps even lonely when she started, and this would be the way the rest of the children would be feeling and that if a child gave her an unhappy look she should recognize it for a sign of her own inner turmoil, not as something personal: that if she would concentrate on being happy and helping the other children be happy she would have a very good time at camp and find many new friends. My mother felt the conversation unnecessary and confidently turned to Martha saying, "I'm sure you'll be very happy"—not an apparent contradiction, but very decisively closing the subject and letting me know that these were unwelcome hints. I remember all too well my own

first horrible unprepared moment of homesickness at a particularly poorly chosen camp. No one, most of all my mother, had wanted to put into my head the possibility that I would be unhappy or lonesome at camp, in fact I was miserable and completely unable to cope with the many new experiences and trials. I don't want this to happen to my children. Perhaps they will escape all unpleasantness, but I doubt it, and feel that sound preparation, adequate warning, and affectionate suggestion as to acceptable behavior will provide a far sounder basis for successful adjustment than will a shutting-out of "unpleasant discussion."

I was too young to have any "sound preparation" for my mother's death. Ironically, though I've never mentioned my effort to understand my mother's suicide to my patients, the act of examining the loss has given me a certain stamina with them so that I do not flinch as I did in the early days of therapy. When I started my training in child psychiatry, I observed a play-therapy case through a one-way mirror. The patient was a 4-year-old girl whose father had killed himself. Afraid that the work would stir up my own confusing memories, I watched with absolute dread when this petite pig-tailed girl with a tendency to bite her lip nervously entered the crowded playroom with its dollhouse, furry puppets, and a sink full of water toys. She grabbed a large, plush crocodile and stuffed its gaping mouth with plastic dolls. Then she slammed the crocodile on the floor, delighted when the dolls came tumbling out. Almost immediately, she gathered up the dolls again, this time pretending to flush the dolls down the toilet while singing, "London Bridge is falling down, falling down, we all fall down!"

Session after session, she hid the dolls in the crocodile and then threw them all to the floor. Sometimes she would stand listlessly, arms at her sides, or stare sideways into the one-way mirror as if she could see us. At times, her play disintegrated and she would angrily throw toys around the room and yank puppets off the therapist's hands, then retreat into a corner, collapsing into tears. I watched as the therapist quietly witnessed the girl's combustible emotions, then offered words to the girl to help her order her chaos. It was unsettling for me as I observed this girl but now, years later, I can make the plunge when my own patients choose to share something painful with me.

My 17-year-old patient Ellen can have debilitating panic attacks, and she came to see me to get a handle on her overwhelming feeling of doom, although she was very skittish to open up. One spring day, Ellen came to my office, her red hair swept to one side, silver earrings dangling against her long neck, a small tattooed eagle on her inner wrist. With studied indifference, as if she had accidentally arrived here, she casually draped her lanky colt-like legs over the chair. She proceeded to empty out the contents of her pocketbook to show me proudly the storage capacity, laying each object on the floor: notebooks, pens, change in a plastic baggie, "pink cotton candy" lipstick, a pair of broken glasses, and a state-of-the-art cell phone. She usually prefers to talk about her best friend ("she is so spoiled") or the wonders of olive oil as a moisturizer than about what may make her feel that a disaster could happen at any moment. This day, she looked out the window and casually started to talk about her first panic attack following the "bizarre national presidential election, where there was a dead heat between the president wannabes Bush and Gore." Her grandfather Morty died before this contested election. He had lived with her family from the time she was little until she was 16.

She cast a glance at me to see if I was listening and then studied her cell phone to see if she had received any new messages. She told me about her grandfather: "The room was always darkened with a twin bed, no pillow and a file cabinet stuffed with papers. Morty would spice things up at dinner, teasing her brothers. When Morty was around we always had dinner together but now we only eat dinner on the run. The night of the election I reflexively set six settings, one extra for Morty, and then I caught myself." She relayed this to me with minimal emotion but her longings were expressed in the minute details she shared, the scrutiny of grief. She said wistfully that Morty had loved to listen to Ellen play piano, "encouraging the music to be in me" and "cultivating an appreciation for minor and major scales." I am learning to listen to her pain and the ocean of sorrow as we build a raft together.

∞

In our study, I have an old photograph of my family together when my mother was alive: my grandmother, my father, my mother, my five brothers and sisters, and me as the youngest arranged on a couch in matching plaid outfits. At one end is Martha, the eldest at 9, somewhat aloof with her hair brushed back into a perfect ponytail. Next is Amy, 7 at the time, with jet-black hair, pale skin, and high cheekbones—she was usually the designated "baby-holder," but on this occasion she is empty-handed and looking toward my mother attentively with wide almond eyes. Judy is my third sister, whom my mother named after her dead younger sister, who had drowned eighteen winters before. She sits next to Amy, a rambunctious twinkle in her eyes and a crowd of freckles on her nose. She is satisfied to be squeezed in the middle.

Then comes Jim, bursting at the seams at 4, with a steady pugnacious gaze; he stands on the couch ready for any battle. Jerry is 3 with baby-soft curls and a tender smile. He is playing on the floor with a toy truck, oblivious to the occasion. Mama is the only one of us who is smiling for the camera, boasting her special pearls and a tweed jacket. Dad is next to her, in a suit, his arm awkwardly wrapped around Jim. He looks distracted. My grandmother is looking annoyed at my mother. She is wearing a tight sweater and sporting vivid nail polish. Her silver hair is pulled back, and the wear of years spent smoking is clear on her cheeks, in a face otherwise composed. Almost 2 years old at the time, I am cradled comfortably in my grandmother's lap, head turned away from the camera. My grandmother's porcelain ashtray is on the low modern table in front of the couch. Even now when I look at this picture, I recall the intensity of the pungent smell of that ashtray and how the smoldering embers hypnotized me.

What we felt as children was too large for any of us to manage, and there were too many of us in need. At the time my mother died, we were living with my father and his new wife Barbara and her three children from her first marriage. What I knew of my mother was what my father and stepmother chose for me to know—this picture that I have now in my study was not on display growing up. My stepmother raised us to think that our mother had not taken good care of us, that she ignored our diapers when they were soiled, that she was self-indulgent. My father and my stepmother wrapped us in an uncomfortable silence and tried to carry on as if everything could be—would be—just fine. We needed to get on with it. As my father has told me: "Your mother died, suicide is a loss. Your mother wasn't ever present, not manifested in your lives. . . . Kids just go on. All of you missed her, loved her, I can't enter into that place. . . . But I assure you at the time there was a lot of life, education, activities."[2]

As a mother, I've come to appreciate how my own children rely on one another and can find a way to communicate, talking in code when there is tension surrounding them. Witnessing Cory, Zoe, and Lila whispering to each other one day made me realize that I had never addressed my siblings about losing our mother. There was an implicit pact I had not been aware of that we did not talk about our mother, and this kept us at a distance. I started to ask my sisters and brothers questions that I had never felt permission to ask growing up. Maybe it was the curiosity I cultivated as a trained psychiatrist; wondering how a suicide would affect an entire family, I had come to appreciate the power of unspoken or disavowed feelings. But now I was ready to find out more.

In forty years I had never asked my sister Martha what it was like for her to lose our mother. We have all grown up, each of us dealing with the loss of our mother in private, alone. As the oldest child, Martha would know best what happened, and although she is a woman of precision and likes predictability, when I asked her, she noted that her memories were vague. Her voice somewhat constrained, she told me that our mother overdosed two days before her eleventh birthday and was in a coma. She died a few days after her birthday. I was not sure how to respond but I thought to myself that this was bad timing, as if there is any right time to commit suicide. Martha, now a prominent woman in Minnesota politics, said: "I can't stand surprises. Surprise birthday parties are fine but I think I am going merrily along, and then, boom, there's something out of the blue that I don't know about. That makes me very frustrated. I don't mind that there are problems. I just want to know about them ahead of time. I don't want to be embarrassed by them." Martha is organized, planning her vacation schedule years in advance. Our mother's suicide may have felt "out of the blue."[3]

Martha can't remember who told her that Mama died. Maybe it was Grandma. Maybe it was Dad. She was old enough to figure out what was going on—she was startled by Mama's suicide, but after my mother's death she was "relieved to not be torn" between our two parents. This new equilibrium, she muses, "really helped at making this new family work [with Dad's remarriage to Barbara and the addition of Barbara's three children]."

In her fifties and in her third marriage, having shepherded her own daughter off to college, Martha has relaxed her formerly stern stance, though she is still cautious about letting people get close too quickly. In past years she was an executive at General Mills and, as she puts it, "a calculated risk taker." Hers was a world of children's cereal lines, "Family Flour," and Betty Crocker cookbooks, a world that is foreign to me. In 1992 her ambitions took a "right-hand turn," and she decided to run for the Minnesota state legislature, which was less than one-third female at that time. My father supported her campaign financially and went door to door putting up lawn signs for her. He felt enormous pride knowing that a Rappaport had been elected to the state senate. Living away from our family's influence on Massachusetts politics allowed her to forge a separate identity in her own way. Martha tells me that it was unnerving to read our mother's novel and to see her perspective on being a state senator, running for governor, and mastering the organizational skills around the political campaign. "The attention to detail, the use of note cards to record information on each individual, how Mama describes 'the secret weapon in the coming campaign that filled nine file drawers.'" Martha remembers that "Mama used to do it also for Christmas cards as well—name, address, names of children, whether a card was sent or received each year. I had the same 'system' when I ran for state senator. The information became critical as I determined who was with me, who wasn't, and how best to approach them." The thrill of strategic maneuvering is palpable as my sister talks, though dread is more likely what my mother felt when she was using her negotiation skills to try to win custody of her children.

Martha teases me that she was the one responsible for brushing my hair into tight pigtails, but Amy, next in line, is whom I remember as my caretaker, reading to me, introducing me to her friends at school, and teaching me that for those who have been given much we have a responsibility to give back. Amy is the sister whom I share the most with about my search to understand our mother, and she still has a fierce loyalty to her. In my mother's papers I found a poem that she wrote to Amy that is adoring and playful, and I was surprised how it made me feel just a bit envious.

TO AMY AMELIA RAPPAPORT,
GIRL WONDER

To Amy my darling dear girl
This child whom I love is a pearl
She's so sweet and so kind
All the words I can't find
All her virtues and good to unfurl.

Oh, Amy I love you, my sweet,
And now for your birthday a treat
You must follow the thread for your treasure
And I hope it all gives you much pleasure
And all of your wishes do meet.

But if in the back of your mind
A need or two you should find
Here's an IOU for your wish
Be it sweater or crayon or fish
Here's my love at the end of the line.

Amy repaid this devotion and adored my mother back. When she was 7 years old, she tells me, she refused to eat in protest of Mama's restricted visitation during the custody battle. She was hospitalized for five days and the doctors prescribed a diet of ice cream frappes. Our mother camped out at Amy's hospital bed, a slumber party of sorts, and Amy wished that they could stay at the hospital forever. She was 9 when our mother committed suicide.

Amy met her husband, Juan Arambula, when they were at Harvard. The son of Mexican migrant workers, Juan arrived at Harvard with a full scholarship and one suitcase. According to Juan, they were both at a party and Amy, feeling mischievous, threw a cream pie into his face unprovoked. "I am either going to hate this woman or marry her," he told friends ruefully at the time.

But for Amy, Harvard was too close to home. She dropped out her sophomore year and fled to California, putting a continent between herself and her pain. Like my mother, she had a baby every two years, in the same effort to fill an emptiness. She also helped to support Juan's political career as he moved from being a member of the School Committee to Fresno supervisor and finally to state representative. During Juan's first campaign, Dad traveled to California to help him get elected; he told me, "Juan was the underdog against two Anglos, and I helped him hire a campaign manager and more TV time." Amy went back to school twenty years later, earning her law degree once her children had grown up.

Today Amy has striking cropped white hair. She shuns physical exercise as a form of torture. She is feisty—her eyes will shoot you a warning look if you cross her—but she is always available to me. Amy is Juan's protective, shrewd, and unofficial campaign manager, although her outspoken manner sometimes gets her in trouble. Juan has charted a thirty-year career in public service through rough-and-tumble California politics. Together, they have raised four children—Carmen, Joaquin, Miguel, and Diego—and her children tell me that she has been very private about her feelings toward our mother and how she died. Amy proudly makes rice and beans, without sacrificing her steady diet of macaroni and cheese, white bread, and sugary coffee and takes great joy in being a grandmother to Carmen's son. I never really appreciated the organizational skills and commitment it took for Juan and Amy to run their campaigns until I went out to Fresno one year to assist them. I watched as my sister helped to orchestrate a victory. In her intensity, I saw a deep and persistent need to even the score. She still feels bitter that my father robbed my mother of what was rightfully hers when he took custody of us. Amy's determination to do battle to vindicate a perceived injustice wherever she might find it comes from the deep wound she suffered over losing someone she could not protect.

Sister number three is Judy—strong willed, dramatic, intense. Of all of us, Judy looks the most like our mother, with lively eyes that flash with a take-charge spirit. Judy tells me that her last memory of our parents together was of a heated argument and that "Mama said she was leaving forever." Her voice sounding forlorn, which makes her seem small, she adds "and then Mama was taken out of the house on a stretcher." She is remembering, I think, my mother's first suicide attempt. Does Judy have her own memories of overwhelming helplessness and imaginary responsibilities, her own guilt at not saving our mother herself? Judy was 8 when our mother died, old enough to have felt the loss acutely, old enough to want to take care of me and her younger brother in a way that she wanted to be cared for herself, old enough to hide her bewilderment, but much too young to make sense of why our family imploded.

Judy loves to perform, and tells me how Mama would direct little plays next to the woodpile in the garage with a troupe that included several neighborhood children—Judy in a pink tutu, the boys in robes. I have always admired Judy's dramatic impulse. She used to have a mercurial temper, but now she is less inclined to flare. After my mother died, my big sister Judy and I took care of each other. She was often my chaperone, fearlessly navigating streets while holding my hand. We would arrive early at school after a bus trip that included two transfers and a couple of sugar-glazed donuts so Judy could sing in the school's Small Chorus. At night we stayed up late playing Hearts and Honeymoon Bridge, and when we were hungry we would sneak down to the kitchen to mix mounds of butter with confectioner's sugar and gorge on the sweet sticky paste. Some nights Judy worried that intruders might come out of the woods and scale up the terrace and onto the second floor. We'd listen, terrified to hear any sound, and to frighten them away we would sing resolutely, "We're not scared of dying and we don't really care." She has often felt overlooked and not given credit for how much responsibility she took for all the children in our family after our mother died. It is touching to me that she has been involved with supporting an organization that provides care for children in disadvantaged situations throughout the world and has set up seven Montessori classrooms in orphanages and public schools in Romania where our father's great-grandfather was born.

Judy is smart and quick to put people at ease. She knows how to build a team and to challenge people to reach outside their comfort zones. She has a confidence about her capacity for "transformation," and she is inclined to think in terms of "unbelievable connectivity." Judy now lives in Sedona, Arizona, where she is receptive to "enlightenment." Not surprisingly, she is impatient with my approach toward making sense of our family history. Although Judy has interviewed many people who knew my mother and father and has constructed an extensive family tree for both sides of our family, she wants to idealize our past and package it neatly in a box, "celebrating mother's mothering." She would prefer to dismiss my incessant curiosity. To Judy, I am simply "stuck in the past."

Judy recently delivered news to me about what she had received during a séance with a psychic in Arizona. The psychic channeled the revelation that our mother had not killed herself after all. "You know how Mama liked to write," Judy announced. "She was writing in the middle of the night and accidentally took a dose of barbiturates with alcohol—she didn't mean to leave us." I'm not sure what to do with Judy's belief and refrain from expressing my incredulity. I can't argue with someone who claims to have direct communication with my dead mother, but I wonder what I am supposed to do with her interpretation. Suicide was our mother's trump card. Both my sister and I are left making a bid to understand. It is not so much about a winning move; it is our effort to put Mama to rest.

As a child, Jim, the older of the two boys, was proud that he could drink seven Cokes a day (my mother's favorite drink) and never get a cavity. He is still amused by the possibility of defying the odds and redefining the rules for clean living. Now a tall, imposing man but compact and looking so much like my dad, Jim has a big presence, a politician's presence—he's hard to miss when he's in the room, and he tends to bellow when making conversation. He's quick to take the pulse of a room, knowing just how long to hold his gaze while he scans the crowd, identifying whom he needs to speak to next.

When I asked Jim to share his memories of Mama with me, he answered that he wasn't sure which would be harder—to cling to the real memories that are left when a person is gone or to have "ghost" memories, memories you know are not accurate and leave you wondering what you missed. He remembers sitting in the bathroom with her as she explained "the birds and the bees." She was loving: "definitely a hugger." He describes going to the Public Garden with her to hand out leaflets for a campaign and swimming next to her in our pool.

Jim was named after his maternal grandfather and great-grandfather. Perhaps in naming her first boy James my mother was bestowing upon him the responsibility of carrying on her family's political legacy. I have an old campaign brochure printed for my mother's run for School Committee and inside there is a picture of her with Jim. He's grinning proudly as her dutiful and unofficial campaign manager, holding a pile of pamphlets. He could not have been more than 5 when this picture was taken, but it's easy to see his adoration of my mother.

She killed herself when he was 7, and as we talk, he looks at me with cold calculation and does an inventory—first Mama died, then Grandma, and then our nanny Bernice, and then his first girlfriend, who killed herself at 15, three months after he broke up with her. As far as I know, however, no one ever helped Jim with his losses until his second wife coaxed him into a little self-reflection.

There is something poignant in the fact that Jim, who loved politics before he could even read, has had such a bumpy political career. Jim served for about five years as the Massachusetts Republican state chairman and has also been a member of the Republican National Committee, mirroring the work of our grandfather, the former chairman of the Democratic State Committee. But my brother's ambitions went beyond organizing, and he has coveted a higher office. Jim's first campaign was in 1990, when he ran aggressively against the incumbent John Kerry for the U.S. Senate. Although Jim lost, he received almost a million votes. At times my brother has wanted to convert me, but we now have a truce and avoid debating our political differences. Jim did not run for office again until 2002, this time for lieutenant governor to Mitt Romney. But Mitt Romney was not interested in having Jim as his running mate and Jim lost in the primary. I often pride myself on being a competent professional on my own terms, but when my brother is getting public attention I am linked to him at surprise moments.

One day when I was pregnant with Zoe, my third child, I got a call from Jim, who was uncharacteristically worried about his 4-year-old son, Joshua. His youngest son, eight months older than my son Cory, was being transferred to the Children's Hospital emergency room. What had started out as a tummy ache turned out to be an extremely rare kidney tumor. The doctors gave Joshua less than a 5 percent chance of survival. I stayed with my brother's wife, Cecilia, overnight in the hospital playroom after the doctors informed her of the diagnosis. She said that she wanted to die, just to not have to deal with an unfolding nightmare. Reflecting back on this dark time, she says: "You wouldn't let me—you told me my son needed me more than ever and went padding off to find bran muffins in an all-night deli."

Joshua was a trouper and not to be underestimated. After surgery and rounds of chemotherapy, he emerged to beat the odds. That experience changed Jim profoundly. I sensed that he made a private bargain with God to spare his son in return for public service. He made good on his promise and is now a major benefactor of Children's Hospital and the Dana Farber Cancer Institute. People turn to Jim, not only to ask for political advice but also to understand how to manage unbearable anguish. When Jim and Cecilia rallied and doted on Joshua—bringing him his favorite food and *Lion King* videos to the hospital, designing a 200-person party for his fifth birthday with clowns and pony rides—they were marking their enormous relief that this potential loss was averted.

But the celebration of surviving cancer is so different from the shame that comes from a mother who attempts or commits suicide—none of us have become the poster child to champion research to discover the cure for suicide. Jim does not talk about our mother's death without my pushing him. He thinks my mother would be proud of the job that Dad did raising us in "adverse circumstances" and wonders whether Mama was bipolar or depressed. "If we knew what we know today and she got treatment for bipolar or depression," he speculates, "would it have saved her?" He tells me that she could be emotional and that there were long periods of her being even-keeled, alternating with periods of crying. He woke up one night to go to the bathroom—

it must have been 2:00 in the morning—and she was frantically making cookies in the kitchen. He says that our mother would obsess over the Christmas tree, putting up and then taking down the decorations. Perhaps Jim's memories have evolved so that he can understand her suicide in a way that eases his sadness. I'm not always sure what to think: Was she frantic and directionless? Or was my mother feeling confined in her marriage?

The baby boy in the family photograph taken on the couch is Jerry, proudly named after my father. Like my father, Jerry is larger than life. Six-foot-two with size 13 shoes, he is powerful and boisterous with an enormous voice. And he has cobalt eyes, like my grandfather Arthur's. Jerry is quite accomplished—president of a successful real estate investment fund. But Jerry is also funny, irreverent, and down-to-earth, often dressed in his favorite Patriots, Celtics, or Red Sox team jacket, impatient with pretense. He can be sentimental and extravagant in a childish way. When he turned 40 he orchestrated a party in Jamaica for fifty of his closest friends and his wife surprised him by showing up in a Mary Poppins costume with a huge sun umbrella. He deploys his considerable skills in progressive urban planning—playing Robin Hood when he can, usually just under the radar. Jerry likes to pursue projects that focus on high-quality, low-income housing, good jobs, and civic pride.

Growing up, Jerry and I spent hours playing tennis in the driveway outside our house, lobbing balls and jokes back and forth. But now my brother Jerry, who was 6 when our mother died, can barely talk about her, even now. I respect his privacy.

∞

I am the youngest in the family portrait. I'm the doctor. I want to help make it all better. Here, I would say, tell me where it hurts. I have wanted to be a doctor for as long as I can remember—even before the moment I realized that there was more candy in toy doctors' kits than there was in the nurses' kits. I would check for fevers with my brothers and spit Jell-O into a spoon and pretend it was medicine. As a doctor, I was no longer a powerless 4-year-old. I was sure I could do something to make it better. But, in fact, I could not.

Caretaker is a role I am drawn to. I feel steady and sure when I am near the dying, the psychotic, the desperate. I'm okay when surrounded with dread, and eager to provide reassurance. A psychiatrist would say that this is a case of reaction formation—the man who is terrified of snakes becomes a snake charmer—and that one of the ways I dealt with losing my mother's comfort has been to provide comfort myself. I need to know I can face the free-fall panic head-on and not be swept away.

I remember driving to kindergarten in my father's big station wagon. We usually passed a cemetery along the way, and soon after my mother died I would announce repeatedly in a singsong voice, jumping up and down in the back seat, pointing out the window of the car, almost gleeful, "There's where Mama is buried, there's where Mama is buried." Years later, Dad was incredulous as we debated whether he responded by finding an alternative route to school. He told me he wasn't invited to the funeral, so he "didn't know where Mama was buried. [He] wasn't conscious of doing something just to disconnect."[4] Like so many children, I blurted out, without inhibition, the unspeakable in my family. If I could have asked, I'd have wanted to know *everything*—What was my mother like, did I look like her, what were her favorite foods, how much did she love us, what did my father love about her, why did they fight, why did she run away, why was she so unhappy that she would kill herself, didn't she want someone to save her and when no one did, was she afraid when she died?

But as a child, I could not be reassured that my mother's death was reasonable. When I was in first grade, at recess I would stand poised on the jungle-gym—the cold metal in my hands—wondering what would happen if I jumped the ten feet to the ground. I would survey the expansive beech tree from my perch on the horizontal bars, watching other kids running in the fields. I tried to get the nerve to jump, wondering if I could join my mother. If I broke my leg, everyone would see how much I was hurting; they would sign my cast and I would get to use crutches.

In fourth grade, I was comforted by a teacher with blue-gray hair, a strict manner but warm smile who wore pleated wool skirts and encouraged me to write. And write I did, a fifty-page paper on Iceland in minuscule hand-writing, presenting it for two class periods and serving up rhubarb pie that I made for my class (rhubarb being a popular vegetable in Iceland).

And then at the end of fourth grade, I wrote a story called "Franny's Trial with Love," which I have safeguarded on my bookshelf over the years. When I reread this story now I can see why. Children often write stories that have a dreamlike significance rather than a literal translation. I wrote about the first four years of a baboon's life, but it doesn't take much imagination to see the relevance to my life. Displacement is the transfer of emotions, ideas, or wishes from the original object (say, a father) to a substitute (perhaps the giant in "Jack and the Beanstalk"). Young children cannot easily talk about how they make meaning about such powerful feelings as loss, love, death, and aggression, but in displacement they have the safe distance to explore more freely how they feel. As I decipher the meaning of this story about a chimp and a baboon and her mother, it conveys that I might have believed at that time that she was unjustly murdered, unable to tolerate that she would choose to leave me:

> Franny was born in the Savannah of Africa. She was bewil-dered at the sight around her. In the three hours that she had been alive, she had seen the whole Chatma Herd. Each baboon had come up to see the princess of their herd.
>
> Franny cuddled toward her mother. Ma licked her warmly and put her big arms around her affectionately. Franny felt her head nodding and in less than five minutes she was in dream-land. She slept soundly in her bed woven of green leaves. She was awakened by a short harsh yap, the yap of danger. The herd

was up on their feet. Franny's mother gently pushed Franny upon her back. . . .

Chimp swirled around. There was no man, but he was sure he had smelled man. They were hiding. He'd find them. He looked around with his sharp beady eyes. Then he saw a spear heading towards him. He ducked. He had missed it. What luck, he thought. But then four spears came at him from all directions.

He sank to the ground and died. "We've killed him," the evil people called and they picked up Chimp and started back towards the zoo. When they went through the gate a loud scream was heard from Franny. They were carrying Chimp.

Everything came back to her mind. All the nice things Chimp had done to her. She thought to herself, "There is only one thing I can do to repay, halfway, all the things Chimp has done for me. Chimp, I'm coming with you to heaven." With a cry, she smashed her head against the concrete and cracked her head and died.

There is not one living thing that is as loyal as Franny and Chimp were, and there probably never will be. Chimp and Franny did go up to heaven and there they live from that day and for every day.[5]

In my child's mind it is the "evil people" who have killed someone I love. It has taken me a long time to realize there are no villains in our family tragedy. Still, there is a violent disturbing death that was confusing to me. Somehow there is no ability to protect loved ones from harm, but after the death there is the solace in the hope to go to heaven and to never leave each other. It is interesting to me that the dead chimpanzee was carried back to a zoo, which is a place for live animals to be viewed. I wonder how I could have understood that there was something very public about my mother's death, that her misery was somehow on display and that there was a real "trial." Yet I know from my own work with families that we often are incredulous at how much children understand without our telling them explicitly.

∞

A December morning, gray sky heavy, and I am out early on the road as I have jury duty in Lowell, an industrial city just north of Boston. I have never been in a courthouse before, even though a court drama between my parents had such an impact on our family. Entering the regal courthouse with its marble columns and mosaic tiles—in a hurry I pause to admire them— I then scurry through the dim halls into the designated waiting room. I am well stocked with knitting for what I anticipate will be a long day on standby. Settling into the waiting area, I survey my fellow citizens.

After twenty minutes, we're escorted to the courtroom and firmly instructed to rise when the judge enters. The courtroom is filled with gray light and a musty smell. Huge arched windows look out on the smokestacks and bridges over the Merrimac River. The judge has an affable smile on his worn face and an intent gaze. He towers at his perch with leather-bound volumes in a wooden bookcase behind him. Clearly in command, he is the director of these proceedings, and we are the extras.

The defendant, a youngish man, sits cowering at an oblong table, the muscle tone of his shoulders visible underneath his white button-down shirt. After a brief civics lesson, the judge begins to tell us the nature of the alleged crime, and the room grows quiet. We are apprehensive and somber in the way that people are before a funeral. The defendant, says the judge, is accused of murdering his infant. The word *infant* hangs out in the stale air, a sanitized technical term for this man's baby son. The infant. The baby. I look at the father. What was the precipitating event? I'm a doctor who sometimes treats teenagers when they have seen or experienced more than they should, but I am not accustomed to holding the abuser accountable.

The judge starts the process of jury selection and there is a visceral sense of unease in the courtroom, as if we are realizing simultaneously that we have just boarded the *Titanic*. He questions us one at a time. I rationalize that it will be intellectually stimulating to see how the trial system operates. It is an honor to uphold justice and to accept this responsibility of determining guilt or innocence. And what if the defendant did commit this heinous crime? Twenty potential jurors have been dismissed, and four are selected. There are twenty of us left as the soft winter light now casts pale shadows. The numbers are not looking great for freedom, as fifteen jurors are needed.

Suddenly there is commotion in the courtroom—one of the prosecuting attorneys has fainted. We all strain to see, and I worm my way toward the bench, stuffing my knitting into my bag, moving from the bench to the judge. I tell the judge as I advance that I am a doctor, and I kneel down next to the prostrate woman who is wearing a trim suit and high heels. Her knee is bent to the side and it looks uncomfortable, so I take her leg and gently straighten it. The lawyers stand around, not sure what to do. Someone calls 911. Abruptly she comes back to consciousness and struggles to sit up, looking slightly bewildered, shaking her straight blonde hair back into position. "I'm Dr. Rappaport," I say, as if to reassure myself that I have the authority to take charge.

How do I make sense of this situation? A woman fainted and even though my emergency response skills are rusty, I was willing to take responsibility. Yet minutes earlier I recoiled from the task of helping to determine whether a father killed his child. And what do I make of the shift of authority I felt as I took the lawyer's pulse, reassuring her that she was safe—safe with me—as we waited for the ambulance? It was deliverance, maybe, or a narrow escape from having to weigh the evidence that a father could kill a helpless child. I am more comfortable with taking care of people, protecting life, than I am in assigning blame.

A few days later, I enter my own therapist's home office through the back door of her house, making my way past the sprawling Japanese red maple and her ever-changing garden. I know the shift of her plants across the seasons, from bobble-headed daffodils to pale pink peonies to somber purple spires of monkshood in September. These weekly sessions, which I have been coming to for over a decade, are natural and comforting to me. Therapy has been a regular part of my life since I was in high school, except for a short hiatus when I was in college and in medical school. My relationship with Dr. Johnson, a psychiatrist and analyst, began during the first year of my psychiatry residency and has continued through the growth of my family. My daughter Lila always looks at me incredulously when I leave for my appointments and shakes her head. "Doesn't therapy ever *end*?" she asks.

Dr. Johnson's small office is stuffed floor to ceiling with books and journals with titles such as *Interpreting Dreams*, *The Psychoanalytic Quarterly*, and *The Family Crucible*. There is a brown leather analyst's couch tucked into the side of the room (I have never used it; I am too active to lie down) and nearby, a solid rocking chair, firm and straight.

Dr. Johnson has skin that is looser for the wear, thin wrists, and a tidy way of dressing in little knit cardigans and brown pumps with buckles. She usually starts by asking if the room is warm enough. She then settles into her rocking chair, listening keenly to what I'm saying, the rocking chair never moving. She approaches me with a surprising nonchalance. During this particular session as December vacation approaches, I tell her I'm excited about a trip we're planning to Costa Rica. We've rented a house on the beach. We're going to hike. It will be Zoe's seventh birthday, too, and I want to plan a party for her while we are there, with pink streamers and a cake. I talk about how when we are together as a family in an unfamiliar place, we grow close, how these adventures bind us to one another, and then I blurt out in a voice that is unfamiliar to me that I would have liked to have traveled with *my* mother, to have known her out of her element, to have seen who she really was.

Dr. Johnson looks at me and asks casually, "What about your fury at your mother for leaving you?"

I dismiss this too quickly, as if to be furious at my mother is to betray her. It's much easier for me to have my mother be a victim. I don't want to rage at her for this hole in my life—I'm more comfortable raging at my father who is still here.

My beeper goes off, distracting me. I push it aside without looking at it, thinking I'll postpone answering the call until after the session.

Dr. Johnson brings the question back into focus. We go on to explore the need to integrate the good and the bad in one individual. We talk about how adolescents learn to see that the omnipotent parents of their childhood are actually parents with clay feet, capable of making mistakes. This perspective also allows us to be more forgiving of ourselves. There is no such thing as pure love and pure hate; we vacillate between both sides with those people who matter most to us. My confusion, she points out, is that my allegiances, my alliances, may shift. Dad fought twice to maintain custody of me, once with my mother when I was 2 years old, and then with my stepmother when I was in seventh grade. Even though he can be impossible at times, he is present. My mother is not even here for me to kill off.

Dr. Johnson goes on to say that if both parents are alive during adolescence, then the teenager can become disillusioned by her parents' shortcomings. The teenager can throw them both out and then reclaim the flawed parents. My beeper goes off for a second time, and this time I look—there is a 911 at the end of the number. This is a code that staff at the teen health center and my kids use to signal me to respond immediately to the page. Realizing that this page is from the nurse at Cory's school, for a moment I can't breathe. I fumble with my phone.

The nurse's voice is small and flat: "Cory fell off a platform while trying to catch a ball during recess and split open his forehead." It's a small cut, she reassures me, but he needs stitches. I close my eyes, praying that Cory is okay, and tell Dr. Johnson that Cory is hurt. Bolting from the room, I run, taking the stairs two at a time, frantic inside, but also thinking that I'm glad I don't need to rearrange patients before running to his side and relieved that I don't have to kick my mother off her pedestal.

I worry that Cory might have a hematoma, a pooling of blood under his skull that could put pressure on his brain and cause a seizure. I know it's a fear grown out of some remnant of worst-case scenarios left over from my pediatric internship and my tendency to catastrophize from my experience of sudden loss. Still, I race down the cinderblock corridor of the school, stopping for a half-second before the door to compose myself. The principal looks oversized in a small student chair as he talks to Cory. The nurse is industriously shining a light into Cory's eyes. I ask anxiously if his pupils are equal and reactive to light, and they look at me as if I'm from Mars. When I wrap Cory in my arms, he begins to cry.

I hold Cory's hand and continue to pray that he is okay as we make our way to the car. When we get to Children's Hospital, my husband, Colin, meets us at the emergency room entrance. The surgeon closes the wound and reassures us that Cory has had no loss of consciousness and does not need a CT scan as his bruise is small and well defined.

In the evening when we are all home together, Cory carries on like a wounded warrior, having survived the numbing shot and sutures. He's shaken from the realization that he's vulnerable to accidents; this is his second mishap requiring stitches, though he is a relatively cautious boy. Colin makes Cory's favorite dinner, grilled hamburgers and pasta. Zoe is fascinated by the bandage over Cory's eye and coaxes him to uncover the wound. Lila protectively drapes her arm around her brother. She gives him a kiss on the cheek and says affectionately, "Poor bro, bro." When I get up to go for a quick run around the block with Zoe, Cory says quietly, "Don't leave me now." I hold him tightly. Clearly, living parents leave; we leave to go to work, we withdraw when we are preoccupied and testy—but we always return. In this raw state, Dr. Johnson's words come back to me. I am furious with my mother, asking her why she didn't resist her rage so that I would not cower against my rage and run afraid. Why couldn't she have managed her fears so *she* could be ready when we needed to call her with a 911 at the end?

Chapter Six

If you lived here, you'd be home now.

—BILLBOARD FOR
CHARLES RIVER PARK, 1967

I pick up Lila from school on a cloudy afternoon. When I see her, now 16 and holding a newly acquired learner's permit, I get out of the car and go around to the passenger's seat so she can practice driving by taking us home. As she slips behind the wheel, she glares at me with a skeptical glance.

"What's the matter, Lila?" I ask, knowing already that I have done something wrong.

"How come you never told me about the West End?" she asks impatiently.

I'm dumbfounded. When in doubt, stall for time and ask for clarification. If anything, I'm usually faulted for giving too much information and for being too transparent with my children. When Lila is really annoyed with me, she says dismissively, "You're acting like a psychiatrist," which is intended to be an insult. I say now, "I didn't realize it was a secret. What do you want to know?"

"Where exactly is the West End?" she asks.

"The West End is where Grandpa built lots of apartment buildings—Charles River Park—across from the Museum of Science, Mass General Hospital, and near the Longfellow Bridge with those salt and pepper shaker towers, and Beacon Hill." Okay, I say to myself, you've outlined the territory, but what about the story?

She tells me that one of her Facebook friends sent her a link to a magazine article saying that in the 1960s Jerome L. Rappaport bulldozed Boston's West End neighborhood and made a "killing" selling luxury condos. Pausing at a stoplight, she turns and looks right at me. "The things it *said*. I didn't know that the Rappaport name was *sketchy*. Why didn't you ever tell me?" Sketchy? I sigh. She seems surprised that I'm at a loss for words.

I feel protective of Dad and don't want to tell Lila a complicated, nuanced story about the West End. Grandparents are supposed to be simple and the details of their lives don't usually get closely analyzed. There are gray areas and I want her to be gentle toward her grandfather—after all, he is my father, and loyalty and pride run deep. I can't begin to pretend to give an objective account of the West End. Teenagers think in extremes and don't always moderate their judgment. I finally say, "There are books about the West End if you are interested."[1]

"Mom," she pleads. "People lost their *homes*." She looks at me, waiting for me to say something. "The West End is public knowledge. You should have told me," she says in her practical and pointed way. She tells me that one of her classmates is doing a research project on the West End—she has the *whole* story. Then her attention drifts away as she changes the station on the radio and carefully shifts lanes.

My father bristles at the controversy that has shadowed him and his children and tarnished his reputation even to this day (though his philanthropic work has helped heal his feelings of being misunderstood). His motivation and his excitement about the West End project were generated by his conviction in those early years that he would have more success rebuilding Boston than changing its politics. To him, Boston at the time was a faltering and dying city and the courageous thing, as he saw it, was undertaking the largest development the city had ever seen to try to help bring the middle class and the professional leadership back in. I tend to believe that his actions were taken also for financial gain, even though there were legitimate urban-renewal reasons to redesign the city to motivate the middle class to return to the city. Some considered the West End a beloved, integral part of the city with 11,000 working-class people that was bulldozed to make way for my father's multimillion-dollar development, displacing the families who called the West End home. Opportunity and destruction. But in my father's view, the protests came from "diehard nostalgic bitter tenants" of the Old West End, a small minority who decried the loss of their neighborhood and yet had forgotten the area was plagued with a high crime rate and gang violence. He is convinced that he had nothing to do with tearing down the West End, that the land reclamation and razing were done by the Boston Redevelopment Authority utilizing the Federal Housing Act of 1949, with the approval of the city, the commonwealth, the federal governments, and the courts. In his mind the BRA did the tearing down and "we were merely the developers selected by the Authority."

In 1990, when my father received a community service award from the American Jewish Committee, the *Boston Globe* published a profile of my father titled "Controversy Is Rappaport's Middle Name."[2] Decades after the West End project was over, it still ignited conflict. The interview was conducted in his thirty-sixth-floor corner office near his "legendary Storrow Drive Sign that announces smugly 'If you lived here, you'd be home now.'"

For the article, he was photographed in a well-tailored suit in front of a canvas of swirling oil paint and a piece of metal sculpture on a highly polished cocktail table with the caption "I have no concern with what people think of me at all!" The reporter invited him to "look into an imaginary mirror and define what he sees in the context of the controversial West End project." She wrote that "he is seen as either the heartless real estate scoundrel, the alien meddler by his enemies or as someone who has taken the bum rap, a mercurial man forced to defend his hard-won victories." My father seemed to respond to the reporter's questions as if he was confident he would gain sympathy during the interview. He came across like a coach explaining his game plan:

- "When I embark on a goal, I believe I can achieve it. Pursuing the Charles River Park project was an act of faith. I was willing to fight those who stood for the status quo. I was willing to fight those who said it couldn't be done."

- "For this I have been called audacious."

- "For this I have been called shrewd."

- "A maverick is a person who marches to his own tune, someone willing to stand alone. I've stood alone more than once. I think of myself as a maverick. But I'm a maverick who does things with a sense of purpose."

- "I'm a leader. At its best, leadership is having the people around you believe that what you're doing and what you're leading them into is a shared endeavor."

- "When you make either a political decision or an economic decision, it's like playing the game of chess. You have to know the consequences that could result from your move."

Just five days after Lila was born, I was invited to speak at the dinner celebrating my father's Community Service Human Relations award. Bundling Lila up with her top-heavy head, I made my way past a small gathering of shouting protesters with pickets stating "We shall not forget." As Milan Kundera said, the "struggle of man against power is the struggle of memory against forgetting."[3] With a neighborhood destroyed, a small group of West Enders have tenaciously fought for acknowledgment of their loss, tangible reparation, and an apology. As I walked past the demonstrators, I worried that I was on the wrong side and that by celebrating this award I was somehow negating their pain, whereas my brother Jim says that the lesson *he* learned is that Dad should have been much more aggressive in presenting his side. He says that Dad should have rebutted the "urban legend" that he was somehow responsible for clearing the West End neighborhood to develop Charles River Park when in actuality this was a federal program of urban renewal to clear forty-eight acres. He is adamant that very little opposition was expressed until after the approval for my father's buildings, although when I pull newspaper articles there is some controversy about the bidding process. I have memories of long afternoons in the Charles River Park pool racing down the slide with my brothers and daring each other to jump off the high diving board. But I also remember as a sophomore in high school standing awkwardly at the last towers' groundbreaking ceremony in the 1970s and seeing protesters, and suddenly understanding why my best friend's grandparents would always say with a bite, "You're Jerry *Rappaport's* daughter." The idea that my father was responsible for a travesty and that he made a big profit from the agony of a displaced community resonated with me. I felt guilt by association. Why was it so difficult for my father to recognize their loss?

During the five years that it took for my father to get approval for the West End development, my parents had three more children. The negotiations with the City Council were sometimes contentious, and it was touch and go for my father to secure adequate financing. My father was on what he saw as a crusade to bring vitality back to a barren land; he saw it as an act of courage to take a risk to build in a city where there had been urban flight and little new construction. My mother kept herself occupied. She earned her master's degree and participated in many local and state campaigns. She and my father launched a campaign for a liberal candidate running for governor and changed diapers and entertained friends. In early July 1960, when I was 10 months old and my oldest sister was 9 years old, my parents took off for California to attend the Democratic National Convention; the candidates included John F. Kennedy, Lyndon B. Johnson, and Adlai Stevenson. My parents were gone for a little more than a week, and my mother wrote home to us almost every other day.

Dear Family all!

What a surprise! It takes as long to get to California as it does to get to Europe! All these years I've known the distance was the same but I didn't feel the actuality of it. Of course, the plane ride was much more fun, though it didn't appear to start that way. . . . When we got on the plane, the stewardess waved:"any seat, please, we're about to take off." And there we were in those luxurious 1st class seats that I envied so all the way to Europe and back! And they're worth every dollar, even though I can get along without a linen tablecloth and shrimp cocktail and a choice of steak or lobster for lunch.

At Chicago, I pretended to be asleep in a lovely window seat while Daddy battled the authorities (he won, claimed we had paid for that kind of seating!). That plus the $30 of extra baggage they didn't charge us put us on top of the world. . . .

San Francisco is beginning very well. The airport is lovely and we rented a car, a white '60 Plymouth (have a convertible on order but may not be able to get it). . . . Amazing to see palm trees in the park in this 60-degree weather and how they built anything on these hills is beyond us. Are we sissies to be leveling the West End?

We went to the "Hungry I" which was interesting though the talent wasn't first rate, and on to a coffee house which was beyond description. Out, man, way out. The cabdriver had taken us to a clean chrome respectable coffee house and Daddy asked for something more bohemian. Disgustedly, the cabdriver said this is it, then reluctantly drawled unless you want something beatnik like this

around the corner. Right down to the dirty clothes, long hair, beards, misce-
genation, and a marvelous jazz trio. It closed on us and we went to a bookstore
full of beat talk and open when we left at 2:30. . . .

I've been writing this in a room full of people so that if it doesn't make sense
draw your own conclusions but I don't think I've lost my sanity. Of course, out
here where there are a thousand rumors a minute it looks like Stevenson still
has a chance, but I suppose everything is all sewed up at home. It will all be over
and we'll be on our way home by the time you get this so it will all be old hat to
you but the excitement of charge and counter-charge is at its height here. . . . We
saw both Kennedy and Stevenson in the lobby this morning and they were both
being followed by people looking like ants after sugar!

We love your letters and are so happy that everything is running smoothly.
We're having a wonderful time and Martha's lovely letter has made us even
gayer and more carefree. How happy you all sound at camp. It is so good to
know that you are in good hands. We love you all.

Mama and Daddy

It was the last trip they would take together. When they returned, my father and Mayor Hynes gathered a small group in front of reporters and stuck a shovel into the ground to start the construction of Emerson, the first of the West End's new towers.

The sheer magnitude of the project kept my father working late, and I wonder if he resented being apart from his family, isolated in all the details of such a mammoth undertaking. When he talks about it now, he never complains about the grueling politics and he leaves out the inevitable self-doubts he had while undertaking such a venture. He never complains aloud, at least to me, that the demands of the West End were too much for him or cost him his marriage. "All in a day's work," he says.

I wonder if he was discouraged by the controversy. But my brothers Jim and Jerry are also developers, and when I ask them what it is like to imagine and then realize something so large, they laugh. You don't understand it, they tell me. I see building a new development as loaded with risks, with management and financial challenges that I'd find daunting. What I don't get, Jim explains to me, is the "rush" that comes with solving problems and getting things done every day. You're dealing with demanding schedules, big contracts, monstrous egos, and large sums of money. If you're lucky, you're getting a chance to make a difference and leave a legacy, something that will stand for hundreds of years in brick and concrete. You're changing a neighborhood or a city *permanently*. It's thrilling, he tells me. What I don't get, Jim says, is the "jazz" of the deal, and that, he believes, is what Dad loved best. The jazz elated him: It was addicting and irresistible.

I am not sure how my mother felt about this controversial development, but I know that if she was going to run for political office, she would need to recognize that some might be suspicious of her motives because they thought that Dad had profited from his political connections. In her novel she seems to be wistful for a shared passion:

> Oh, what I would have given to see him again, faintly shabby in a baggy tweed suit and the traditional pipe of the intellectual young man in politics, his ideals intact, his enthusiasm un-challenged, his energies channeled so magnificently into worthwhile, practical reform. Where had it all gone wrong? Where had the turn come so that he too ended up the suc-cessful businessman with no time left for crusading, with no courage left to climb out on limbs, with no freedom left to do what was right rather than expedient? He felt that his manip-ulations, because they were grandiose, were honest, because they were successful, were virtuous.[4]

My mother wasn't part of the development jazz. My mother's friend Sydell describes her as a good mother to her kids at home—yet she had aspira-tions that went beyond the household tasks: "She had dreams to fulfill. Her focus was elsewhere. She was incredibly efficient, but not exactly the kind of person that I would talk about diapers with or ask if she had tried a wonderful recipe."[5]

Over time, my mother's interest in politics intensified. With my father's encouragement, she decided to run for the Boston School Committee herself, challenging candidates like Louise Day Hicks, who would go on to oppose the desegregation of Boston's schools. She focused on the 1961 election and got to work. She promoted herself as a "clear-thinking, hardworking candidate whose sincere interest has been proved by years of extensive volunteer service to a greater Boston Community." She kept letters of solicitation that my father sent to potential contributors in which he said that "Nancy is working very hard. I think she has a good chance of winning and you and I both know she would make an exceptional public servant."

Peggy Melgard, one of her best friends at this time, describes a small brunch, a political gathering that took place when my mother had started to run for the School Committee:[5] "It was the wrong time—July or August—and only three or four people showed up. Your mother was sitting on a pink stuffed chair and as people were asking questions about her election, she carried on as if fifty people were there. She had grown up with politics in her family. She knew what went on behind the scenes, and she loved the intrigue and gossip. She had a strong organizational self."[6] But as the pace of election preparation picked up, a man by the name of Richard Sears accepted the position as my mother's campaign manager. It would soon be an alliance that undid my mother.

Somehow Lila has challenged me to explore a history that cannot be unlived. I want her to dream and be unfettered by family legacy and take some grudging pride in the heritage of enduring strength that can lead to achievement. Of course, I have come to appreciate that I am out on a limb as I try to understand this complicated story that is not always mine to tell. It is like driving a car at night. I can see only as far as the beam of my headlights but I can make the whole trip that way.[7]

Chapter Seven

Those who talk most about the bless-
ings of marriage and the constancy
of its vows are the very people who
declare that if the chain were broken
and the prisoners left free to choose,
the whole social fabric would fly
asunder. You cannot have the argu-
ment both ways. If the prisoner is
happy, why lock him in? If he is not,
why pretend that he is?

—GEORGE BERNARD SHAW,
Man and Superman

Tucked away on a side street in an old Cambridge neighborhood, our house with its cobalt-blue shingles and sloping lines reassures me whenever I come home. Our neighbors include a Nobel Prize–wining physicist who wanders off to work wearing headphones and a backpack; a passionate gardener, her entrepreneur husband, and their lumbering black Lab; a woman who marks spring's arrival by carefully laying window screens on the ground to keep birds from devouring the grass seed. The slope of our roof and tight quarters on the street create the effect of houses shoulder to shoulder with other houses, old friends standing together.

There is equanimity to our house even after two substantial renovations; every time I enter, I have a rooted sense of permanence. The house's Yankee exterior with a slate roof dissolves in an interior of light and glass—sunlight on an oak floor. In renovating this house, my husband, Colin, knew what we needed most. Colin, an architect—lover of luminosity, the strength of steel beams, the different forms of wood—designed the house to be our home, a backdrop of security for our energetic family. Left to my own devices, I'd probably stuff it full of treasured trinkets from our travels and use bold colors. But Colin has a different vision. He's headstrong, and although he incorporates some of my suggestions, design is mostly his domain. And so our house is subdued and calm, with cherry and stone and spare details.

As a California transplant, Colin finds the overcast New England winters challenging. He has made it easy to access the garden by adding large glass doors in the living room and a glassed-in kitchen nook that pushes out into a small green space. Our family migrates to the nook with hydrangeas nestled against the glass outside as Colin delights in preparing breakfast pleasures, tortillas or waffles, sustenance for the day. The evenings are often ours alone. Sometimes on a moonlit snowy night, Colin and I will sit there in the stillness.

I knew when I met Colin for the first time that he was the man I wanted to marry. Less than a week later, he invited me on a ten-day wilderness hike in the Sierra Nevada with some thin excuse that it was hard to find a fellow backpacker. I knew I wasn't alone anymore. The trip was dangerous—we were lost for two days and had to scramble across a glacier that sloped precipitously toward a river turned menacing by the unprecedented summer snowmelt. I was ready to take his lead—cautious, but trusting him.

Four years later, as I prepared for the stresses of my internship, we decided to get married. Right before the ceremony in Vermont at a country church, my father threatened not to walk me down the aisle because he was outraged by some confusion that had delayed the arrival of my sister Amy, her husband, Juan, and their young children. My sister Judy tried to salvage the situation. In her glossy green dress and protective bossy way, Judy instructed Dad to get in line. Colin did not blink when one of my brothers-in-law remarked under his breath that it takes a lot of courage to marry into the Rappaport family. When Amy arrived twenty minutes into the ceremony, it was Colin who encouraged me to start over so that Amy's daughter—8 years old in a multilayered dress of white lace and with fingernails painted cherry red for the first time—could walk down the aisle too, as our flower girl. With the wedding party at my father's farm there was a reggae band and dancing in the fields, and the reminder that our family could celebrate the hope of new beginnings.

Twenty years later, I know that Colin is the right match in ways that I could not have predicted. He is an astute measurer of character and has the kind of warmth and animation that draws people in. His enthusiasm is infectious— I am more likely to curl up for hours and read to the kids, but he can galvanize them to head out on a camping trip or to play soccer in a local park in the rain. His energy daunts me sometimes, as he manages coaching the kids' teams while orchestrating our renovation and running an architectural firm. But his energy isn't frenetic. Colin is focused, persistent, pragmatic, and intense.

He gets annoyed by my habit of interrupting, a survival skill developed over the course of a childhood spent jockeying for position at a dinner table that eventually included eleven children. I interrupt him when I am exuberant or particularly anxious, and then Colin will withdraw, perceiving me as dominating the conversation. I wince at his annoyance. I'm invested in his approval, and even though he's annoyed, I want to feel loved. I wish he saw me more as a rambunctious girl at these times, clamoring for affection.

But usually, we balance each other well. We both need the predictability of routines, but he is meticulous, whereas I can be scattered. He will often give people the benefit of the doubt, and I am more suspicious and judgmental. I can over-interpret—he stays cool. I work with words, looking for pathways to an inner world, while he works at capturing an aesthetic, creating exterior space and security. He needs time to respond and is precise and observant. I am transparent, immediate, and decisive, best in a crisis.

There are times when I'm haunted by my family's perplexing, intrusive demands and disappointing absences. Colin has helped me negotiate these situations. He is able to maneuver within my family without getting lost. His admirable restraint is a balance to my shoot-from-the-hip, take-no-prisoners attitude, and his diplomacy inspires my family's respect. As a result, my father and Phyllis have been magnanimous and kind to Colin. Architecture and real estate provide their common ground.

A few winters ago, Phyllis and my father organized a family gathering in Florida to discuss their estate planning and charitable giving goals. At the time I was quietly working on trying to make sense of my mother's legacy and I opted out. But Colin chose to participate, straddling that fine line between being loyal to me and wanting to understand the information that my dad and Phyllis were sharing. Colin listened conscientiously, providing a filtered connection for me from a safe distance.

Even if Colin doesn't often choose the head-on collision, he has a calculated strength. He doesn't need me to be orthodox, to color inside the lines. He gives me the room I need to feel more confident about who I am without feeling that I have to apologize.

My customary (or reflexive) suspicion that intimacy is somehow dangerous and that you shouldn't completely trust or rely on anyone has abated over the years with him. When I was pregnant with Zoe, Lila and Cory were two young toddlers who would consume anything their hands could grab. I was devastated when Colin announced that he wanted to plant spires of alluring but deadly foxglove in our garden. Bathed in indignant pregnant hormones that exaggerate parenting instincts, I was sure that Colin was being callous. My irrational fear obscured how caring he is of me and of our children. I now am confident he will not hurt us.

In our bedroom, we have a picture of Colin as a child, about 4½, staring at the photographer and brimming with affection. He is an adorable boy with a puckish, mischievous, contagious smile, a turned-up nose, and eyebrows with a distinctive thick, wavy quality expressing permanent astonishment. He is at ease and cooperating with the pose because the picture was taken by his mother. About a year after the photo was taken, she died unexpectedly—a brain hemorrhage cutting off her life at age 32. She left behind Colin, his older brother, and their father.

The disquieting truth is that we both have the same absence in our lives, the experience of growing up without our mothers. We were both encouraged to pick up and move on, and so we did. When we met each other and learned what we shared, we recognized our mutual sadness, even if we have chosen to deal with it in different ways. Once Cory looked at me and astutely observed, "Mama, just because you talk about losing your mother doesn't mean that Papa doesn't miss his."

When the nights grow darker and longer in the weeks before Christmas, Colin can become moody. This is the time of year when his mother died. His irritability is epitomized by the yearly struggle to fit the Christmas tree into that always-too-small Christmas tree stand. We have resolved this now by bringing the stand with us when we go looking for the perfect tree. If only we could remember that the inevitable sense of loss each of us feels around the holidays has its source in memories we cannot reconcile and cannot fix. Yet the mind has an interesting way of migrating back, a shadow that is not so easy to define but is unsettling.

One winter day, I was on edge as I plodded through my routine of an early morning run, dropping off the kids, and getting to work. I was just going through the motions, as I tried to check my spiraling worries and keep myself glued together. Colin took a sleeping pill the night before. It's something that would seem relatively trivial to most people, perhaps, but for me, it is a crack in the sky: Is he really okay, will he leave me, am I too much for him? I know the answers, but they don't reassure me.

He's been having trouble sleeping, and he wanted to be rested as he had a big presentation that morning. I should know better. I should trust him. I'm over-analyzing. But this kind of preoccupation is part of who I am. Ironically, I make my living deciding whether and when to prescribe medications. I know that one sleeping pill can help with the anxiety and insomnia Colin is experiencing. I know this is a rare event for him. But that night as he finally found relief and drifted off, I sat up alone with my worries, bothered by an exaggerated dread that comes from the fact that my mother overdosed on the same type of drug. Colin is my safe harbor. I worry, too, that in my anxiety I am not sympathetic enough.

Our kids know when we are tense, and they hover. They watch us, quiet and concerned. I want to let them know that we are "stressed," to assign a word to what is obvious. If anyone asked how I'm doing, I would say I'm trying to be strong, determined that I'll comfort Colin when he feels forlorn and embrace his tenderness, but the truth is at this moment, I feel vulnerable and inadequate. But over the years I have come to trust the wilderness of our heart, "safe beyond the bounds of what we know," growing confident we can weather the storms.[1]

∞

A few days later, during a routine physical, my doctor interrogated me about my family history, and when I mentioned that my mother had an affair during my parents' marriage and my mother committed suicide, he cautioned me that affairs could be "hazardous to my health" because I might feel so out of control that it would be inordinately destabilizing. I told him that I didn't have any intention, I was happy in my marriage to Colin. But it was a good question: why do people have affairs? I am left wondering what went wrong.

In my mother's novel, Diane finds herself sexually attracted to another man: "Niles was ineffectual among his friends, and among strange men, he was a positive deterrent. With women, because of his almost unconscious flirtation and flattery, he was more dangerous than a nuclear bomb."[2]

In another passage, she provides more detail:

> She looked closely at Niles to see if there was anything that she had missed. He wasn't tall, about 5'8", maybe 5'9", and he was certainly not good-looking, with that huge nose, and receding hairline, and selfish mouth, but there was something about him that was appealing, sort of defenseless. He had beautiful brown eyes, with long, Valentino-like lashes. There was something seductive, almost immoral, in Niles's eyes. . . . She decided that Niles was a ladies' man, not a bad thing to have around a headquarters, to convince the girls to come in and write envelopes, and make telephone calls, but certainly a bad type for a woman's campaign manager.[3]

In the novel, the married Niles becomes Diane's driver, shuttling her from one campaign stop to the next, adoring her from afar. Diane brushes off his attentions yet flirts with him when she feels rejected by her husband. Though she doesn't commit adultery until the end of the novel, she struggles with her attraction to Niles. She avoids her desire throughout the book until it finally wears her out.

Psychiatrists have traditionally understood affairs as a symptom of a deeper problem in a relationship, not simply as a problem with the straying partner. From this perspective, an affair is more complicated than an exciting escape from the confines of a suffocating or disappointing marriage. In *The Family Crucible*, Augustus Napier and Carl Whitaker describe the complex meanings of the "unholy triangle" of adultery as a desperate, often impulsive, and sometimes unconscious plan to break a marital impasse.[4] An affair can be a risky quest to infuse energy into a dead relationship. Although it may be an act of betrayal, Napier and Whitaker postulate that couples decide unconsciously or tacitly to have an affair and that there are no real secrets in marriages. The catalyst for adultery is often set in motion by a married couple having "activated in each other anxieties that plunge them back into the central conflicts in their respective families of origins." The affair can be a dangerous distraction from confronting the "person whom we really love, who touches our very roots, has the capacity to drive us crazy, and it may be only this person who has the capacity to help us find our deepest strengths." They suggest that in a practical way an affair may provide potential for growth if a couple is supported and encouraged to reflect on its meaning. Otherwise, if it leaves an open wound, it is often the beginning of the end of the marriage. A fight polarized around guilt and innocence typically ensues, and while each partner may want forgiveness, the situation may crystallize into a bitter, uncompromising standoff.[5]

Nevertheless, family therapists have largely discredited this view as perpetuating myths about extramarital affairs. Frank Pittman, a psychologist and author of *Private Lies*, posits that affairs are not all alike. Rather, they fall into four broad, distinct categories: accidental affairs that are careless acts; habitual, compulsive philandering where someone enjoys the conquest and the notch on his or her belt; the crazy romantic falling in love (often prompted by a crisis); and the rare marital arrangement in which the couple tacitly agree to satisfy their needs with other partners while remaining married (this last is an infrequent occurrence).[6]

Pittman advises therapists treating couples where infidelity has occurred or where there is a risk of infidelity to address the myths of infidelity and marriage.[7] The mistaken idea that affairs are inevitable is countered by the fact that most married people do not choose to have affairs.[8] He disagrees that an affair is a collusion by partners, and he argues that this erroneous belief (shared by many therapists) takes the responsibility away from the cheating partner. Many therapists assume a fairly neutral stance about the momentous decision to have an affair and do not warn that this decision can seriously derail a good marriage. Rather, they choose to focus on the guilt that can plague their patients. Pittman argues that when affairs occur, it is not always because of unhappiness in the marriage; rather, there may be a faltering in the marriage commitment and a decision to abandon this bond in pursuit of an illusive romanticized love. The choice to have an affair can often lead to confusing the act of betrayal with a problem in the marriage, and he sees affairs as jeopardizing the marriage. Drawing from forty-five years of experience treating couples, Pittman identifies the corrosive aspect of an affair not as the act of sex with another partner but as the secrecy and lies involved in covering it up.

Pittman is relatively optimistic that, if affairs are exposed, with commitment and effort it is possible for marriages to survive. If the therapist can keep the couple relatively calm and focused on the marriage, the affair can begin to look "ridiculous and insignificant."[9] The partners can begin to concentrate on a constructive course of action and avoid the potential fallout for their children. Repairing the marriage may involve developing the confidence that their love can endure and that they can manage conflict and anger without the relationship imploding. They may come to understand their self-destructive patterns by examining what they learned about relationships from their parents' marriages. They can clarify what has motivated their past choices and reflect on how they may avoid infidelity in the future, rebuild their intimacy and compassion, and tolerate each other's imperfections.

My mother had an affair with her campaign manager Dick Sears while she was married to my father. The circumstances leading up to my mother's affair are a mystery to me, and my father is understandably reticent to explain. The likelihood is that there was something not working in my parents' marriage, though it is also possible that my mother was depressed and lonely and that her affair came from a desperate need to fill a growing void. I will never know with certainty. Whatever the tangle of factors, one thing is for certain: Dick Sears was flesh and blood and trouble. And my mother found him appealing enough to leave her husband and six children.

If Dick were *only* my mother's lover, the matter would be complicated enough. But Dick is more than just her ex-lover. Dick Sears is also the ex-husband of my first stepmother, Barbara. He is father to Dickie, Carter, and Andrew—three boys I grew up with as brothers. They moved in with my father and his new bride Barbara about one year after my parents' divorce was final, when I was 5 years old. This intricate arrangement looks to me like a form of payback inspired by the twisted plot of a Greek tragedy—my father's response to my mother leaving to be with Dick was to marry Dick's former wife. My father says it was not revenge that motivated him but, rather, that Barbara and he were "thrown together." After all his hurt it allowed him to feel good about himself.

I can't pinpoint when I realized that my mother had an affair while my parents were married, but it was not a dramatic discovery, and was probably passed on by one of my sisters when I was a teenager. But after reading my mother's novel and wanting to know more about her, I decided that I should talk to Dick Sears myself. If he loved her, and I suspect that he must have in some way, if his sense of her differed from my father's, then his perspective was worth understanding.

It was complicated for me to talk to Dick. He has been a cipher to me—I know him only as the object of my father's disdain—and Dick, for all intents and purposes, disappeared about forty years ago after my mother and he split after living together for six months. He drifted off to New York City, and I rarely saw Dick when I was growing up—he appeared only at the occasional graduation. Yet the idea of talking to him started to feel compelling. It felt wrong at first, but persistence is both my strength and my downfall.

⚮

I call Dick Sears and I'm surprised when I get him on the phone. He seems pleased to hear from me and quickly offers his cooperation. I have rehearsed a few questions: "Who was my mother as a person?" I ask tentatively, and his refreshingly plain response is "Your mother was the finest person I have ever known." When he hears I am writing a book, he grows reluctant to answer my questions—maybe he's a little flustered because I have caught him off guard. He says he has just come back from a run and has not eaten lunch.

I offer to call back, and when I do, he is more gracious and composed. He encourages me to come for a visit. Perhaps he's as curious as I am.

And so, surreptitiously, I arrange my field trip to meet my dead mother's ex-lover from forty years ago. In the days leading up to the trip, I have sleepless nights and worry that I'm disobeying my father by yielding to my insatiable curiosity, that I'm pursuing something illicit, and that my father will be threatened and hurt if I tell him. Colin is angry. Colin doesn't like Dick even though he has never met him. He's heard the family stories about how Dick was an absent father to my three stepbrothers. He left when my stepbrothers might have needed him most, having newly joined our family. And Colin suspects that Dick isn't exactly trustworthy, given that he "lured" my mother away from her marriage. He thinks I'm imagining Dick as a grand knight who can rehabilitate my mother's reputation. I tell him my eyes are open.

Dick's house is on the Hudson River, just north of Manhattan. My flight to Newark is thankfully short. From the air, the Hudson shines like chrome and the few clouds in the sky drop their shadows on the green hills. Newark Airport is loud and hot. Am I making a terrible mistake? I brace myself for disappointment, knowing Dick might be evasive. We are supposed to meet outside of the baggage-claim area at the curb, where he said he would be parked in a blue BMW. And when I step out onto the curb, there he is, disarmingly dapper and charming.

Dick Sears, at 72, is fit and lean. He has chiseled straight teeth, thin lips with a quick smile, and a "beak," as he refers self-deprecatingly to his long nose. He has the air of a man who has done a lot of crazy things in his life, and is now too old and too wise to be embarrassed by any of them. He says his best asset is his skull—its structure is undeniably prominent and gives him a distinguished look. In the back of the car sits Bianca, a pure-white, perfectly coiffed poodle. Immediately, Dick tells me how much I look like my mother.

He starts right in as we make our way from the airport to his home. "I met your mother on Patriots' Day in April 1961. She invited me out to her house to meet her and discuss whether or not my group, Citizens for Boston Public Schools, would endorse her for School Committee. She was such a breath of fresh air, outgoing, bubbly. And you were like a puppy, lying on her lap. She had so much energy, so much life." Then he says with conviction as if he is reading my mind, "My first impression was that she was a good mother. I came from such an austere, WASP-y home, and, oh, she was something else. I appreciated her warmth."

We make our way along the New Jersey Turnpike past chemical plants—he has the intake fan on and the car fills with an acrid smell. He rambles, "The Boston School Committee was such an awful group. They had no real interest in education. They all used it as a stepping-stone to city council, possibly mayor, and took payoffs under the table." I glance at him as he drives, trying to see who he is, trying not to be obvious. He is doing the same, taking my measure while he offers his observations about my mother and about Boston politics in the 1960s.

He is a confident driver, even as tanker trucks bear down on both sides of us. But I am stiff in my seat. He shoots a knowing look at me. "Things started rapidly with her. At first, we spent a lot of time talking on the phone." He pauses. "You don't mind hearing this?" I answer steadily, "That's what I'm here for."

"She always said she fell in love with me talking on the phone. She said she could have an orgasm just listening on the phone." He pauses again, creating some space for my reaction. But I'm not exactly sure what to do with this information. It's stifling in the car. He apparently plans to be more forthcoming than I expected, and I'm not sure I'm ready to hear what he might say. I force a chuckle—*too much information*, I am thinking, an expression my kids like to use when I talk to them about awkward subjects like sex. Then I say facetiously that it wouldn't be the first time someone responded to phone sex. "My analyst said that wasn't possible," he adds with a grin. "But I don't know. Ostensibly, we were strategizing about her election for School Committee. But it was much more than that." I didn't bargain for disrobing my mother on this visit. He grows quiet, and then for a moment he is back in time with her.

He sighs, feigning modesty and pretending to be mystified, but I know he believes his own PR. "Your mother always said that when she was around me she felt calm. I don't know what it is, but all kinds of women are drawn to me, almost as if I had magic powers." I don't feel calm, however, and I'm questioning what I'm doing here.

"In the end, the group did not endorse your mother. There were a number of complicated reasons for that, and your father was definitely one of those reasons. On the surface it was the picture of your father as someone who could not be trusted and if she was married to Jerry then she couldn't be trusted. Your father had been involved with an early reform movement and helped get Mayor Hynes elected to office. He was probably in favor of tearing down the West End as part of urban renewal and liberal city planning. At some point Jerry became personally involved to make money. That, and it was too early for a woman to be so liberated, so forceful. It was prejudice. Your mother was a piece of work—for example, she wouldn't let people smoke cigars around her or in the house. In those days it was outlandish for a woman to tell a man not to light a cigar in her own house." Never mind that the infamous Louise Day Hicks was elected to the School Committee that same year. I want to say that there's no reason to think my mother couldn't have done well as a politician if her life hadn't become such a train wreck. If. If. If. "So I quit when she did not get the endorsement and even grabbed a headline in the newspaper, 'Citizens' Group Director Quits in Huff'[10] or something like that, and then soon after I became her campaign manager."

I don't want to talk about politics, so I force a new subject. "How old were you when you met Barbara?" I ask, knowing that Barbara and Dick were married at the time he met my mother.

"Barbara and I got an early start; I was in an enormous hurry to get on with my life. Freshman year at Harvard I hadn't been doing as well as I wanted, so I took a year off. When I returned the following semester, Barbara got pregnant. So I dropped out and started studying to be an actuary at John Hancock. Nowadays, it would be the end of the world if you dropped out of Harvard, but in those days it didn't matter. So I worked at Hancock and studied sixty hours a week for the grueling actuary exam."

I ask him what an actuary is, remembering that my mother too had planned on being an actuary at one point, and he tells me that actuaries determine life expectancies for insurance companies by weaving together statistical probabilities and mathematical formulas. I'm tempted to ask him if he would have predicted my mother's suicide, but I restrain myself. He continues, "When I was finished with the exam, I was looking around for something to do, and thus began my brief phase of being a do-gooder. So, in addition to working at Hancock and raising babies with Barbara, I got involved in local politics.

"The first time I went to Quail Street to see your mother about the campaign, I was talking with her down by the pool, and your father strode in wearing riding britches and boots—he had just finished horseback riding. He was glamorous with his fake British accent. Your mother used to always say that when she first met Jerry he had no *savoir faire*, no experience with people. According to your mother, she taught your father how to dress, how to eat. She gave him flair and finesse. She molded him."

Dick grows increasingly animated as he speaks. "The four of us started going out together—your mother and father, myself and Barbara. Once or twice a week, one night to dinner, one night to the movies. Your mother and I had an open flirtation going, but Barbara and Jerry were just thrown together." He glances at the rearview mirror before changing lanes.

"I never had an affair before your mother," he says suddenly. "I love women, I admit, but I'm not a womanizer." He wants me to believe in his character, or perhaps he is seeking preemptive forgiveness before he tells me something painful—he wants a kind of bargain. He knows what he is about to tell me will be shocking, but he is excited, enjoying this. "Your mother and father were eight years older than me. They had a lot more money than we did. I was 23, with a wife and three sons. And they were other-worldly."

He goes on, "Then, one blistering July weekend, they invited Barbara and me to go with them to Cape Cod. We stopped for a casual dinner, and we were all having a grand time and then, at some point, Nancy and Barbara came out of the women's bathroom and announced we were going to swap partners for the evening. And Jerry and I looked at each other and then at them, and we agreed."

I am sick and incredulous. My mother and my stepmother concocting this unseemly exchange together—it's impossible to believe that this is how it unfolded. That my father was complicit, that he went along with it too. That this was no accident, and although it might have been fueled by a few bottles of good wine, it was still considered, premeditated, *thought through*. That four people with nine young children between them could be so irresponsible stuns me. I think to myself that it cannot be true, but there is no obvious reason for Dick to mislead me, except to stick it to my father. Yet what he has told me so far has seemed honest. I say numbly, "So this was a 1960s-swingers, Playboy-mansion sort of thing."

He is displeased. "No," he says, annoyed that I could be so dense. "That implies a one-night stand. What I had with your mother was more serious than wife-swapping."

"When we got back to Boston after that weekend, we all felt terrible. And the four of us together went to see a psychiatrist, who advised each of us to get into psychoanalysis."[11]

Dick checks my reaction again, but I'm stone-faced—my regulation psychiatrist's mien. "Your mother and I both chose to go into psychoanalysis, which she did only for a year or so after she broke it off with your father. Your father went, too, but only briefly. He was disgusted because he thought the analyst was just prurient and into talking dirty and, well, what was the point, anyway. Barbara never went—she thought that she could rely on her own inner resources." (Maybe that is what he remembers, but Barbara had told me that she went briefly for a few weeks when her parents were paying for her to see a therapist. They stopped paying because they wanted her to return to Illinois with her three boys.) Dick shakes his head as if reliving an old frustration. "For me, though, it was important. I didn't want to live that crazy kind of life. My parents had divorced, and I knew Barbara and I didn't have a great marriage. I had no thought of getting out of it at that time, but I could see that I wouldn't achieve what I wanted in life if I kept going the way I was going. I needed psychoanalysis as a way to move on. I stuck with it for three years in Boston, then tried to make a go of it on my own, and then did nine years of psychoanalysis in New York. After Barbara, I was married again for fourteen years, and we had two sons. And that ended badly, too."

I wonder whether Dick is telling me about his psychoanalysis in order to establish some common ground or if he is looking for more than that. Is he trying to flatter me by showing respect for the profession I'm in, even though I'm not an analyst?[12] "I am the poster boy for psychoanalysis," he says with satisfaction. "In analysis I went through a process of abandoning some of my childhood ambitions as unrealistic. It was liberating. Now, I have been married for twenty-five years, and have a wonderful relationship with my third wife, Debbie. I was reluctant to get married again after being a two-time loser." Dick is proud of the work he has done and wants to communicate that to someone who can understand what it means.

By now we've made our way onto an imposing tree-lined street. We pass the occasional estate and expanse of perfect lawn, then pull into a circular drive shaded by the long and heavy arms of a weeping beech. Dick's stone Victorian mansion is called Cliffside. It is a grand house overlooking the Hudson, built in the late 1850s as a wealthy family's summer retreat. I seem to have walked onto the set of *The Great Gatsby*. He is pleased by my reaction. "Somehow, I eked out a good living," he says, satisfied. He is slightly amused by his own good fortune and conveys a sense that he is grateful for it although he seems a little smug.

The house has large common rooms, a grand piano, and the largest pipe organ ever built in a residence. Its understated Victorian exterior hides a wildness I rarely encounter in New England. Dick's house is filled with folk art—a painting of Adam and Eve jogging together naked by a primitive lollipop tree and a large, muscular serpent; a sculpture of a man with a large bowler hat featuring a naked woman on its crown; a mermaid with prominent breasts. Dick said he likes folk art because a Victorian house can come across as too formal and somber and the folk art makes it cozy.

Dick gives me a quick tour of the house. There is a fireplace at one end with handmade tiles depicting musicians and their instruments. The dining room has two buffets with two antique silver candelabras and an open wooden chest filled with silver settings. The room is dominated, though, by a large oil painting, a portrait of Bianca, his princess poodle, painted in the style of Monet.

He leads me to his smoking room, a dusky pungent room of leather and rich wood dominated by a mounted bull's head. A brass plaque identifies the bull as Latiquero, who apparently weighed in at 638 kilograms. A matador's cape, photographs of bullfights, and a matador's *estoque*—the sword used to kill the bull—are displayed alongside.

We head toward the kitchen. There is a framed picture of Dick in a glossy advertisement for *House Beautiful*. He is perched out on the limb of a tree, in a striking white suit and a bowler hat. The grand trees, the bloodied bull-fighter's sword, the jasmine-scented air—Where on earth did I land?

Dick invites me to spend the night, but this isn't my intention. He leads me upstairs and shows me to a guest bedroom. I'm distracted when I notice a copy of *A Question of Character: The Life of John F. Kennedy* on a shelf and put my bag on the bed as if I am settling in. As he leans against the dresser casually talking to me, I stand awkwardly a few feet from the bed, suddenly all too aware of how weird my visit is. I would prefer a long table between us to this strange intimacy. It makes me uncomfortable that I remind him of my mother, and I resolve to leave as soon as is feasible. I pick up my bag and let him know I have to get back.

We make our way outside to the wrap-around porch and nestle into wicker chairs with large pillows. I regain my equilibrium and resume my inquisition, knowing that he can talk with ease about the past. But Dick wants to talk shop. "You know, my analyst was always critical of your mother's analyst. Her analyst was too demanding—stuff would come up faster than she could incorporate. He should have put the brakes on." He heaves a sigh that does not seem forced or apologetic. "I used to always feel I caused the whole mess, but my analyst would tell me, there were three other adults. I shouldn't feel I caused it all. I shouldn't blame myself for everything."

He pauses and looks at me. "I never felt ill-treated. Rather, I felt I let your mother down. I never wanted our marriage to break up. That's not what I wanted. We were young kids, Barbara and I. Nancy and Jerry were powerful people and your mother always knew what she wanted, and I wasn't resisting. Barbara and Jerry's feelings began to play a bigger role as time went on. Then Barbara threw me out and wouldn't take me back." For a fleeting moment he looks dejected and adds, "although my analyst said that I wasn't someone to fight. It was a bitter divorce, initially, before Barbara and Jerry married. I paid her 60 percent of my salary. I don't know what Jerry was thinking when he married Barbara—they were married how long, ten years? But my kids told me it was not a happy place, Quail Street."

He looks out toward the river. "Your father has a lot of fine qualities. But his tragic flaw has always been his excessive sense of competition. When he is competing for something, anything goes. Your father was dependent on your mother, and he was enormously disappointed and angry with her and under tremendous psychological pressure. People can get aggressive around a divorce. Even mild-mannered people in the experience of divorce get so frustrated that they do things they would not normally do."

I ask him to tell me more. He says slowly but firmly, "Your mother was afraid of violence, the threat of violence. Once Jerry punched her in the breast. I saw the bruise. We took photographs. It might have been the cause of her leaving you all and the house, and it was around the time of her first suicide attempt." It is hard for me to take this in as I did not know this before. I feel dread.

I don't want to distract him with my reaction and I try to appear stoic. "When your mother left the house, she did not want to be married to Jerry anymore. She wanted the children and she assumed she would get the kids back. But there were a lot of villains in that custody battle. A number of people gave false testimony—including your grandmother." I ask him what he thinks my grandmother's motive was to go against her daughter, saying that her decision to side with my father in the courts gave my father added credibility in the custody battle. His eyes narrow a little. "Your grandmother was a lush. And it is a small world, you know—my stepmother, Hazel, was a drinking buddy of your grandmother's." He looks hard at me. "It's not unusual for parents to want to see their children's families stay together, to blame your own child for screwing up. Especially if you have your own problems. Maybe that's why Edith lied."

I ask whether my mother cleaned out the joint account as my dad has repeatedly told me she did. Why did she sign over custody of her children and file for a quick divorce stating cruel and unusual treatment? Did Dick go with her? He answered that my mother might have been worried that the state would intervene with her children after her suicide attempt. She probably cleaned out one of the accounts, but my father had others.

Bianca the poodle pads out to join us on the porch and stretches out at Dick's feet. "We moved into the Beacon Street place. I'm not sure how long we lived together, must have been about six months. She bought a Volkswagen bus and used to put all of you kids in it. You all would come to visit, often two at a time, and spend the night. Life seemed tolerable. We used to talk about starting a new life in Australia or New Zealand. I never saw her have big highs or lows, but then again, I had a strange ability to calm her."

If they had stayed together, would I have grown up halfway around the world, or would she have disappeared from our lives forever? I ask if he wanted to marry my mother. He admits, "We never talked about marrying. Your mother knew what she wanted, and it wasn't to be married to me; I was more torn. I was always aware of people repeating bad patterns. You know the classic college story of a girl falling in love who keeps on choosing abusive partners. I thought that I needed to restructure, hopefully from psychoanalysis, if I wanted to make something out of my life, live up to my potential. I just wanted to be. . . ." He trails off. "I wasn't thinking beyond the moment." I ask how it ended, and he tells me that her analyst said she shouldn't see him anymore. He seemed resigned that the cards were stacked against them and he didn't appear up for the fight.

"We bumped into each other once, soon after she had married Alex Stanley. She told me that she needed to show that she could provide a stable home or she wouldn't get the kids back. Alex was mild-mannered and wanted to help her, but I always thought that it was a marriage of convenience."

Feeling betrayed by all of these self-indulgent parents, I tell Dick that sometimes my friends, when they hear the story, are judgmental, outraged that my mother left six children, and Dick left three. He responds, "You cannot control whom you fall in love with. It may depend on how desperate you are."

Dick reaches down to pat Bianca, who looks up at him with adoration. He goes on. "I remember once she accidentally put her arm through a glass door and she went white as a sheet. She had a big V-shaped scar on her arm, I remember." He looks distant now. "I found out about her suicide in the newspaper after I moved to New York. I had not been in contact with her for over a year. A friend of mine showed it to me—it was a full page on the front of a tabloid: 'Rappaport's Ex Slays Self.' That's a hell of a headline."

We are both exhausted from stepping into this time warp and decide to take a break for lunch with Debbie, who has graciously given Dick and me two hours by ourselves. She is willing to host me despite our unusual connection. As she greets me, she says, "What a terrible situation with your mother," as if it happened yesterday. I am relieved that she is not afraid of the topic.

"Does she look like her mother?" Dick nods in agreement, and for the moment I'm self-conscious. He senses this and tries to include me: "You're smaller, right?" As we sit for lunch, they are warm with each other, attentive, describing for me the recent lawn party and talent show they hosted for fifty neighbors. Debbie reveals that early on she realized she was not going to have any children with Dick; he already had five boys, two ex-wives, and too much animosity. She says proudly, "I made it my life's work to bring the family together. Four sons have gotten married in the last decade, and at each wedding Dick's ex-wives gave me a toast."

Clearly Debbie understands the complexities of family interactions and is able to manage even among long-standing hurts. She asks me with a mischievous smile, "So how does it feel to be in Satan's house with the boogeyman?" Now that I am at ease with her, it's my turn to answer questions, and they come fast and furious. "Do you get along with your father?" I tell her I love my father and that I used to get along with him until he read a draft of the book I've been writing. Why am I writing this book, she asks. At one level it is to pay homage to my mother, at another level it is for me—but I also hope that sharing my experience might help families who have lost someone. "Do you remember your mother?" she asks. I know I must have known her long enough to love her, or I wouldn't be working so hard to try to understand who she was.

It has been a long morning. Dick lights a cigarette—a thin Fantasia cigarette, gold and blue. "I started smoking after a forty-year hiatus when Mayor Bloomberg banned smoking in New York City." He shoots me a sly look. "I like this mix, healthy activity with unhealthy activity. I'm a harmless rebel. When you get older, you see things your own way."

Dick smiles. "I am not inclined to think deeply, at first, but then I tend to ruminate. I can go through twenty drafts for an invitation, refining things." He says the secret to life is learning from things that happen, from turning them over in your mind, drawing conclusions. He muses that he loves this stage of life. He says he is pleased at not being a central figure and at stepping back, although I'm not sure I believe him as we sit here in his theatrical house. He's still out on a limb, being so open with me.

I ask him what was it like for him when his sons were living with my family. He said that he always felt like a stepfather to his sons. "Boys need a father," he says to me. "And I hoped your father was doing the job." Dick says he would see his boys every couple of months, growing up, and they would come down for a couple of weeks during the summer. But I know that as boys they longed for a father and were angry with Dick for failing them too often.

Dick has seen my father several times in the decades since my mother's suicide. "Once I was at the Coral Beach Club in Bermuda and some fellow was blocking the sun. It was your father. In a bathing suit." He laughs, and I have an uneasy smile at my father's expense. "And then once when Deb was with me, and we were checking into a hotel in Vienna, there was your father with Phyllis. It must have been their honeymoon. We spoke as if we barely knew each other." He wants me to tell my father he wishes him well, but I can't imagine that conversation. "I hope that he won't feel threatened by this visit. I still have fond memories of the good times we had together before the trouble began, and it is clear, looking back, that all four of us share the blame for what happened. Whatever grudge I might have had has long since evaporated."

What do I make of all this? I know that he is no saint, but Dick is not as diabolical as I imagined. I can see all too well the consequences of his affair with my mother. The real Niles was no match for what my mother needed; he was young, and their affair was short-lived. His adoration offered her some temporary sanctuary, but he could not provide the antidote to her turmoil.

On the way back to the airport, I suddenly remember the bull's head in Dick's smoking room and ask about it. Dick is clearly pleased. A true aficionado, he has been going to Spain to see the bullfights once or twice a year for decades. He explains that he was first exposed to the tradition of bullfighting when his parents lived in Majorca. From the moment he walked into the arena, he fell in love with the excitement, the heat, the smells, and the tragedy. "The bullfight to the Spanish," he declares, "is like opera to Italians. It is an art form, not sport. But an art that is more impromptu. No rehearsal. And the bull is a real threat."

As he speaks, I can see his excitement. He explains about *corridas*—long, hot summer afternoons in Spain in which six bulls are killed by three different matadors. After the third bull, the crowd feasts on grilled sausages, shellfish drizzled with oil and lemon, and glasses of wine.

"It is not a bad life for the bull, even if it is hard for most people to get over the brutality," Dick says casually, but I know this must be a well-rehearsed speech meant to shock and amuse. "They have an incredible life for a bovine. Your average bull here is castrated and slaughtered. But the bulls heading to the arena live like kings. They spend four years in beautiful pastures." He describes to me how magnificent the bulls are with their thick hides, glossy coats, and sharp horns, how they are 1,000 pounds or more of fierce muscle and power.

"Once they go into the ring, they are ferocious and will seek to kill," he says. "They know how to conserve energy for their charge. A charging bull can toss a horse and rider over his head. One must learn to control the bull gracefully and imaginatively," Dick instructs. "If it goes well, it is wonderful. If not, he will kill you."

A bullfight lasts less than fifteen minutes. "The whole idea is *hot* blood," Dick says, and although his expression is vivid enough, I am not sure I know what it means exactly—Isn't all blood hot? "I don't think that the bull feels much pain. I won't say pain is a uniquely human concept, but we might be bringing our own baggage. We might be anthropomorphizing the bull. The bull is making a good living. In the lottery of domesticated animals, the bull is really the winner."

Dick emphasizes the danger to the matador so I won't mistakenly assume that the fight is one-sided. "Every top torero gets seriously gored," he reassures me. "I have a picture of Manolete, one of the greatest bullfighters of all time, taken at his last fight right before he was killed." I wonder if Dick imagines himself as the bull. Or maybe he identifies with the matador, flaunting his cape and escaping danger.

I try to sleep on the plane, but I cannot get comfortable.

I am relieved to arrive home after my visit with Dick Sears, home to my street, my house, my family. The house is quiet and dark when I arrive, but there is a reassuring chorus of crickets in the yard. I step into the garden full of white lilies and remember a picture we took of them with Lila, their caretaker at the time, so proud of their bloom. I dodge the sprinkler and with relief open the front door. Colin is glad and relieved to see me. Later, I will tell him the whole story and reassure him that I was not deceived. Colin doesn't ask for details: He provides the solace I need. My curiosity brought me to the edge, but I wasn't consumed by the visit.

How do we safeguard what is most valuable in our marriage? It is easy to slip away from each other with the demands of a busy life or when we are bored by familiarity. It can be hard to compromise and I am often reluctant to admit when I make a mistake. The stamina of our love comes from the private rituals of renewal: hiking a mountain, relaxing by the fireplace, finding each other in the middle of the night as our bodies fold into each other, sealing us together with the promise of more days to come. As I settle into the stillness, I focus on Colin's steady breathing. All I want to do now is be home.

Chapter Eight

I know that you are going to be lenient with mmmmeeee because of our common bond of having noone else to looove us. Amirightorwrong?

—NANCY VAHEY RAPPAPORT,
LETTER TO JEROME RAPPAPORT

Choosing to leave a marriage is never a casual move. When two bodies come together to make one and then many more, how is it possible that they can separate without an explosion? Even blessed marriages have their crisis moments, times when it is hard to believe there is a way around an apparently permanent impasse. It is easy to worry whether love can inform the art of reconciliation or if the impasse is a sign of impending loss.

Research psychologist John M. Gottman analyzed the patterns of marital success and failures in order to identify difficulties and teach couples more productive ways to communicate. He devised a questionnaire he humorously called his marital "poop" detector to assess how life was going in the partnerships he studied. His diagnostic tools can sometimes seem as if they've been pulled from the pages of *Cosmo*, in that they involve checking to see if a partner feels "emotionally distant" or "irritable" or is "fighting more than usual," but Gottman's methods are actually based on twenty-five years of longitudinal research on more than 600 couples as well as detailed analysis of 3,000 additional marriages.

Having observed so many marriages, Gottman claims he can predict which marriages will fail. He says that marriages in crisis share key behaviors—the "four horsemen of the apocalypse," which are "corrosive to marriage." These are *criticism*, especially the kind where one spouse starts a diatribe with "You always" or "You never"; *defensiveness*, or the evasion of responsibility for one's action; *stonewalling*, in which one or both partners become impassive or withdraw from the communication as a form of self-soothing; and *contempt*, which is characterized by sarcasm, eye-rolling, and teasing that are experienced as humiliating by the partner. A high degree of contempt expressed between two partners is seen as the single best predictor of divorce, "the sulfuric acid of love." If negative exchanges also outweigh the positive ones, the marriage is doomed.

Couples in trouble, Gottman writes, have repeated "failure of repair" whereby the partners feel that the same problems keep coming up again and again with little progress toward resolution. One partner may feel that the other is making unreasonable demands or may feel attacked unfairly or disregarded. It can feel like gridlock—every argument heats up and interactions grow nastier and more intense. In these situations, Gottman asserts, solving problems (as some couples' therapists try to do) is not the answer. Instead, he recommends that couples learn how to live with differences, figure out how to de-escalate, keeping things lighter and more humorous between them. If each partner can give up some power, the couple may find a compromise and move forward. Over time, they can develop greater flexibility.[1]

But what Gottman recommends is a tall order. I wish my parents could have pulled it off. Looking back at their relationship, I wonder if their divorce would have been averted if they'd had good referees like Gottman. Once there is irreparable damage, the decline is rapid. It follows a somber, three-phase pattern described by noted divorce researchers Judith Wallerstein and Shauna Corbin.[2] This well-trod path will be familiar to anyone who has been involved in a vitriolic divorce.

The tone of the first or "acute" phase is set by the fact that divorce in a family with children is rarely a mutual decision. This acute phase is filled with drama, highly emotional responses, and escalating conflict. Sometimes there is physical violence between parents—even if neither spouse has been violent before. Wallerstein and Corbin note that both parents may have thoughts of suicide.[3] They may accuse each other of betrayal and revenge. They may misinterpret what the other intends and have exaggerated responses to minor insults. In addition, parents in the acute phase of a marriage breakdown often have lapses of judgment, act rashly on sexual urges, and behave immaturely. This acute phase may be brief, or it may last several years. Some couples remain trapped at this stage, reenacting the drama over and over again in a futile effort to change the outcome.

This acute phase is followed by a "transitional" phase in which the couple disentangle from each other's lives. They may find increasing satisfaction with new friends, work, and time for self-discovery. However, as families readjust, this stage can be stressful. The "final" phase involves the establishment of post-divorce households with single or remarried parents—households that are relatively stable but may experience awkward adjustments along the way. I don't know if my parents ever actually got to the supposed second phase, much less the third, but then again, I'm not sure *divorce* is even the most apt term for their conflict.

It's difficult to read anyone else's marriage or conflict from the outside. In my parents' case it can also feel particularly intrusive, as I try to piece together something that happened forty years ago, which was further complicated by the fact that my mother made a suicide attempt right after their separation and killed herself after the divorce. As my father says, exasperated, "Who are you to rekindle a mishmash of events that are not pictured in entirety?" I will never know why my mother gave up on her marriage or why she needed to leave in a way that hurt and shamed my father. It is easier sometimes to make up a script about why the separation and divorce happened, and what role each partner played, to make it more under-standable.

The sequence of events I find are sketchy. My mother left our home after the affair started with Dick and she temporarily moved in with a neighbor, Elaine Werby. She made a suicide attempt during a fight with my father,[4] and it is hard for me to place what was going on when this happened—she had returned to our home to see if she could reconcile with my father. He declined and she took an overdose. After this suicide attempt, she made a financial settlement and signed a custody agreement that gave custody to my father and my grandmother Edith and also allowed her liberal visitation at our home. She then moved into a two-bedroom apartment with Dick Sears, and during her visitation with her children the negotiations with my father became increasingly contentious. She returned to court to fight for the return of her children.

My father, who was reticent with details until recently, noted that one of his biggest mistakes was not to reconcile with my mother. From his van-tage point, here was someone (Dick) who came into his household and had an affair with his wife. He didn't think it was fair to the kids that their mother was wandering in and out of their lives while she was having an af-fair. When he found out she had gone off with Dick to Tanglewood, Dad was hopeful that he could get her to end it, but she chose to stay with Dick. He told me that he "cared most about you kids, and [he] was willing to give her financially what she needed," but he was too hurt to take her back later.[5]

Elaine Werby reappeared after thirty years (she says that my father had discouraged her from having contact with us while we were growing up) when my sister Judy arranged for a visit to my mother's grave. It was the first visit with my brothers, sisters, and father together, and Elaine joined us. I kept her phone number for ten years after this memorial service, and when I was trying to understand more about what happened with my mother I decided to see if Elaine was willing to talk with me. She was.

Elaine Werby was my mother's close friend and knew my parents for nine years; she is 77 now, with a warm smile, an elegant dress, and a hoarse voice.

My mother stayed with Elaine and her husband after she left my father. She told me with great enthusiasm,

> I was crazy about your mother. She was very smart. Such good times. . . . We would sit around the pool in summer and the kids would swim and we would yak and talk about politics. We were on the board of the League of Women Voters and we were ·drawn together by geography since we both lived in West Roxbury. We were the two ethnics on the League, your mother representing the Irish, me the Jewish, and most Brahmins saw us belonging together. As two couples we would go to movies, go to dinner, go to the house. One evening, your parents came back from Paris; it was your mother and father's first trip, she was absolutely gorgeous, she wore a purple cloche hat. They had brought back dirty books that were contraband at the time and we sat around—my Jerry, your dad, and your mother— and we were hysterical reading.
>
> After your mother finished the fund-raising drive as chairman of the United Fund, she needed something that was hers. She wanted to be more interesting to people. She liked being *somebody* whenever she felt let down and she conceived of the idea of running for School Committee. She had an idea of strategy that was wonderful. She never really articulated it but she always felt a mission to carry on what her family did—she felt that they had shaped Boston politics. Your father had made such a name as a do-gooder at the beginning with Hynes; this was something where she needed to be on her own. She was proud of her family and political role all tied up also with her own ego. She had enormous charisma. I always felt that either people were drawn into her orbit or they didn't like her at all. I raised questions to Nancy when she chose to have Dick run her campaign.

I was naïve and it took me a while to figure out what was going on. The summer that she was running for School Committee, I saw your mother every day and I didn't see anything. Dick was in and out. Your father called me and I was startled because he was crying. That was his first open emotion and he said that your mother was gone and he didn't know where.

The sequence is fuzzy when your mother came back from Alabama, where she had gone to get a quick divorce. She asked to stay with me. I remember for three weeks she was living up on the third floor in our attic. Dick Sears came to visit in the afternoon. . . . My husband was annoyed that I had taken your mother in . . . afraid that I would get in the middle and advised me just to not get involved. I remember wondering where she was going to get the money to move. She got a financial settlement when she signed an agreement giving custody to your grandmother and your father [she had daily visitation]. When she signed the agreement that allowed her to move with Dick Sears into a beautiful small apartment, on a corner downtown in a walk-up on the second floor, that was the beginning of the end of our friendship. . . . She was so engrossed with Dick.

She continued, her voice heavy: "When she moved into the apartment in late September, she was *so* convinced that she would have no trouble getting the children back. During six months she worked out an arrangement of kids coming to her apartment and her visiting at the house.

"Those visits intensified. She kept going back to court and each time she would think that she was going to get you back. You couldn't dissuade her. And it would be another blow. It was more than she could bear. She was leaving you all with your grandmother. Edith would supervise your care while your mother figured out her next move. I couldn't believe it at the time how Edith could back your father." She paused. "I am not sure what her finances were but your grandmother was living on Jerry's largess and she wasn't going to threaten it."

I asked her about Dad and Mama's marriage.

"It was very hard to tell with your Dad and Nancy. . . . They were very competitive, which was a problem. Your mother and father loved kids, and loved the idea of having a lot of kids. Your dad had a quick temper. Your mother may have had unrealistic expectations. It must have been difficult that your grandmother was there all the time though she was an integral part of the household running smoothly. She had a major role with the kids but it must not have been easy to have her around."

Yet my investigation into my mother's life as I read her journals and look at court documents adds to the complexity. She was struggling with excruciating decisions. She worried that, if she followed her desire for Dick, it would kill her as the person she was and that she would damn herself. In her journals, she's caught in depression's torment, losing her equilibrium, knowing that she was making an agonizing choice that seemed to eat away at her natural self-preservation.

> All my life I've been like a peeled onion with all my nerve endings exposed, and all sorts of feelings have rushed through. . . . I'd say that I have had a marvelous life, with all sorts of wonderful sensations coming through me, until lately. And now someone has put the skin back on, and I can't feel the pain, because I won't look at it, but I can't feel the pleasure, either. . . .
>
> Long and uncertain stretched the smooth black road, urging one into forgetfulness, deceiving one into day dreams, long, long, long—long black insomniac nights broken only by the white line of consciousness and . . . hateful solitudes, as indistinguishable from one another as curves and crossroads before the headlights. Consciousness, uniqueness, slowly drains away from the asphalt and from the cottony, lonely wakefulness until finally there is nothing but the black road ahead and death. . . . Death is a change in degree rather than

in kind, and for many of us is a blessing in neon rather than in disguise.

On September 12, two weeks before their divorce would be final, four months after the affair with Dick had started, and one month since she had dropped out of the School Committee campaign, my mother went to the Quail Street house to talk to my father. By some accounts, she was there to reconcile with him, to apologize and ask forgiveness—perhaps defiance was too difficult for her and came with too much risk. My father could not forgive at that time. My mother swallowed three handfuls of the sleeping pills that she had been prescribed for her insomnia and "nerves." Dad found her, groggy on the bed with a bottle next to her. He immediately knew there was something wrong and called for an ambulance. It scared the hell out of him.[6] She was taken out of the house on a stretcher, my sister Judy remembers. Dick Sears told me that Dad called him to meet them at the emergency room, which is somewhat mystifying to me. Dick told me that when he arrived at the hospital he "was desolate, shocked. She came close to killing herself that time. I had never seen the panicked side of her before. It was all a mystery to me.... I never had an understanding of why, and she did not tell me anything beyond that she couldn't take it anymore."

My older sister Amy adamantly insists that my mother was simply "distraught." She spent five days at Faulkner Hospital. When she was released she returned to Elaine's house where she signed an agreement to give custody to my father (with Grandma Edith as co-custodian) and reached a financial settlement. She needed time to recover and to work out a plan. I am puzzled as to how Elaine can remember so many details about spending time with my mother but remains "blocked" about my mother's suicide attempt when I ask her.

It's hard not to look at my mother's writing as an ominous prediction of her eventual suicide—as a long suicide note to her children. But I also realize now that writing was a way she had of working out her first suicide attempt that September, an honest effort at trying to understand who she was and how she had come to that point—her way of comprehending so she could find strength not to do it again. As my parents fought, as she downed the pills, my father was terrified by my mother's recklessness. Now, as a parent, I can sympathize with my father's fear and his desire to protect us from her behavior. In that moment, she was capable of anything.

In my mother's novel, Diane wonders whether her husband Peter would accept her death guilt-free or if he would be "overcome with remorse and self-disgust" after her suicide. Remorse does not come easily to my father. If my mother had been looking for this reaction, she did not get what she wanted from him. Instead of bringing remorse, her suicide attempt only distanced them further.

It must have been frightening to her, too, to realize that she could swallow so many pills so easily, and so easily punish my father by dying. If she sometimes could not stop herself or even recognize what she was doing, then surely she was at risk of dying. She needed to quiet her racing thoughts and take time to think them through.

The divorce was finalized on September 25, 1961. The next day, the preliminary elections for Boston School Committee were held, and Louise Day Hicks was victorious.[7] By this time, my mother had no thought of any political victories—she needed to steady herself.

Curious to find out more about this period in her life, I requested the divorce decree from the state of Alabama. It starts out innocuously, specifying that my parents had lived together for ten years and had six children and that they had agreed on a separation agreement with reference to the support, custody, and maintenance of minor children. But I was stunned by what I read next: that my father "committed actual violence on the person of complainant [my mother]; attended with danger to her life or health or from his conduct there was reasonable apprehension of such violence." In a response, my father protested this characterization and "denies allegations" and demanded "strict proof." Dad recently explained to me (when I got up the nerve to ask him about this), "The laws of divorce were archaic in the '60s. There were only limited grounds for divorce—it had to fit within circles. There was a long mishmash, and somebody took the hit. There was nothing like irreconcilable differences; someone had to have an affair or somebody got hit... stupid way to get divorced. Alabama and Nevada were the two states that competed to be the divorce capital to expedite the process, and your mother went to Alabama."[8]

As she took time to heal in the autumn months, my mother started seeing a physician regularly and a psychiatrist three times a week, documenting the appointments in a leather-bound date book. My grandmother Edith had a hip fracture and needed to be in the hospital. With my grandmother's role as caretaker temporarily suspended, my mother became more vigilant to safeguard her children at Quail Street, following our every move to the extent that my father permitted. My father made sure that there were always two or three adults in the house when he was working and tried to help us accept the change and get used to the comings and goings. However, even with the best intentions he was bound to miss Martha's homework assignments or little Jerry's performance or when I required a nap. My mother yearned to share our daily routines—she wanted to bathe us, talk to us about school, and comfort us. I know from working with children that parents draw their children close when there is a crisis, and in my mother's case she might not have known how to explain what was hard for her to understand herself. My sisters and brothers could not understand why my mother had moved out of our home even though she was visiting most days. Amy remembers that my father told her that my mother had given away her children. But Amy knew better. In my mother's papers I find short notes—proof of love—written by my sister:

Dear Mr. Sears and Mama,

I love you very much! I hope you both see us all soon.... I like to be at your house, I like the toy I have.

Love, Amy

My mother writes wistfully, "Only the mother can hear the cry of her child." She details the small and large conflicts she was having with my father, who only grudgingly conformed to their arrangement that I find archived in the courts: "[D]uring such periods as the custody shall not be in the wife, the wife shall have the right to visit all said children at all reasonable times, free of supervision, control or the presence of any person.... The wife shall be consulted in all substantial matters affecting their health, education, religious training, and summer camp and the decisions relating thereto should be by mutual agreement." Yet the access did not happen easily. She was allowed to come to our home only as an unwelcome visitor. Her entries capture the intensity of my parents' antagonism and mutual hurt. After Thanksgiving, as my mother's strength and frustration increased, their situation escalated into a high-stakes tug-of-war over decisions about parenting and visitation. The affair between my father and Barbara had become more serious. Everything—the money, the punch bowls, visitation arrangements—triggered another confrontation. I read through her diary with the sad realization that their bitterness was allowing no room for cooperation or compromise.

THURS. DECEMBER 21ST

[He] refused little Nancy any time because it was too difficult to get her in and out on her schedule. He hung up and called back and apologized. Agreed that he hadn't been letting me see Nancy enough and she'd be coming Sun. and Mon., so Sat. wasn't the best possible day.

Never told me about school recital or Mother's Visiting Day 11/9. I said so and he said he figured the children would tell me. Little Jerry is just four and lisps and wouldn't know time anyway. He agreed that he should have told me about Mother's Day but nothing important. GRR.

Said he'd give me $1,800 for a $2,500 car, I said no, $2,500. And he could have that back if he'd give me the car plate. He said he'd do it for $2,000. I called him a cheap bastard, which he is.[9]

Refused punch bowl and cups (we have 2 and 150 cups, none of which will be used over weekend).

On Christmas Day, despite the constant bickering, my mother embraced the festivities of a family tradition. She prepared a feast and wrapped piles of presents. This was "her holiday," and she forged ahead, never mind that my father was holding hostage the punch bowl with its matching cups. She and Dick hosted a small tree-trimming party in their apartment. She welcomed old friends and held her head up and looked vibrant. When she was complimented on her appearance and asked if there was something different, she quipped that the improvements had come from divorcing my father.[10]

But the brief festivities quickly deteriorated.

THURS. DECEMBER 28TH

Called at 11:15 am, not having heard from the children yet. Jerry still refused to let me talk to them, but agreed to let me have little Jerry. When I arrived at 1:15 was told that little Jerry was going to the movies (he's only 4!!). He wanted to do that instead of be with me. Jimmy decided to come instead. I started toward my mother's room to get some things she needed in the hospital. Jerry told me he'd get what I needed. I said don't bother. . . . I said all I want is some clothes for Mother. He said you can't get them and turned and pushed me. I pushed back and he started hitting me hard around the head.

We were then at the banister and Bee [our housekeeper] tried to separate us saying, "Watch out for the banister," at which time I realized he was pushing me halfway over. He let go when Amy and Judy came out of Mother's room crying and begging him to stop. But then he started in again twice more. . . . He then refused to allow Jimmy to come with me, screaming and trying to pull Jimmy out of my arms. Jimmy as often cried "Daddy I wish you'd get the divorce and leave me with Mamma." He took him aside and said, "Don't let your mother make you choose between us, Jimmy." Jimmy told him, "But I do. I love Mamma. I hate you." I told him he didn't hate Daddy and that because he wanted to be with me didn't mean he didn't love Daddy. Jerry screamed at me for about fifteen minutes with Judy, Jimmy and Amy clinging to me and crying. . . . He was saying things like, "You're crazy, a lousy mother, always were, never loved them. . . ." He was VERY upset. Finally, he let Jimmy come with me and Judy will come tomorrow, though he had been saying I wasn't fit to see them.

No one deserves to be hit; it upset me to know that my father hit my mother in the head. No one in my family had ever talked about hitting, so I asked my sister Amy if she remembered. Amy remembers the hitting. Martha tells me it doesn't matter if he slapped her forty years ago.

During my next meeting with Dr. Johnson, I read the entries to her in choked despair, indignant for my mother forty years later and struggling with my loyalty to my father. Trying to understand what happened to my family, I have to acknowledge with sadness that my father was apparently abusive at that moment.

James Gilligan, a researcher with extensive experience working with men who have been violent, contends that "the first lesson that tragedy teaches us is that all violence is an attempt to achieve justice, or what the violent person perceives as justice for himself." But Gilligan cautions that "explanations are not to be confused with exculpations." Just as it is important for me to understand my mother's sorrow and fear, it is also necessary to examine my father's rage. Gilligan writes that he has "yet to see a serious act of violence that was not provoked by the experience of feeling shamed and humiliated, disrespected and ridiculed, and that did not represent the attempt to prevent or undo this 'loss of face' no matter how severe the punishment, even if it includes death."[11] Dr. Johnson reminds me that none of this seems fair.

When my mother left my father, she injured him profoundly. When she chose so publicly to live with Dick Sears, it was a special form of humiliation aimed at my father. She left, but she did not make a graceful exit.

I think of myself as well schooled in the tragedies of violence. I make my living trying to understand why children are aggressive and how to prevent this behavior. I appreciate how shame can fuel anger, and I don't want to be judgmental of my father. I do not write about this incident as an act of betrayal, though I fear he will see it that way. I will not overlook his devotion, his dignity, his love, his steadfast interest in the people his children have become, or his presence and involvement in our lives. My father has a fierce and justified pride in his parenting and by any standard he more than managed to balance the demands of work and family while we were growing up. I don't want to reduce him to nothing but a man who used his physical power to intimidate my mother. He can be more generous than that and he has learned from history.

Anna Freud emphasized that children may not have perfect recall and that there is a dynamic force that shapes how they construct their meaning. She wrote that "human beings are acquainted with only a fragment of their own inner life, and know nothing about a great many feelings and thoughts which go on within them, that is to say, all these things happen unconsciously without their awareness. . . . [T]he importance of any event is by no means a guarantee of its permanence in our memory; indeed, on the contrary, it is just the most significant impressions that regularly escape recollection." I know that if I were at the banister watching, at an age when I was too young to have verbal memory (the language of affect), I would be left with an unspeakable fear that my father could use force and intimidation. I have often worried that angering him could be dangerous, threatening to my security, and I've been frightened by the consequences. My mother's words leave me with the visceral dread that I did see this, peering down the hall, holding Amy's hand, terrified of the yelling and hitting. I feel as if I have traced an insidious fear of my father (which has tempered over the years)—what Anna Freud described as "the forgotten act of the inner world [that] has the curious characteristic of retaining its dynamic force when it disappears from memory."[12]

I hate to think of my brothers and sisters as being actively involved in this acrimonious battle and witnesses to physical violence.[13] I now know that they were excruciatingly vulnerable as they watched our family breaking apart. Many of the most significant findings from clinical case studies highlight the intense reactions of children exposed to conflict between their parents. Family researcher Ava L. Siegler writes that children who witness domestic violence "live in terror that they or their parents will be hurt and in guilt that they are helpless to do anything about it. This terror makes children... feel ashamed about their inability to stop the hostilities between their parents." This terror can be worse if the abuse is chronic. Such experiences exaggerate the sense of weakness of the children in the face of adult power and can "erode their self-regard."[14] Siegler cautions that children learn "bitter lessons" when they are "caught in the crossfire of intimate aggression." Most learn that a parent they love can frighten them; many learn that a parent they love can hurt.

During the time that I was finding out this upsetting information, my stepmother Phyllis and my father were concerned that I was growing increasingly withdrawn. I agreed to meet with my father to figure out how to explain my distance, and also wanted to ask him why he hit my mother when he knew she was so fragile.

It was devastating to talk with my father. He told me that my mother was a big woman and capable of defending herself. He was furious that I would question him. I left him and went to the bathroom. Putting my head against the cool wall, I went down on my knees; torn with my loyalty to my father and disappointed that I was on the defensive, I begged for strength from God, from the love for my mother, to go on.

When I arrived home spent, there was a package from my mother's best friend Peggy Melgard. She had written me a note saying that she'd found a few more of my mother's papers that must have fallen out of the trunk that Peggy had sent to us before and she thought that I would want them. There were more diary entries that spoke of my mother's frustration at not being able to comfort us. The battle between my parents had escalated to the point that her children were like human torpedoes, and she seemed thwarted even as she appealed to the courts and the police for help. The urgency and immediacy to reach us had added meaning when she lamented in court, "No mother can imagine what it means to be separated from her children."[15] Although she admits that my father "had said that I would always be their mother," there is a tragic sense that her authority was undermined:

TUESDAY, MARCH 20

9:30 I called my mother to see which children were still sick, having promised Martha and Amy on Monday that I would visit them again on Tuesday. Mother said JLR [my father] thought he was sick too and I said that was too bad but I'd see her around 11:00. Immediately Jerry [my father] called. "Nancy it doesn't make sense for you to come out today. Come out to-morrow." I told him I had promised the children and would see him soon then hung up. Ten minutes later he called to tell me he had spoken to the court and the police and if I appeared at the house I would be evicted. I asked if he had spoken to Judge Casey himself and he said yes. I said I'd call and see about that, which I did right away. The judge was already sitting and I left a message, calling again at the noon recess. The court officer said the judge would speak to neither party in the case and could do nothing but if a law had been violated it was a police matter and I should inform them.

About 1:30 I arrived at Div 17, W.R. [West Roxbury], asked for Cap. Hogan and showed him the agreement and told him the story. He said he'd see if he could get a plainclothesman to accompany me to the house and went to the poker room returning with Det. or Lieut. Jerry Sweeney. He said JLR was a lawyer and knew his rights and could throw any cop out unless a felony was in progress. I burst into tears and asked if I had to be beaten again to get their help. They all commiserated then. Jerry Sweeney, after much talk about using reason, called JLR and requested permission for me to visit my sick children. JLR refused them. Sweeney went in another room. JLR called him back and became convinced by him to give me an hour with the children. He was alright at the house but my mother and two oldest children were furious with him. ALL the cops thought he was extremely unreasonable but claimed the Alabama decree had no validity and they couldn't help me unless he hit me again, but that I should hurry and get to court.

Also in the envelope were a few handwritten pages given the title "Problems of a Long-Distance Mother": To me it could almost have been an article in a parenting magazine. She instructed about the importance of "setting up the atmosphere in which the children can grow—warm, loving, unsophisticated, relaxed, yet preparing them for each new step in their development and presenting that step at the right time—in the right way. This requires intimate knowledge and frequent 'lightening' supervision of myriad minor aspects of their environment which, actually, are the whole." Then she set down a list of "typical day's problems," which conveyed her anxiety that she was not able to create the kind of nurturing that comes with the small decisions that weave a durable protective connection.

- What to wear to school?
- Whether a cold is severe enough to remain at home?
- Getting there on time
- Practicing piano, etc. Should it be continued if it is sloughed off too often?
- Who picks up sick child from school?
- Must naps be taken today or will earlier bedtime suffice?
- Bath and supper-time quietly and quickly observed (whose slippers? Bathrobes today?)
- Warm or cool pajamas?
- Peanut butter and marshmallow held to a minimum
- May we swim today?
- Who fed the chickens?
- Whose bike may I borrow?
- Birthday plans and their carrying out . . .
- When should the dentist look at those teeth, which NOW need brushing?
- Public or private school?
- Local recitals, parents' days, conferences with teachers, scout leaders, etc.
- Does the baby's diaper rash need the doctor's attention or just the diaper-changer's?
- Gamma-globulin for measles?
- Television figures on pajamas?
- Coloring or wrestling after supper?
- Pigtails or pony-tail?
- Who needs aspirin?

- Who needs a little extra time alone or with a parent?
- Why doesn't Martha do her homework sooner and more carefully?

I consider similar questions almost every day. I have had to be fairly resourceful in finding good advice to guide my own parenting—sometimes I think that if she'd stuck around, my mother would have provided useful counsel around the endless and sometimes agonizing executive decisions parents make. These are the small, intimate details of children's lives, the things that should matter. By making such a list, I think my mother was holding on to a hope, reassuring herself that she was a savvy mother, not only well-intentioned but also sure-footed, one who would not be willingly banished or seen as "unfit." I sense that in writing her list, Mama realized she had created an absence by moving out. She seems hell-bent on reassuring herself that she will be good to her word, that she will be there when we need her. If only she could have delivered.

I have questions of my own that she might have considered:

- Why are the parents so mad and fighting?
- What is it about?
- Who should the children live with, mother or father?
- How to explain suicide attempt?
- What should children call their parents' lovers?
- Who is watching when children are in the pool?
- Why can't the children be with their mother?
- When can I let you go?

Chapter Nine

There is a higher court than courts of justice and that is the court of conscience. It supersedes all other courts.

—MAHATMA GANDHI

My parents' battle reached a climax in June 1962 when my mother and father spent six days in court. Until the 1980s, it was common practice to award mothers sole custody of the children while relegating fathers to the role of a visiting bystander. But my mother's suicide attempt, along with my father's vigorous opposition to her having custody, forced convention aside. The fact that my maternal grandmother, Edith Vahey, supported my father having custody and agreed to continue living at the Quail Street house reconfirmed the decision.

There are few surviving documents and records to peruse, and my father has never talked about how the custody battle played out in public. I am forced to rely on what the newspapers reported, with their lurid headlines and peculiar observations, to make sense of an outcome I could never understand. In the newspaper accounts, my father is presented as reasonable and concerned and hoping for a reconciliation. He is described as generous, and as protective of the children. My mother is portrayed as hysterical, free-spending, and unstable, with the question looming of whether she is "fit" to take care of the children.[1] My mother's physician testified that she was "suffering from secondary anemia, loss of vitality, severe migraine headaches, and depression." The doctor acknowledged a bruise he'd noticed when he first examined her, but he asserted that "Mrs. Rappaport is now capable of caring for the six children as far as her health was concerned."[2] In the newspaper articles, evidence of my father's violence is rationalized and justified with examples of my mother's own angry outbursts and suicide threats.

TELLS STORY IN CUSTODY BATTLE, PILLS FELLED MOTHER OF 6
(*RECORD AMERICAN*, THURSDAY, JUNE 7, 1962)

. . . Mrs. Rappaport seeks custody of their six young children. She testified she had gone through a crisis in the past two years and "I know now I should not have signed the agreement."

She told the court she has since discovered she had a "blood deficiency," that she was "desperate, felt horrible," and could not "stay in the same room with Jerry without bursting into tears."

Mrs. Rappaport testified she "just had to sign that agreement because I did not feel I was a fit mother for the children at the time. I decided the only thing I could do would be to get away and pull myself together as best I could. The only reason I signed the agreement was because my mother was co-custodian.

"The only thing that Jerry wanted was to get me out of the house. He always said that I would always be their mother."

Mrs. Rappaport, who won a divorce in Alabama in September, 1961, on grounds of cruel and abusive treatment after 10 years of marriage to the Boston attorney, told Judge Keville that since the divorce she has had two doctors, one a psychiatrist and the other a physician.

"I know now what happened to our marriage and what drove me away from Jerry," she said. "I've been through a crisis the past two years. I know now I should not have signed the agreement."

She could not tell the reason for her illness.

Her testimony was interrupted to permit the court to hear Dr. William A. Dixon, of Milton, a Beacon St. pediatrician, who has treated the children since birth.

Dr. Dixon, a witness for Rappaport, testified that the care and maintenance of the children at the present time, "considering the upset of the home, is that they are adequately cared for. Their care at this time is no better and no worse than it was before the divorce."

On one occasion since the divorce, Mrs. Rappaport testified she went to the 17-room Rappaport home at Quail St., West Roxbury, to pick up her son, "Jerry," and the father shoved and pushed her, so that the children had to step between them. At one point, she said she feared they were going over the stair railing.

Under cross-examination by Atty. Jackson Holtz, she testified that although she was having a visitation problem, at no time did she ask anyone to arbitrate her visitation rights.

The fact that this story made it into the papers heightened the drama for spectators, but the problem was that there were kids involved in the media circus. What is lost in the conflict is the fact that six children needed and wanted both their parents—even if imperfect.

WIFE WASTED CASH
(*RECORD AMERICAN*, THURSDAY, JUNE 14, 1962)

Atty. Jerome Rappaport Wednesday pictured his divorced wife, Nancy Vahey Rappaport, as a woman with a violent temper, who talked of suicide and spent her divorce settlement money at a lavish rate.

The prominent politician-attorney testified during the fifth day of a hearing before Judge Edmund V. Keville in Suffolk Probate Court on her suit to regain custody of their six children who had been given to him as part of the Alabama divorce settlement she received last September.

Rappaport testified that Nancy would storm out of their home in Quail St., West Roxbury, and when he would coax her back home, she would throw books, a radio, dinnerware, glasses or whatever was at hand at him.

. . . Rappaport said he promised to give Nancy $52,000 as part of the divorce settlement, part of this sum to be considered a "loan."

He said she wanted the entire sum at once but for tax purposes he insisted on paying it in installments. Last month, he testified, they had a discussion about money. She said she needed more and admitted she had a little more than $1,000 left out of the $21,000 or $22,000 he had given her to date.

Rappaport said he tried to tell his wife that she was living beyond her means. He said she took an apartment at $385 a month and told him she did not intend to look for a job until after the custody petition was heard.

The lawyer testified he was willing to give her money until she remarried.

A bruise on Nancy's body, which her physician, Dr. Samuel Kowal of Beacon St., Brookline, had testified to seeing, may have been caused by him striking her, Rappaport admitted.

He said there had been an argument Feb. 2, 1962, when she was visiting him and when he tried to prevent her from going to a telephone, she kicked him and he struck her face. He was not certain where the blow had landed, however.

At the suggestion from Nancy's lawyer that Rappaport had ordered her to leave the house during a Mother's Day visit with the children, the lawyer declared that to the contrary he had insisted that she stay. The visit lasted from 11 a.m. to 4 p.m., he testified. . . .

My grandmother was the closing witness, portrayed in the newspaper as sympathetic and doting. It is not clear to me why my mother would have thought she had the support of my grandmother before the trial, as the newspaper described Edith as willing to "share custody of these lovely children with anyone"—a decided blow to my mother's bid.

GRANNY TELLS LOVE FOR 6 IN CUSTODY ROW
(*RECORD AMERICAN*,
FRIDAY, JUNE 15, 1962)

. . . Edith Vahey, trim and active at 65, spoke of the failings of both her daughter and her son-in-law, Atty. Jerome Rappaport, during her testimony as the windup witness.

She made it clear that she was neutral as far as they were concerned but she emphasized that she loved the six children whose custody she shares with her son-in-law.

(Mrs. Vahey . . . spoke with conviction when she was questioned about her concern for the children who live with her and Rappaport in their Quail St., West Roxbury, home.) She was asked if it was true, as maintained in her daughter's petition, that she no longer wishes to share custody of the children with her son-in-law.

"I would share custody of these lovely children with anyone," she said with finality to the Judge Edmund V. Keville. Asked if she would assume full custody, she replied, "I certainly would."

"The children are my life, "she said simply. "I have no outside interests besides these children. They have my entire attention. I have had many arguments with my daughter and
perhaps always will. But I have been happy living in the house
with Jerry, although there have been times when I left when I
did not approve of his visitors."

"The children are the ones that are important."

Mrs. Vahey, who looked and played the part of a loving
grandmother, carried a cane into court but explained she does
not need it but carries it for support. . . .

Near the end of the testimony, Judge Keville took the six children into his
courtroom and questioned us—Where did we want to live? My older siblings remember this and I find it confirmed in the court records. Martha
and Jim wanted to live with Dad, Amy and Jerry asked to live with Mama,
and Judy could not decide. At 2 years of age I was spared as being too young
to understand or answer the question. My sister Judy says that her indeci-
siveness that day has haunted her—if only she had been able to weigh in
confidently and let the judge know she wanted to live with Mama.

Today, a judge would never invite children under 12 years old into his
chambers for this purpose. People who work with families and children
know that this question is too great a burden for children so young. Nowadays, court evaluations of children consider each child's developmental history, what the children have witnessed, the separations and losses each of
them has experienced, the children's reaction to the parental separation,
and their attachment to each parent.[3] But in the 1960s, most judges were
not as knowledgeable about children's psyches as they are now.

At the end of the six-day hearing, Judge Keville considered the testimony
and made his decision awarding joint custody to my father and my grandmother except for one month in the summer when my mother would have
us. He added the unusual provision that neither Dick nor Barbara Sears was
allowed to be in our presence. We would still live with my father and my

grandmother but if Edith was not able to serve as custodian, my father would not be able to assume individual custody of the children without a further hearing. My mother would be allowed to see us Monday through Friday at Quail Street from 11:00 a.m. until 4:00 p.m., and she could visit our home on the holidays and on the children's birthdays and have us come to her apartment on "alternate weekends." The probate court documents also state that "she shall be informed and shall be allowed to visit the children without limitation whenever they are ill."[4]

Elaine Werby tells me that my mother was devastated by her loss and felt deeply betrayed by her own mother. The only reason she initially signed the agreement when she separated from my father was that she trusted her mother. "I think that she truly thought she was going to get you children back," Elaine says. "That is what she lived on.... She counted on it. She was so sure." Elaine's voice is heavy. She sighs. "She left for self-preservation but your mother couldn't see it as it seemed to an outsider. No mother deserts her kids and gets them back."

Mama around 1937, all dressed up in her petticoat.

Grandma Vahey, my maternal grandmother, in a formal portrait, around age 50.

Photo published in the March 1952 edition of Redbook magazine. The original caption read, "Founder of the New Boston Committee is Jerome Rappaport, young Boston attorney, shown here with his wife, Nancy. The romance blossomed during the early days of the committee."

Mama's 1956 graduation from Boston University with a master's degree in English language. She holds Jim, who was just three weeks old at the time.

Photo of Mama printed in the October 1958 edition of *Boston Evening American*. The original caption read, "United Fund Chairman Nancy Rappaport: Stitch during work time gets many things done." (Photo courtesy of FayFoto/Boston.)

Family portrait on the couch in 1960: Jerry, Amy, Martha holding me, Judy, Jim.

Front view of our home on Quail Street.

Lined up youngest to oldest on the diving board the summer of 1966. I am third from the left.

Our new blended family in the Fall of 1968 on the terrace with our dog, Winsor: Dickie is on the far left, then Jerry, Amy, Martha holding Debbie, Judy holding Elizabeth, Jim, Carter, me, and Andrew.

1970 family portraits on the couch. Front row: Jerry, Martha, Andrew, Barbara, Dad, me. Back row: Carter, Dickie, Judy, Elizabeth (perched), Jim, Amy, Debbie.

June 20, 1987: Colin and I at our wedding on Dad's farm in Vermont. We invited 110 family members and friends to help us celebrate.

Chapter Ten

Once upon a time there was a mother and a father who had six children. They had a big house and two maids and five dogs. They had a swimming pool. Now they were very happy until one day they started to get very angry at each other and one screamed and another yelled the opposite to the other's answer and a few months afterwards my mother went to Alabama to deforce my father. We were very sad. My mother is very pretty, kind and she loves everybody in one way, so do I. I wish I could live with my mother and father both at the same time. It wouldn't be happy without father or mother. I wish they could get along together so they could live together again and live happily ever after.

Sincerily Yours, Your Daughter Amy Rappaport, age 8

I started treating Katey, a spunky 15-year-old, when her parents were in a bitter divorce battle. While she was living with her dad, Katey was superficially cutting her wrists and had poor grades. Her mother was worried and asked her to see a therapist. Katey refused, so her mother worked to convince a court to order psychotherapy. In response, Katey stonewalled her mother and would not speak to her. Unable to win Katey's cooperation, her father risked being in contempt of court unless he forced Katey into both treatment and visitation with her mother.

So on this late April afternoon, Katey's father brings her to see me. She enters dressed in a V-neck T-shirt and loose-fitting Harvard sweatpants, surveys the room critically, then quickly informs me that she will be reading throughout these mandated sessions. Further, she announces in a loud voice, she will *not* talk about her standoff with her mother. Katey settles into a chair and picks up her book. I ask her a few questions, which she ignores, but eventually, when it's clear that I don't intend to ask about her mother, she eases into conversation. I question her about school and she starts to warm up as she talks about her debate club—and soon puts her book aside.

"We are *awesome*," she tells me. She's proud that her team went to the state championships. She tells me that she's the "mad dog" in her group, the one who will construct the most aggressive arguments, and that she loves to win. "I have a reputation," she confides. "I can be pretty intimidating."

I wonder as I sit with her if I'm sitting with a future judge: She delights in the nuances of legal arguments. Emboldened by my sense that we're making progress, I ask a gentle question about her mother. Katey shuts down instantly, and there is a sudden coldness in the room. I quickly backpedal, adding that I have faith—she'll know if and when she wants or even needs to talk about her mother with me. I have grown to trust that my patients have good reasons for making their decisions. I'm not interested in pressuring her. She needs to know that she is in charge of what she chooses to share.

She arrives at our next session with her debating notebook, and we begin to peruse the details of one of her arguments. I gently ask if we can choose a debate topic for our next session. She looks surprised when I hand her a real case from a professional journal. One week after starting an antidepressant, a man killed his wife and then committed suicide. We inspect the different positions about whether drug companies should be held accountable for rare but tragically adverse effects of popular medications. I say quietly, sensing an opening, "I'm going to need your help because I'm probably going to need to go to court to explain why you shouldn't be forced into therapy." She sighs, a little defeated, and for a few minutes we are quiet. She seems to retreat into her chair.

Katey then explodes, tortured: "She doesn't know me! I haven't seen her in three years except for emails; she calls me on my cell phone at night when I'm with friends and leaves me stupid messages." She looks disgusted. I ask, "Why do you think she's so persistent?" She responds sharply, "I don't know—you're a mother, you figure it out."

I'm caught in a maze of sympathies; I can't imagine the anguish of being completely rejected by one of my daughters, unsure whether it's temporary or whether there is a possibility for reconciliation. I know that thinking in extremes and absolutes is a trademark of teenagers. I need to help her find a middle way. She will be wary of betrayal, but I like working with strong kids like Katey.

Katey goes on indignantly, "My mother *provokes* me. She forces me into therapy and then when I get pissed about it, she says I'm not okay. My aunt wrote me a long email, telling me how I needed to fix things with my mother and that everyone needs a mother. But I'm fine, day to day, when I am not reminded of her. Not like before." Before she was miserable, self-mutilating, getting C's. "But now look at me," she says, holding her arms wide, showing me her healed wrists. "I'm better without her, *right?*"

I say again, quietly, looking away, "It's hard for your mom to think you're okay if she's not in your life." I tell Katey she's a hot ticket, and that I'm sorry her mom didn't have the time with her to see that. If she could have some flexibility and compassion for her mother's position, this wouldn't become a permanent standoff. I support Katey's right to choose whether or not she'll be in therapy, but also want her to recognize how she may have options other than icing out a mother who clearly cares about her, and I want her to know how hard it must be for her mother not to have day-to-day opportunities for reparations.

"We're running over," Katey says, beleaguered. "If you go to court, tell my mom this isn't forever, if she can back off. She should let me decide when I'm going to contact her. Maybe it'll be in college, or when I have a child: I'm not sure," her voice trails off. "But," she looks at me with all the resolve that she has, "*I need to be able to choose and not be forced into it. Okay?*" She wants it to be clear that she won't be cowed into submission by court mandates.

I'm left feeling slightly chagrined. I want her to move forward. I want her to make small overtures to her mother, call her, and appease her in some way. It's not good to lose a mother, I want to tell her, and it's terrible to lose a child. I worry, too, that her mother will vilify me. The best I can do for Katey is have her grudgingly acknowledge that this isn't necessarily a "*forever* decision." I appreciate Katey's strong defiance and the fact that she resists her mother's negative outlook. She is smart and she knows what she needs.

Neutrality is often hard to accomplish; the family can be polarized and children can act in ways that take attention away from the sobering reality of the family changing—a sacrifice of sorts. Katey may have been the voice of protest about how her parents divorced, a protest that I was only beginning to understand. I am reminded of my sister Amy's "happily ever after" wish for our family; her effort to create a sensible story is so often what children try to do when their parents divorce. Amy seemed wise beyond her 8 years to know that, despite our parents' fighting, "it wouldn't be happy without father or mother." Katey reminds me that when teenagers have space to reflect on what has happened and the confidence of people who care for them, they often arrive at a clarity that allows for a loosening of the battle lines.

My husband and I are both children of divorce, but neither of us thinks of the other that way. If you're going to create a hierarchy of childhood traumas, then clearly the loss of our mothers was more traumatic than the speed bumps of our families' divorces. Some psychologists advise people who have lived through divorce as children to seek spouses from stable homes if we want a better chance of staying married. But love and psychiatry do not operate the same way.

In the 1960s, almost 90 percent of American children were raised in homes with ostensibly intact families with married parents.[1] Nowadays, divorce is much more common—only 57 percent of marriages in 1995 made it to their fifteenth anniversary, and over 1 million children each year are witnesses to their parents' divorces.[2] The causes of this apparent rise in divorce rates are unclear. Some argue that the dramatic increase in divorce is a sign of the deterioration of the culture, while in my field it is widely acknowledged that reforms in family law have made it easier and safer for partners to leave unhealthy marriages and have legal protection when domestic violence has occurred. Divorce is an increasingly familiar part of the culture and it is now more socially acceptable for women to initiate divorce. Divorce books with titles such as *What About the Kids?* and *Raising Your Children Before, During, and After Divorce* fill the shelves of self-help sections in bookstores, and there is a widespread assumption that the relatively common dissolution of a marriage may not necessarily cause lasting harm. Yet the particular meaning and fallout of a breakup is unique to each family. Today we know better how to help families manage divorce. In books, therapy, arbitration, and legal reform, families can find pragmatic suggestions gleaned from decades of observation on how to minimize the damage and provide security for kids during the divorce and transition.

Two of the best-known long-term studies of divorce examine the effects on children. In *The Unexpected Legacy of Divorce: A 25-Year Landmark Study*,[3] a book about sixty divorced families in Marin County, California, authors Judith Wallerstein, Julia Lewis, and Sandra Blakeslee conclude that a small minority of children will be permanently scarred by divorce. These children will grow up with a greater risk for depression, delinquency, and poor grades. The authors further warn that most young adults will recall their parents' divorce as a major trauma in their lives and fear that it will color their relationships as they repeat the pattern established by their parents.

The second important study, described in *For Better or For Worse: Divorce Reconsidered*,[4] was led by E. Mavis Hetherington and John Kelly, who for three decades followed about 1,400 families and more than 2,500 children. Hetherington and Kelly found that 25 percent of children of divorce have serious social or psychological problems in contrast to the 10 percent of children from intact families with similar difficulties. But they also note that most children of divorce experience little lingering damage. Within two years after their parents had divorced, most of the children examined in this study were doing reasonably well, and as adults they were able to choose and sustain satisfying careers and relationships. Furthermore, more than two-thirds of the divorced parents were living happier and more fulfilling lives than they did before their divorce.

The most devastating consequences of high-conflict divorce lie in what psychiatrist Diana Siskind identifies as "the interplay of hatred and dependency between the parents juxtaposed with their pain and loneliness at not being able to share with each other (or, perhaps with anyone) their love for their children."[5] Divorce can also bring with it the erosion of parental authority. In the midst of conflict, parents can lose their identity as adults in full charge of the care of their children. According to Siskind, the erosion of parental authority as a tragic consequence of divorce is unavoidable when legally imposed terms and conditions replace the naturalness of parental prerogative. Sometimes this can also cause parents to feel awkward with their children.[6] For some parents, mine included, "divorce is a critical developmental moment"; their secure attachment to their children was disrupted and the way of life that shaped each parent's sense of identity was threatened. Some parents may be so devastated and preoccupied that they are temporarily blind to the needs of their children.[7]

When custody becomes contentious, the meaning of the divorce takes on even more unsettling dimensions. Researcher Janet Johnston has built a career on empirical studies of 200 families in entrenched custody disputes. Her work reveals the nature of the damage caused in intense, high-conflict divorces where some parents in custody disputes are vulnerable to the stresses of loss and rejection that are inherent in the divorce crisis and its aftermath. She explains that some separating spouses who have experienced traumatic losses such as the untimely death of a child, parent, or sibling are at risk of re-experiencing this earlier helplessness and grief along with the pain of the divorce. For them, the marital separation can trigger panic and intolerable anxiety about abandonment. In order to manage the unbearable "bad" feelings, they project the unwanted aspects of self onto the former partner so that the self can be experienced as invulnerable and "good." Often these spouses then come to see the other parent as increasingly "irrelevant and irresponsible, even dangerous, whereas the self is seen as the essential, responsible, and safe caretaker."[8]

The reorganization of divorced families can move in a positive direction if separating spouses are able to create "limited partnerships," as described by Constance R. Ahrons in *The Good Divorce*.[9] In her longitudinal research on ninety families, about half of the couples were able to provide continuity and stability for their families (she calls these couples "perfect pals" and "cooperative colleagues") by accepting joint responsibility, being flexible, prioritizing the children's needs, and making it clear that the children benefit from having a constructive relationship with both parents. The remaining half of the divorced couples (whom she calls "angry associates" and "fiery foes") were consumed by power struggles and a sense of unrelenting bitterness. Ahrons motivates divorcing couples to find a common ground by asking them to envision future occasions in their family such as attending birthday parties, sending their child off to college, or celebrating the birth of a grandchild to help them recognize that on some level they will continue to be kin.

Sometimes I think about how my mother might have felt as our family fractured. It makes sense to imagine that my mother's loss of her bid for custody and her seemingly permanent separation from us would have evoked intolerable anxiety. She might have long harbored a fear that at any moment

life could take a catastrophic turn and felt a sense of tremendous comfort
that, until her family collapsed, she had a stroke of good fortune with her
flock of children. When my father portrayed her as unfit to care for us, my
mother might have been enraged that she was seen as irrelevant and irresponsible and that my father took on the appearance of the essential, responsible, and safe caretaker. Did this custody battle evoke other times
when she might have desperately wanted another outcome—a sister who
could swim, sober parents, and time to heal?

My father, too, was devastated by my mother's departure. Anger is sometimes
easier to bear than sadness. Janet Johnston—who, in addition to her research,
provides parental counseling and resolution with families—describes a destructive pattern in custody disputes where parents are acting unilaterally,
without prioritizing the child's needs, and not only sabotaging but also undermining each other's capacity to parent and protect the child. The ad-
versarial legal system, she notes, can heighten each parent's experience of
"the other's rejection, custody demands, or accusations, as a devastating attack, and in defense develops paranoid ideas of betrayal, conspiracy, and
exploitation by the ex-mate."[10] The children, in order to receive any semblance of nurturance and to avoid their own sense of abandonment, or even
psychic destruction, may feel pressured to express what the rejected parent
feels and perceives.[11] My parents, consumed by their own fight, were blind
to what was happening to us.

   After the first court decision in June 1962 to have the children live with
Edith and my father, the summer wore on as my parents bickered, battled,
and maneuvered. Though she'd lost the first round, my mother persisted,
braving my father's fury—and perhaps even exacerbating it—by diligently
visiting us as much as the custody agreement allowed. If she were ever to
get her children back, my mother would need to show the court that she
was secure enough to provide a home for the six of us, and she set to work
building that foundation.

The first step was to say good-bye to Dick. My mother also began trying to win back Edith's support. She made incremental progress and put aside her own sense of betrayal. She knew that at least she could count on Edith's concern for the children. She also knew that Edith despised the Searses and that this could be used to her advantage. Edith couldn't stand it whenever my father insisted that she leave Quail Street for the weekend when he had plans to entertain Barbara, and she complained about being "kicked out of the house so he could be with that woman" to anyone who would listen. And with Dick moving on and Barbara moving in with my father, Edith was now much more sympathetic to my mother.

In November 1962, my mother took a job at the Harvard Business School as a research assistant. As her life began to assume a modest rhythm of normalcy around the scaffolding of daily work and visitation, she grew more confident and self-sufficient. Over the fall and into the winter she strategized with her lawyers. She changed lawyers, she kept detailed notes, and she prepared for another round in court. In February 1963 she filed a petition to revisit the custody decision. A new hearing was scheduled for June. And she also started a new romance that had no connection to the breakup of her marriage.

Alexander Stanley had married twice before he met my mother. He had written a dense text on trade, and in the late 1950s he was invited to join the Harvard faculty as a visiting instructor at the Business School, where he met my mother. She had come to work for him as a researcher. His niece tells me, "I remember when he met her. He told us, 'I've met someone and I'm in love.' He was glowing. And I remember that he lost weight because he wanted to be svelte for her.... He was in love with your mother, truly and deeply, and he was awed that he was going to be stepfather to six great kids; he wanted to embrace this because he didn't have children."

She describes Alex as an intelligent man, fastidious, full of energy, but with a temper. "He wasn't the type to speak openly: he was stoic, and the kind of guy to look forward and not look backward. But he was fond of all of you." Alex had problems with money. "He wasn't a gambler, but he had terrible luck with the stock market. And he wasn't good about managing his money. He made money at times and then at other times he was out of money."

Alex Stanley and my mother married in a Catholic cathedral, St. Cecilia, in March 1963.[12] My mother's friends share mixed reviews of Alex. Some tell me that she loved him, that he was a supportive presence in her life, that he was good for her. Others are more suspicious; he made them uncomfortable, and they suggest he took advantage of her vulnerability and perhaps what he thought would be a solution to his financial problems. They wonder if it was a marriage of convenience, necessary for my mother's custody claims. Alex had been raised Catholic, though as an adult he was a lapsed Catholic at best. When he met my mother, he recommitted himself to Catholicism, and my mother (who had converted to Judaism after she married my father) returned to her roots of Catholicism when she married Alex.[13]

Elaine Werby thought that Mama was starting to lose a sense of who she really was when she married him. Elaine noted that others were curious if not somewhat suspicious about why Alex had two dead wives and he was only 50. She says dryly, "We used to joke to your mother, three strikes and you're out. It wasn't so funny after she died."

Sydell Masterman offered yet another perspective when I reconnected with her after seeing her at my father's seventy-fifth birthday. "I think the real love of her life was your father. He was intellectually challenging to her— they were equals that way. I think that Dick Sears fling was just frustration. It turned out so wrong, and she knew that. She was devastated by her mistake and by the fact that your father was with Barbara. I don't think she wanted to be with your father, but she couldn't stand that he was with Barbara—woman to woman, it would have bothered me, too. My impression is that she didn't love Alex but that she knew she needed someone to keep her afloat."

Sydell's voice was soft. "She didn't have a way to know that she might have messed up her life, but she could still be a part of yours. I think marrying Alex was her way of trying to get you back."

For whatever reason, and I will never know for sure, my mother believed that her marriage to Alex would appear to the court as a sign of her stability. It would, she rationalized, at least increase the odds of winning in court. This is what mattered to her the most. Yet within weeks of my mother's marriage, my father asked to have the custody agreement modified to allow Barbara Sears to be in the presence of my siblings and me, and then, dealing yet another blow to my mother, he decided to marry Barbara in May.

When the time came to begin the depositions, my mother was by all appearances a recovered woman—physically healthy, married, employed, and making progress with her therapy. Though the court proceedings were not recorded,[14] I was able to retrieve a copy of my grandmother's deposition. In a large cavernous courthouse I find the transcript in faded black ink printed on brittle pages. It provides me with one more perspective as it captures the dramatic turn of events when my grandmother was finally ready to give my mother the support that she needed. Reading the transcript, I can't help but wonder if she had a premonition of her fate and if it made her more determined to settle matters. Perhaps she realized that my stepmother Barbara Sears, the new Mrs. Jerome Rappaport, would not welcome her continued presence at Quail Street, thereby limiting my grandmother's access to her grandchildren. (Less than six months after she gave these statements, Edith was diagnosed with advanced throat cancer.) My grandfather, Arthur Rappaport, was also at my dad's side during the deposition at my grandmother's apartment. My grandmother's lawyer was Willard Lombard.

Representing my mother was Roger J. Donahue. He worked to establish Edith as a credible witness who lived at Quail Street with my parents when they were married and then stayed after my mother left. To establish her as someone who has seen what was happening with the children at Quail Street, he described her as having shared custody with my father of the six children. She was a well-trained witness, answering the questions and not elaborating.

Donahue was testing whether Edith would provide evidence in her testimony that my father had brazenly violated the previous judge's order to keep Barbara Sears away from the six of us. The court had prohibited her from being in our presence until the previous April, when my father engineered his legal change. And, as Donahue must have known, Edith could not stand Barbara Sears. Edith was a force to contend with, poised but all too ready to show her disapproval of Barbara.

> *Donahue (my mother's lawyer):* Are you aware that in February of this year your daughter Nancy has brought a petition for a modification of the custody order of the Court in which she is seeking custody of the six children?
>
> *Edith:* Yes.
>
> *Donahue:* And you are aware, of course, also that your daughter Nancy married Mr. Stanley last October; is that right?
>
> *Edith:* March 1963.

Donahue was setting the stage, introducing the cast of characters. Maybe he was also aware that although Edith was cooperating, willing to help my mother at this time, she was unpredictable and not a reliable ally.

As I study portions of the testimony looking for nuances of meaning, it seems to me that Edith was anxious not to alienate my father. It is interesting to see how she qualified her testimony—she made sure to acknowledge him as a father. She was upset that he chose Barbara over her as a custodian of her grandchildren, which meant that Barbara's children, the three Sears boys, were added to the Quail Street household. But even with all that she'd seen, Edith still loved, and even feared, my father and was cunning enough to play both sides depending on what was to her advantage. My grandmother was not entirely won over by Alex Stanley, but she was apparently grateful for his sensible influence on my mother. She gave him credit for calming her.

Donahue: There has been a difference in Nancy since her recent marriage to Mr. Stanley?

Edith: Yes, quite a difference in my opinion.

Donahue: What have you observed about Nancy that was different from her condition before she remarried Mr. Stanley?

Edith: Well, she is a lot happier.

Donahue: You feel Mr. Stanley has been sort of a stabilizing influence on her?

Edith: I certainly do.

Having established that there was some degree of normalcy in the home of my mother and Alex Stanley, Attorney Donahue tried to have her expand on her reservations about the disorder and turmoil at Quail Street. Jackson Holtz was up next. He represented my father. Holtz knew Edith well, having socialized with her at my father's house. His style was markedly different from Donahue's. He had an ingratiating manner. He wanted more from Edith than the facts. He knew that she cherished the children and loved Jerry, and he wanted her love to come across. He started out disarmingly:

Holtz (my father's lawyer): Just a couple of things, Edith. This being a holiday, I suspect we all want to leave and I don't want to trouble you any more than the proceedings require. I think you told us, told Mr. Donahue, that Mr. Stanley represented a stabilizing influence on Nancy. What was her problem that needed stabilizing?

Edith: Well, I don't think—

Donahue: Note my objection to this.

Edith: [continuing] I don't think Nancy—I think Nancy has been very emotionally upset and very upset, and she is a, well, as you know, a very emotional type of person anyway.... And I think, as I said before, married to Alex, she is—well, he just seems to handle her very well, and I think she is happier and just in much better condition. She will still flare up, as I said before. She will always flare, just as I will, or anyone else with that temperament.

Edith appeared flustered, elaborating too much. She was looking for Holtz to help her out, but he was not on her side this time. He was adept at insinuating that Edith was minimizing her daughter's outbursts. Holtz seemed confident that he could get Edith off balance enough that she would suggest that my mother was too volatile to care for the children. It had worked before.

> *Holtz:* Will you give us some illustrations of what you refer to as a flare-up?
>
> *Edith:* Well, I don't know at the present moment, any more than another argument. She is a very vehement sort of a person.
>
> *Holtz:* Would you mind giving us some illustrations of it, Mrs. Vahey?
>
> *Edith:* Well, I don't know what you would want me to give or what you want to bring out. Perhaps if you'd ask me a question, I could answer it better.
>
> *Holtz:* All right. I think you told us she was quite emotional before the divorce and after the divorce I think a little more so, in substance, I think you said. I would like to know what you mean by that so we could have it a little clearer rather than just characterize it at this point.
>
> *Edith:* Well, what else do you want me to say? Emotionally upset. I don't know how else you'd describe it or what you want me to say. Any more than anybody else being—the whole thing was very much of a mess and everybody not knowing whether they were coming or going. Not Nancy any more than all the rest of us.

People remember my mother's stability in different ways and it is unlikely for me to find the complete truth amidst the confusion. My father has a deep conviction that he was protecting us, generous with Mama's visitation but the better primary parent. Dad claims that she had emotional tantrums before she was married. He saw her tantrums as potentially dangerous. When her water broke with the birth of Amy, my mother was disappointed that her doctor was not available. She locked herself in the bathroom and finally came out when he called her two aunts. He says that she threatened suicide and it was hard to know how far she would go.

Amy, who was only 9 years old at the time of my mother's death, says adamantly that she doesn't remember multiple suicide attempts. Martha remembers that our mother had extreme highs and lows and would "disappear" for a time, needing to be alone. No suicide attempts prior to the one in 1961 are mentioned in any of the papers. But if it is true that she struggled for years with depression and that she had previously tried to kill herself, then I am sorry for my father. Her threats must have terrified him. He would not have known how to manage. If it's not true, then I must try to understand his claims as being self-protective. The transcript gave me the false hope I would find the definitive truth.

Returning to the proceedings, I find Holtz persisting in his interrogation about my mother's mental status. Edith sounded as exasperated as I am feeling.

> *Holtz:* I think you said she was a girl of vehemence, so that whatever you
>   can say as to what you mean by vehemence, with illustrations and so
>   forth?
> *Edith:* Would you rather that I said that Nancy has a very quick
>   temper? And, as I have always described it, an Irish temper, when
>   she can say a lot of things, and the next minute she has forgotten it
>   and everybody else is supposed to have forgotten it too. Now, that is
>   typical of Nancy.
> *Holtz:* And this is true of what we call flare-ups, too, isn't it?
> *Edith:* It is. That has been true all her life, and I am very sure will be the
>   rest of her life, regardless if I say that Alex has a very quieting
>   influence on it. I don't believe he is going to change that part of it
>   very much. But he does handle her well.

Holtz: Even over the last two or three months, she will go along for a little while on a plateau—

Edith: She still flares. As I say, she will always have these flares. . . .

Holtz: I think you said that she was emotionally upset and after the divorce even more so. Can you help us on that?

Edith: I don't know whether she was any more so after the divorce. If you are talking immediately after the divorce—

Holtz: Let's have that.

Edith: I think it took her some time to get a hold of herself. I am sure it did. Until after June, when she got out of this mess with these people. She began to calm down and—

Holtz: You say June. You mean June of '62?

Edith: Yes, the last June after the—

Holtz: Well—

Edith: After those people were out of the picture and she wasn't with the children, and so forth.

Those people. Edith had such distaste for the Searses that she wouldn't even deign to identify them by name. According to Ed English, who was one of our babysitters but more often Edith's young companion, she believed the Searses had poisoned my parents' marriage. She refused to see that my mother and father were responsible for their own problems and harbored the hope that, with Dick and Barbara out of the picture, my parents could reconcile—that somehow my mother's poor judgment would be forgiven and that my father would take her back and all would go back to normal.

Dad recently told me that if he hadn't married Barbara, Edith would have been there: "I married someone I loved and Edith wouldn't stay. She probably would have stayed if I had married anyone else."

Holtz soon turned to the question of the children. Edith's opinion was that nine children made for too big a family and that these nine were not an ideal mix. She acknowledged that the last time she saw Barbara was when my parents had "their big break-up" in July 1961.

Holtz then managed to get Edith to praise my father. Edith had no ax to grind with him—it was Barbara she had a problem with. And maybe, Holtz tried to suggest, that problem was irrational, vindictive, and without any basis in facts.

Donahue redirected. He wanted to make sure Edith portrayed my mother as stable. And he wanted to make sure she communicated her opinion that a woman of Barbara's character should not be in charge of such a large brood.

Donahue: You object to Mrs. Sears?

Edith: That has been the whole thing in this whole case for two years, as far as I am concerned. And that is in the other case, in the decree.

Donahue: What is Nancy's feeling and attitude towards the children, as you observed it in the past six months or so?

Edith: Well, Nancy has always loved her children, you know.

Donahue: And you have been with her and the children, have you, recently?

Edith: Oh, yes.

Donahue: And as far as this Irish temper that you spoke about, which I also possess to some extent, did you ever see any of this vehemence displayed towards the children, that is, since her marriage to Alex?

Edith: No, not since her marriage to Alex, I haven't....

Donahue: Would if be fair to say, Mrs. Vahey, that the influencing factor as to your feelings towards the present custody situation, is not just Jerry Rappaport's remarriage to Mrs. Sears, but also the other factors, that Nancy has remarried and more or less is settled down?

Edith: To this person.

Donahue: Yes.

Edith: Had it been the other situation [she means, if my mother had married Dick], then, well, I can't imagine. I would have been really sick. The influence on these children—in the first place, Nancy has settled down. It makes a great deal of difference. And with the people—naturally, there is an awful lot of feeling, as you know, from two years. It started two years ago. It hasn't changed, in my opinion. Marriage doesn't change that sort of thing. And as I brought up last June in court, those people were a bad influence as far as I was concerned. I didn't want the children under their influence.

Donahue: And that was Mr. and Mrs. Sears?

Edith: Yes. It would have been the same thing had Nancy ever married him, as far as I am concerned. I do feel that as far as Nancy's health is concerned and the situation and her marriage, that she is in ... a position to take those children now, take care of those children.

Donahue: And prior to the time there was any trouble between your daughter and Jerry, your daughter was a good mother to these children, was she?

Edith: Why, I certainly think so.

Donahue: Took good care of them?

Edith: Well, yes. If you mean washing their diapers, or washing their clothes, Nancy didn't do that. But Nancy was, as far as looking after those children and the discipline of those children and their welfare was well taken care of.

Donahue: I take it at the time when Nancy and Jerry were living together and apparently getting along that there was help to do the washing?

Edith: There has always been help. Jerry has always seen to that. And even though I lived there, why, I wasn't any more of a help as far as washing the dishes.

Donahue: I have no further questions.

Holtz wrapped up. He turned to Edith and asked about my mother's health, knowing that she had an ulcer. He also acknowledged that he had known Edith for many years.

⚭

In the trunk I was given, I found a baby picture I had never seen before. It is a picture of me at about 15 months, wearing a white, frilly diaper cover, hoisting myself to a standing position holding onto a chair for balance— as the legendary British psychoanalyst D. W. Winnicott says, "alone in the presence of others." I am standing just a few feet from the edge of the back-yard pool, and my grandmother, the mother of a drowned child herself, is sitting on the grass anxious and eagle-eyed. She will do whatever she needs to do to save her grandchildren. And I see this deposition as her effort to se-cure us a safe landing.

On July 26, 1963, Judge Keville made his ruling. It read:

> The petitioner, Nancy Stanley, is awarded custody of her six minor children commencing September 1, 1963. Thereafter, Jerome Rappaport may take the children on alternate week-ends from Friday at 5 p.m. until Sunday at 5 p.m. commencing September 13, 1963. He may take the children during the first half of regular school vacations including the summer vaca-tion. On Thanksgiving, Christmas, Easter, and on the children's birthdays he may take them at 2 p.m. for the balance of the day. He shall be kept informed with respect to the health of the children and shall be allowed to visit them without limita-tion whenever they are seriously ill. Until September 1, 1963, the children shall be in the custody of the Respondent Jerome Rappaport.

Miraculously, my mother had won.

Chapter Eleven

*Govern a family as you would cook a
small fish—very gently.*

—CHINESE PROVERB

Sheishere sheisgone sheisgone she must be here. . . . Itiptoeintotheirbedroom she is not sleeping shrill laughing newmother playingpianoendlesssound. I am in the bathtub I can see my faceonthefaucet thewateriscold goosebumps. IfIcomeout itwillallbeasbefore. Bee makes me warm tomato soup . . . the doll can't cry–shewatchesme with a stone face long eyelashes.

Three little kittens they lost their mittens
And they began to cry,
O mother dear,
We sadly fear,
Our mittens we have lost

Iwillnotsink if I holdontightenough.Tight. Tighter.

Butweonlyswim towards a landing of quicksand . . . quicksand . . . someonesaveus . . . saveus Hushhushlittlebaby. Hush little baby don't you cry. Hold on fast.

I wake up and prepare for work as I shake off my unsettling dream. I am seeing a patient, Sunil, whom I have seen for four years. I always look forward to seeing him as he nods his head respectfully, his voice warm with the recognition that he is not alone with his sorrow. He tells me, his head bowed as he avoids my gaze, that today is eight years and twenty-five days from when his wife died. Counting each day somehow marks his loss. The ashes of Sunil's bride sit in a small silver urn stashed away in a dingy closet behind the clutter of the day-to-day. He couldn't bear to part with her saris, her combs, or her grey dust, although, over the past eight years, on auspicious days, he would measure out small spoonfuls of ash into plastic sandwich bags and take her with him to the river. Thin in his worn shirt, jet-black hair brushed back with precision, he would crouch low on the bank, then scatter her ashes over the water and weep, tears and ash falling into the river together. Dust on water, she slipped quickly downstream.

I met him only after he went to the hospital by ambulance. He had thought that he too was going to die. He hadn't been able to stop weeping, and the nurses, disconcerted at finding him so inconsolable, had asked me for a psychiatric consult. He had been so tired, he mumbled, hardly able to move out of bed, so immobilized that dressing, shopping, even collecting the rice from the stove, had become too demanding. It hadn't always been this way, but he found it hard to imagine that life had ever been different. In the hospital, we learned that he was anemic. The doctors prescribed a series of shots to make him feel better and to give him energy. But Sunil did not get better. Depression like this cannot be cured with shots. He was gracious and polite as we talked that first time, and he was reluctant to reveal anything that would make me think less of him.

He had grown up in a rural part of India, the eldest son in a lower-caste family. His mother had mostly stayed sequestered in her room, while his father, a factory worker, enjoyed drinking with his comrades at the end of the day. His sisters and brothers worked to keep the house functioning while he was expected to study and practice his computations. He attended a regional school for advanced students, and each day his father would arrive halfway through the day carrying *dabbas*, silver containers, one carefully placed on top of another, filled with curry, rice, and yogurt. His father would stand at the gates of the school, and Sunil would ignore his presence and devour the food. As he grew older, he began to tell his fellow students that his father was a wealthy man from a small village in India who sold silks and gold trinkets—the man bringing the food was merely a servant sent to check up on his son's progress.

Applying to Stanford came as a challenge. A friend bet him that he wouldn't get in, so he had resolutely filled out an application. To his surprise, he was accepted with a full scholarship. Privately he carried the sense that he was a fraud, that these lucky breaks were somehow undeserved.

When he arrived in Palo Alto, he quickly found a small community of Indian students. They egged each other on and shared the comfort of firsts together. The firsts of breaking the meatless code and eating hamburgers at McDonald's, and of seeing a baseball game. They competed into the night, solving impossible problems and telling jokes, sharing their ambitions for the future. Sunil felt like part of something and was hopeful about his future. Then one of his fellow students killed himself. He hanged himself just a few months into the year, and the reason why was never clear. The stark confusion Sunil was left with marked the beginning of his inability to concentrate. Now when he looked at a math problem, the numbers started to collide with one another. Unable to proceed, he would focus on one strategy and repeat it over and over again. As he began to slip, he stopped going to his classes and would drift through the campus. He withdrew from Stanford, never finished his PhD, and returned to India.

He told no one what had happened. The new doctor of mathematics was simply home for a visit as far as anyone knew. Back in India, the summer heat bore down on him, and in the thick afternoons, he would escape to a cool, dark bookshop and sit so that just a sliver of light from the window could catch his page. It was here that he met the woman who would become his wife. She was living with her father, a well-known Bollywood executive. She pursued him at first, intrigued by his stories of California and his American expressions. Sunil told her he was thinking of going back to the States, to the East Coast this time, because he'd been asked to join the faculty at MIT, and she was impressed.

They started dating. His brother's friends warned him—she was notorious for her volatile temper. Sometimes, she would barricade herself in her room, or throw things impetuously—but Sunil saw that she could also be vulnerable, and her deep-brown eyes had a way of drawing him close. She found the idea of escaping to America intriguing—she could be free of the burdensome restrictions she faced living with her father, and it was appealing to marry a professor at MIT. So they married and together they moved to Cambridge.

Initially their life together had a dreamlike quality and was full of tenderness: They went to the movies and stayed up all night talking and discovering each other intimately. Each day Professor Sunil would leave to teach his mathematics students, although in reality he was working as a temporary typist. In the evening when he returned, he would talk with her about the politics of the math department and his pretend students. And this pretense went on for months.

One day, though, she needed him, and she called what she thought was his office. The math department secretary told her there was no Professor Sunil. Confused, she went to the office where she thought he worked, but again the secretary told her no such person existed. When he returned from work in the evening full of details of his students, she would have none of it. She broke all the dishes and let fly a string of invectives. It seemed to Sunil that there was no hint, no possibility of forgiveness, and for the next few days he resigned himself to the silence that pervaded the apartment, a silence devised to provide her with a way of separating her dream of who he might have been from the pitiful, contemptible man he felt he was. A few nights after she had discovered his betrayal, he awoke to hear her tight wheezing—she was barely able to ask him to call the ambulance. And he watched panic-stricken as she struggled for air and then went limp as they waited for the ambulance to arrive. At the hospital, the doctors informed him that there was nothing they could do; her lungs were too constricted and the asthma attack severe. She was dead.

He was unable to believe that there was no hope for reconciliation, numb that she had never forgiven him for failing to be more than he was. And since that time eight years ago, he lived from one anniversary to the next—cataloging all the events they had shared. Each time he wrote something down, he would question what was true and what was not. He would sift each detail for truth and meaning. But nothing was true in retrospect. The details of their life together did not add up—they made no story. He started again and again, revising, retooling, reimagining what it was that could be known. All night he would pace and write and try to remember, and try to repair a half-stitched heart. He remembered missed opportunities but worried that these might be illusions. By the break of dawn, he was exhausted. In the mornings, he always knew the same thing: Somehow, he had to let her go, but he wasn't sure how. Under the weight of his despair, he faltered. Grief and guilt together can make for a dark prison.

How did my own father escape it, I wondered, if, in fact, he ever did? I opened the curtain a little, but even with a little light, the depths of Sunil's sorrow speak to me of love and abandonment, the unfinished absence.

Leaving without closure (or having a chance to say goodbye) can sometimes lead to frozen grief, where we are left baffled and confused.[1] Our task together, as Rilke poetically describes, is to "be patient toward all that is unsolved in your heart and try to love the questions themselves like locked rooms and like books that are written in a very foreign tongue. Live the questions now. Perhaps you will then gradually, without noticing it, live along some day into the answer."[2] As I listen to Sunil, I wonder if he will ever tame his longing, but with my comforting encouragement, perhaps he will glance backward while moving forward, building a learned optimism.[3]

Within days of Judge Keville's ruling to return us to our mother, my father made a desperate appeal to the Massachusetts Supreme Judicial Court. Appealing to the SJC was the only way one could stay the court order and not have circumstances change. My father wanted the court to determine that the decision was wrong because he had a signed agreement from our mother that the children were better off with him. They needed to establish that he was an inadequate father; they had the burden of proof. He was appealing to a higher court because he didn't want circumstances to change. Once the court stayed the probate decision, which was very unusual in those days, the children would remain with him until the case was argued before the SJC.

My father's lawyer submitted a letter from our pediatrician, who was of the opinion that our mother was questionably stable and was married to a relatively unknown new husband. He cautioned that moving us from the luxury and spaciousness of the country, where we were living with a happy, wonderful, devoted father to whom we were deeply attached, as well as a loving stepmother and three stepbrothers, was a frightening proposal. He thought that the move to my mother's household was ill-advised and dangerous; he saw it as a strange, confining home in the city and as causing an unnecessary change to new schools and the loss of old friends.[4]

Elaine Werby tells me that this change in venue shocked my mother—that before this she had firmly believed that each time she went to court, she'd get the children back. This last time, there was such a build-up, and it looked like she had won. But with the change of courts, she worried that my father had personal and professional relationships with several judges and that he would be able to sway them against her. There would be no recourse for her after that and she would lose her children. She felt trapped and helpless, hopeless that she would ever get us back. Why bother living? After talking with Elaine, she drove out to his house. When she came home, she asked her husband, Alex, to play a game of chess—and after a few minutes announced that she had taken an overdose of sleeping pills.

The only way I suspect that my father knew to survive after my mother died was to carry on as if she were invisible. He had difficulty acknowledging that we missed our mother and that she would be a lasting presence, as if any love for her was a betrayal of him. He still thinks our missing her obliterates his presence and his role as our father, and I cannot reassure him that my search to know more about her does not outshine my love for him. He has repeated to me that he loved my mother, but he never talks about his own shock and loss. My sister Judy asked our father why he didn't help us grieve, preserve my mother's memory better, and bring us to visit her grave. He told my sister only that he was relieved for my mother—relieved that she was no longer tormented.

My father married Barbara Sears just months before my mother's death. The harried 26-year-old Radcliffe student with long, straight, chestnut hair, no money, and three young boys of her own, married my dad because, she says, she loved him—although my memories are of her exasperation with him. The addition of the three boys brought the total number of kids in the family to nine—with another one soon on the way after ten months of marriage. We were supposed to welcome Barbara and these new boys into our family and love Barbara as our new mother and follow her rules. Her son Dickie recalls the jarring change: "I remember suddenly being part of a bigger family. One day, I was the oldest and the next day, I was right in the middle." Her son Andrew remembers the thrill of seeing the new green swing set and the sprawling backyard on the day he and his brothers moved to Quail Street—quite a contrast from their modest two-bedroom apartment downtown. Soon, Barbara became the only mother we had.

Barbara was several months pregnant with Debbie when my mother killed herself. We celebrated when Debbie was born in March—our new sister provided a welcome distraction—new life challenging death. By late fall, my father and Barbara felt they needed a break from our home life and took a trip to Moscow on an extended and belated honeymoon with a group of architects and other developers. Our nanny Bee had to take care of the *baby* now, not me. I was terrified that Barbara and my father would not return. I cried in my bed and frightened Andrew, who was now sharing a room with me. It seemed to me that Dad and our new mother were gone forever, as I was 5 years old with little sense of time. Their three-week trip was an eternity. When they returned, I was so relieved but also confused because I had thought that Mama might somehow return, too. Young children often think that death is not permanent and if Mama had gone to heaven it seemed reasonable that she had a return ticket.

After that summer, Barbara and Dad began to settle us into a routine. In the fall, I was off to kindergarten with Andrew. Barbara sewed a red jumper with a pocket in the shape of an apple for me for the first day of school and only baby Debbie stayed at home. Though Barbara says nine children and a baby didn't faze her ("I just bought a bigger table"), she was only 26 and, I understand now, felt under siege. To be fair, it was an enormous task—a baby, a pile of children, a husband, and a new large home (which, just a few years before, she had visited with Dick Sears to socialize with my parents). She was reduced to enforcing crowd control over her unruly crew. The first truth was that my mother was gone. Barbara's view, and my father's view too, was that now we needed to move on.

Barbara was our mother now, but my sister Amy refused to call her that and took the heat. There is a recurring scenario in many stepfamilies of conflicts of loyalty in the aftermath of loss. There are multiple loyalties and the conflict can quickly escalate. In our case, the conflict was heightened by my mother's suicide. It was key to honor Barbara without dishonoring my mother if the family was to move forward, but instead it became a pissing contest. Amy was our instructor in defiance. Dad would smack her for refusing to call Barbara "Mummy"—as if he could force the word out of her mouth. He underestimated our spunk and tenacious loyalty to Mama's memory. Now we needed to learn to live as a new family. But Mama was not gone because every day we missed her. Our mother had not been a good mother, they told us, because she was the kind of person who could abandon us. They would not tolerate any idealization of her because it misrepresented who she was. Barbara often told me that before she died, my mother ignored the day-to-day details of our lives; with obvious disapproval she said that my mother once had left me filthy in a crib, forgetting to change my diapers—she delegated too much responsibility to Bee and others. "But I *wanted* to do the grocery shopping, I *liked* sewing you a new dress," Barbara tells me proudly. This was a task she would not delegate to others—proof of her superior parenting skills.

With such a large brood to oversee, my stepmother could be seen as an overwhelmed drill sergeant who'd stepped up to a demanding task. No noise. Keep our rooms clean. Chores were assigned and needed to be completed in a timely way. Boys' chores were feeding the dogs, mowing and raking the lawn, and taking out the trash; girls' chores were emptying the dishwasher, matching mounds of socks, and washing grubby fingerprints off all the surfaces. Martha recalls that when Fantastik debuted, she viewed it as a godsend because before she had had to "arm-wrestle" to erase so many children's grubby fingerprints, which came at several different heights. Barbara would inspect surfaces. Inside the house, she would sort through our cubbies in the crowded changing room, throwing smelly bathing suits and stale towels into a laundry basket, and searching our pockets for evidence of our transgressions.

My father essentially dismissed Barbara's rules. He didn't share her need for discipline, for setting boundaries and expecting compliance. She tells me, "I used to say in the morning 'tabula rasa,' because he'd say he agreed with my discipline strategies and then counteract everything I did. Once, three of you kids were bowling in the attic right over our bed, and I was tired and I told you to stop and go to your rooms. He took you to a movie." One time Barbara called our pediatrician and asked him to recommend a parenting book, then left it on my father's bedside table. She tells me he growled that he wouldn't read that "Republican rag."

Barbara feels that my father undermined her effort to impose discipline. "I got a lot of glory at parties for managing all these children," she says, "I would describe how you sorted your own socks. He'd say, 'Yes, Barbara strings them up by their thumbs,' and there would be this awkward silence." My father, she tells me, was determined to raise his children and be in our lives much more than she expected. "I had all the responsibility but none of the authority."

The children, Barbara liked to joke, came in three flavors: "yours" (the six who were my mother's children), "mine" (Barbara's own three boys), and "ours," referring to my half-sisters Debbie and then Elizabeth, who were born in the first three years of her marriage to my father. The eleven of us did not always fit together easily. Andrew with his wry wit likes to joke that he and his brothers were crunchy peanut butter while we six were smooth. They were PB&J; we were fluffer-nutter. There was vigorous argument about "real mayonnaise," Miracle Whip versus Hellman's. Still sounding as if he's in the debate today, Andrew explains, "It says right on the label *mayonnaise*—Miracle Whip says *salad dressing*." He sighs. "But there were too many to fight it out."

We both know that the divide between our families ran deeper than what to have on a sandwich. Dad's new role as father to the three Sears boys presented challenges to him. He is a man who has ancient tribal loyalty. He felt that their father had abandoned them, and although he did the best he could, he still felt that they needed a relationship with their real father. Dickie was the same age as Jim, and Carter was Jerry's age—they were older than me and resentful at being outnumbered. But growing up, I felt that Dickie, Carter, and Andrew were our brothers just as much as Jim and Jerry.

Andrew and I were close in age and temperament. Dorothy Newell, the wife of my father's law partner and a close friend of Barbara's, tells me: "Andrew and you were very much brother and sister. You were like two little puppies." I was comforted by his company. I still enjoy his good nature and am indebted for his friendship, in spite of our family dramas.

Even Quail Street's big rooms could barely contain us. Our house was an overgrown turn-of-the-century stucco house—the kind of capacious house

that had eight bedrooms and seven baths for a growing family. The big common rooms on the first floor had a long stretch of windows full of light, and
upstairs there were bedrooms for everyone. At the end of the long hall on
the second floor was the master bedroom with its thick carpets and muted
colors. The room had a large screened-in sleeping porch, which was so
crammed with old furniture that no one could get past the door. This is the
bedroom where Mama slept before she left, when she was alive, and it was
where Barbara was sleeping now. Four bedrooms lined a long hallway, and
Andrew and I mischievously loved to scribble on the floor; illicitly rubbing
our crayons into the dark wood, we could hear with panic and fear the click
of my stepmother's heels as she came looking for us. If we were fast enough,
we could hide in the *linen closet*—words that always sounded so proper to
me when I was young. Andrew and I liked to crouch in its shadows and
smash together chunks of quartz we had collected from the yard to see if we
could create sparks. Once in a while, I would find Jim in the closet, hiding
so that no one could see him when his feelings of missing our mother were
too much. Another flight up, in what had once been an attic, were the big
boys' bedrooms—Jimmy's, Dickie's, and Jerry's. They thumped the floor
when they fought and wrestled, and they took long showers that sometimes
leaked down into the hallway.

Our big house sat at the end of a long uphill driveway that ended in a
loop. In the middle of the loop were purple and magenta rhododendrons.
The front entrance had an imposing oaken door but we never used the entrance except when we were leaving for or arriving from school. Instead, we
entered through the back door, carrying groceries, past Winsor and Phillip,
our two large German shepherds who stood guard, and past the stairs to
the basement, which was home to our dyspeptic, belching oil furnace. I did
not like the basement or its cool, mildew breath and rumblings that
sounded like a monster.

The basement flooded frequently—Andrew remembers using a raft one
time—and there was a door down there leading to what I imagined was a
storm shelter, although it was actually where the coal for the furnace was

stored before it was converted to oil. If there was a weather disaster, if we all had to pack shoulder to shoulder into that small dank room, I worried that there was not enough room for all of us. Behind the furnace, high in the wall, there was a small access hole to the crawl space, and we all believed that if you crawled far enough through the crawl space all the way to the other end of the house, there was a secret office hidden under the main stairs above. We believed that the office was inhabited by the ghost of the house who worked there every day.

Once in a while, the house's bones trembled, sending fine cracks branching like veins in the stucco walls, and I would hold tight to my blanket, worried that the end was near. Barely a mile through the woods, there were distant explosions as workmen dynamited a quarry, making gravel and sending it off.

Our love and memories of my mother were supposed to be buried in our new, blended family. But instead there were cracks in the foundation, blasted one too many times. From the outside, we may have come across like a fun-loving *Cheaper by the Dozen* family. When I see photos from that time, even my childhood memory does not overestimate the scale of our home, but that home was also filled with a numbing grief.

By the end of the summer of 1965, less than two years after my mother's death, my father decided that it would be a great opportunity to take a trip across the country. Neither Barbara nor Dad had ever seen the national parks. An added bonus was that a promotion was offered by the Holiday Inn chain: No matter how many kids were in a room, they could stay for free as long as they were with an adult.[5] So from Buffalo to California, the boys stayed in one room and the girls in another for a bargain.

Even better than cramming so many kids into two hotel rooms, Dad had also decided to drive us across the country in our new Dodge Polara station wagon with its three rows of seats, shag carpeting, and sticky vinyl interior. Each child packed a small suitcase that was strapped to the luggage rack along with a full-size crib. The nine of us kids piled into the back seats, while baby Debbie got to sit up front with my father and Barbara, and we headed west.

Barbara wanted to make sure that no one forgot the trip. She handed out notebooks and told the six oldest (Martha, Amy, Judy, Jim, Jerry, and Dickie) to write about our adventures. To inspire our literary talent, Barbara promised a reward of going to the local bowling alley on our return. Amy's first entry reads: "It was ten-thirty. Everything was packed and ready. We all loaded up with our parents and Debbie up front. We had arrived at the fork in our road and Daddy said, 'Where are my sunglasses?' It was the first of many things that we would realize that we had forgotten across the continent."

My brothers and sisters were serious about recording the trip. Martha, writing from her vantage point by the car door, her cheek pressed to the window, noted the many kinds of farms and reveled in the wildflowers that lined the highways—lupines, Indian paintbrush, cactus flowers. "What is so strange about the West is that the moment you are outside the city, you are in farm areas again." Amy wrote with a dash of melodrama. She tells of our "long last look at the house and the people to whom we would return" as if we ourselves were captains embarking to exotic lands. In rich detail, she described Montana glaciers, painted canyons, and "a very rare trumpeter swan." Jim, almost 11 years old, gleefully confided that Teton was French for "breast" and recorded every pike, trout, crappy, and bass he and Dad caught, and Jerry scribbled about meeting some random relatives and landmarks we visited such as Custard's last stand.

It was more difficult for Barbara to give in to the rhythm of the road trip—she had Debbie to care for, and parenting out of a station wagon was not an easy task. Each day she rationed Ritz crackers for snacks, and insisted on all of us going to the bathroom every time we stopped for gas. To make sure we were all accounted for after each stop, there was a count-off—oldest to youngest. But this was not foolproof. Once Amy called out Carter's number, and it wasn't until fifteen minutes later that Barbara and Dad discovered they were missing a child and had to turn around to quickly retrieve him. I liked stopping for ice cream dips at Dairy Queen restaurants, drinking soda from real root beer mugs at A&W, putting our toes in the Pacific Ocean, and driving through a hailstorm. The big green neon Holiday Inn signs with the flashing star on top were a welcome sight at the end of the day and I loved the small soap bars and the Gideon's Bibles that seemed strangely exotic with their undecipherable letters and translucent paper, and the turquoise swimming pools. We always had adjoining hotel rooms with two double beds— Barbara would have one room with all the girls, and my Dad would have the boys. We'd leave the doors open between the rooms, and Dad would send us off to sleep with scary ghost stories, not always sure how to finish.

This was a trip that often had learning destinations: Minnesota with the beginning of the "mighty" Mississippi river, the great cliff dwellings at Mesa Verde with campfire talks, and museums where we looked at dinosaur fossils. "I've learned more on this trip than I could in a thousand books or a year of schooling," exudes Amy at the end of her chronicle. "It was great fun traveling around this vast country." Jim remembers, still animated, that when we stopped in Las Vegas, Dad had a windfall playing craps and he told the kids the next day that he had stashed the money in the engine for the night, afraid that someone might come for it. Andrew says that Dad got a speeding ticket in Kansas clocked at 110 miles per hour. Dad says proudly he made it back home in five days. Speeding tickets, the occasional "slap" for being "mouthy," and lost children aside, it was so much fun that the next summer we did it all again. But soon Elizabeth was born, and with another baby, ten older kids, and Martha getting ready to go off to college, it was hard to imagine another trip as a family. And the next summer, the strain of Barbara's Herculean efforts at household management was rewarded by my father with a trip to Europe—grown-ups only. While they traveled abroad, they would leave the eleven of us in the care of Bee and Barbara's sister Marcia. Travel adventures have always been rejuvenating for my father. Traveling satisfies my father's intense curiosity and sense of exploration.

However, Barbara hadn't traveled much at all before meeting my father. I can imagine that her enthusiasm was appealing to him, who could assume the role of the knowledgeable tour guide. Abroad, she appreciated my father, and he appreciated her. Their European trip lasted three weeks, and Barbara sent us a postcard from each European capital on their itinerary. I hoarded all sorts of postcards and stored them in a Wonder Bread plastic bag, keeping not only the ones she addressed to me but also those she sent to my siblings and various random postcards picturing icons such as Batman or grizzly bears whenever I could get them. I studied the glossy photos of Notre Dame, the Eiffel Tower, the Tower of London, the Spanish Steps, Stockholm's Royal Palace, and the Parthenon. Sometimes it seemed that she was checking that we were behaving. Other times I wondered if she missed us. It didn't matter to me if the cards were addressed to my siblings. To me, they were reminders of her wanting to be present to us and she sounds playful and attentive. Now I peer at her neat cursive handwriting to see if there is a clue of her marriage strain. Now I admire how conscientious she was to take the time to write to all of us as I know that it must have been quite an undertaking to keep us all posted.

Spain
Dear Andrew,

I saw some young boys surfing before, today. It looked like such fun I just might try it. Are you being a good boy? Are your shoes tied?

Love, Mummy

London
Dear Kids,

Daddy bought himself some very dandy clothes in London, so much so that one of the young ladies said he was the grooviest lawyer she'd ever seen. This is a very swinging group but Daddy outdoes them all, what with asking questions all the time and all his fancy boots, scarves, leather jacket (long) etc., he's the star of the group. I hope you're not giving Pat too much trouble. Give her our best and our power and authority over you.

Love, M& D

Madrid
Dear Carter,

This is the hotel we're about to leave. We've had a lovely time in Madrid. I hope you're not being silly or throwing Carter-style tantrums. Spain is a glorious country, oddly enough. The larger the city, the lovelier the trees and bldgs. The countryside is so arid. Now we go to Italy for two days to Venice, where there have been floods. Only one more week and then home again. We miss you.

Love, M&D

Cordoba
Dear Bee,

I hope you are doing well. We did some early shopping in Lisbon, a gold neck-lace and an opal ring for me, and a Madeira table cloth (yes, another fragile one, but this will fit the table). He's been FAIRLY pleasant, even when driving those treacherous roads, so far, so much fun.

Love, J&B

Portugal
Dear Nancy, Debbie and Elizabeth,

Doesn't this look like a Sleeping Beauty castle? We saw it in a mist, which made
it even more beautiful and mysterious. We miss you all very much. Today we fly
to Majorca. We've ridden in horse carriages and had dinner on high mountains.
Last night we went swimming at the pool on the roof of this hotel. All's well.

Love, Mummy and Daddy

They came home with a suitcase stuffed full of gifts—hand-carved me-
chanical bear toys and fuzzy creatures made out of pine.

Meanwhile it was Bee who was the steady, constant comfort who kept
me going. Barbara certainly tried and for that I am grateful to her. But she
had an impossible task. Bee provided a continuity of care and fortified us.
To me, Bee, not Barbara, was our "other mother." We fondly referred to
her as Bee, but her real name was Bernice. Bee suited us because she was
busy and kind and she loved us. As Elaine, my mother's best friend, told
me, "When your mother married your father, Bernice came with your
mother the way your grandmother Edith did. She was not a maid, although
she was a marvelous cook. She was more of a nanny than anything else, and
she seemed to be very happy in the household when your mother was running it." Bee could tell stories and knew almost by magic what I needed—
she was always there in a starched white uniform like a nurse, the fulcrum
of our household.

Bee, like Edith, had stayed with us when my mother left to live with Dick
Sears. She loved my mother, but we needed her. We were *her* children, too.
Years ago before I was born, Bee had herself been married, but before she
could have her own kids, her husband fell into an elevator shaft and died.
As a child, I sometimes felt sad for Bee as I understood that she had sadness
as well, but I was happy that she was our other mother. I remember when
I came home from school in second grade crestfallen, and listlessly picked

at my favorite lunch of Campbell's soup with rice and grilled cheese on Wonder Bread, and Bee asked me what was wrong. I burst into tears because I had been banished from the classroom by my teacher, who told me to sit in the hall. The teacher had an oversized pink eraser with bold black letters that declared, "We all make mistakes." When I asked if she made mistakes, she replied, "Yes," and I told her flippantly that this proved she must be stupid. In my family, mistakes were regarded as a sign of weakness. If you made a mistake, my brothers teased, you were stupid. Bee stroked my hair and consoled me, and that afternoon, she bought me a life-sized doll with long eyelashes—a mountain of joyous plastic. Bee taught me about taking care of people, about listening for what was going on underneath. She could discipline us because she didn't play favorites—she knew just what to say to set us right. We did not argue with Bee because we understood that she was wise. When I was sad, we would go into the neighboring woods to look for sassafras roots, and when we returned with our prize, she brewed a pungent pot of sassafras tea for us to share. Then we'd curl up on her bed and watch her "stories," as she called them, *As the World Turns* and *Days of Our Lives,* and laugh at the soap operas that people were living.

Bee *knew* things, somehow. Secrets or thoughts you weren't even aware of or didn't understand yet yourself. She knew how much I missed my mother, because she missed my mother too. She used to tell me that she slept with me tucked on her pillow in a blanket after my mother left. I remember how her soft skin smelled of Bengay, and how Bee had a wig that she wore to cover her short hair and dentures that she would remove at the end of the day and put on the bureau in her bedroom in our home. From the threshold, I watched anxiously and wanted so badly to help as every day she would take a needle filled with a strange liquid and jab it into her thigh. Bee was full of mysteries. Much later, I learned that Bee was diabetic.

Whenever I missed Mama, I would go to Bee's room and stare at her wig and dentures and needles and starched uniforms. I would fling myself onto her white bedspread belly first and wait for my tears to stop.

I would watch Bee in the kitchen as she prepared favorite dishes like apricot soufflé or ham with mustard, spices, and brown sugar—she would let me stick the cloves into the ham. Then she would make something special for herself—collard greens, dark and bitter, shiny with a pat of butter. Sometimes while she cooked or scrubbed, I played jacks with Judy or Andrew on the crooked floor and snitched Fudgsicles from the freezer when no one was looking. Most remarkably, Barbara says gratefully that she wouldn't have survived those years without Bee. My daughter Zoe's middle name is Bee, my small way of honoring how important she was to me so long ago. Indeed, many children look to someone who can help them make sense of a complicated world; having a trusting relationship with an adult provides substantive strength for them. With Barbara managing so many children, Bee was able to make me feel special, buffering me from an aching loneliness.

Right from the beginning, Bee told Barbara that she and my dad wouldn't last. Many otherwise sensible people believed that Bee was psychic, and for years she would take a taxi downtown to the Tremont Tea Room where she would read tea leaves. Sometime Bee would pour strong tea into cups for me that she would sweeten with sugar and lots of milk. When I was done, she would look into my cup at the leaves and smile. She was not afraid for me. Her smile was reassuring—I would have a happy life, she believed, and I believed her.

Bee died in 1968. I was 9 years old. Dad organized the funeral and brought us to the service that morning. We sat in the front pew, nine bereft children in the storefront funeral parlor, united in our loss more than ever before, and definitely more than we have been since. Everyone was dressed in our Sunday best as we sobbed inconsolably, drowning out the gospel choir.

With Bee gone, Barbara's need for order intensified and she became more rigid. Now there was no longer any buffer between stepmother and children. Now Barbara would do the cooking and six o'clock was to be the start time for dinner. Every evening we watched the minutes tick down. If my father was delayed, which was often unavoidable (or, later, because he did not want to come home), Barbara would storm into the living room and begin to play Rachmaninoff's "Prelude in C-sharp Minor" on the grand piano, banging out those chords. I preferred to retreat to the kitchen with Judy, where we willed Dad to hurry home as soon as he could.

When the two families blended, at first Dad had done the shopping on Saturdays. We would migrate through the aisles, filling at least two carts at Roche Brothers, and we would share with Dad his raw hamburger snack and ice cream. Barbara insisted that no one was allowed to snack between meals, probably to make us more manageable, but also to stem the never-ending grocery shopping that later had become her responsibility and her torment. Eventually Monday became grocery day, so whatever she brought home had to last all week. We, however, wanted our snacks and we weren't fussy, so we found what we could. Dickie ate packets of tartar sauce, others would spoon mayo out of the jar (some of us had a mayo addiction, Andrew tells me ruefully), and Judy and I would mash butter and sugar together and eat as much of the paste as we could. We would sneak down to the kitchen in the middle of the night and steal Oreos and Pop-Tarts, tiptoeing back to our rooms worried about punishment if caught by Barbara.

Barbara redesigned the menu, and dinner quickly became a minefield. Gone were the spiced hams and sweet potatoes that Bee had prepared. Instead, dinner became Barbara's opportunity to educate our palates by feeding us frozen scallops, boiled liver, and frogs' legs that my father brought home. Sometimes she cooked roasts or served us bread and steak and gravy. On Fridays, we had fish sticks, one of many convenience foods she introduced. I wanted Bee to come back.

To ensure order, Barbara formalized a seating arrangement that would change every month when she put names in a hat and allowed us to choose our seats when our names were pulled. My favorite spot was the seat on the right side of the end table next to my father, as I would have the hottest food or a larger portion (my father served the food counterclockwise). Serving a family of thirteen each night was a logistical challenge. Dad loved technical innovations. Even though there was a fine carving set, he had an electric knife to carve whatever the meat was each night.

The large ornately carved dining table had pull-out panels and king and queen chairs at either end. Looming large at the head of the table, my father reigned supreme, doling out the food. Barbara sat at the other end, eagle-eyed. Dinner was served all at once, and we all made our best effort to enjoy that time together with games such as 21 or Botticelli. While on a trip to Expo 67 in Montreal, we learned a Jewish folk song—a rondelet of one lyric, "Hava Nashira"—and from then on, each meal began in song or was started with a moment of silence. No one was to touch their silverware until Barbara picked up her fork. No one was allowed to leave from the table before their plate was scraped clean. To this day I will meticulously avoid asparagus or Brussels sprouts as I remember gagging on these odious vegetables when I could not clandestinely bury them in my napkin or sneak them under Debbie's chair. One glass of milk per meal at the table. You had to be quick—conversation and food moved fast. Last one done got no dessert. Debbie was a picky eater so Barbara would often end up sitting at the table for what seemed like hours while she waited for the reward of a scraped-up plate. If Bee had been there she would have humored Barbara and gotten us out of the line of fire.

One night, when one of us must have hit someone else during an argument at the table, I was surprised to see how apoplectic Barbara was. Barbara had recently bought a brand-new set of the high-tech unbreakable dishes that had just come out on the market that year. She stood up and grabbed Carter's dinner plate, screamed, "I hate violence!" at the top of her lungs, and slammed the plate full of food down on the table. The plate vanished completely after it bounced up, food and all. We all sat and stared, completely mystified, at the spot where the plate had hit the table. A full second later, the plate shattered into smithereens after falling down from the ceiling. In unison, we all burst out laughing, except Barbara. Barbara tells me now that she went out to the car to cry and the dog was baffled and kept looking in at her.

After dinner, Dad would slide back the wooden doors at the end of the living room with its wall of books, mostly mysteries and histories, a large plush sofa, and three big chairs to lounge upon. We sometimes played board games like Monopoly, Operation, and Life, or had a rock band performance where Judy sang and played piano, Dickie played six-and twelve-string guitar, and Carter played the drums and wrote an environmentalist song about the Yangtze River. Jimmy was the manager.

The Newells were occasional guests in our house, and Dorothy Newell reminded me that my father would quiz us about *Time* magazine. Each of us was assigned a section to report on. "That's one way to keep control, I thought," Dorothy tells me, "but why was he trying to turn you into little Kennedys?" Her remark makes me recall that Barbara once joked about making a match for me with John Kennedy Jr. My father warned, "Don't marry a Kennedy—*be* a Kennedy." He expected us to achieve, and losing our mother was a minor setback.

Sometimes, after-dinner was the time for our spankings, promised for whatever we had done wrong that day. Barbara always sent us upstairs to change into our pajamas. Once we were ready for bed, she would have all of us stand around the enormous porcelain sink in the pantry to brush our teeth while she supervised. Washing out the spit was one of the monthly assignments that I hated.

In some ways, with so many children, family life, when it was good, could be like summer camp. We spent hours on bicycles racing around the large driveway loop, then careening down the driveway toward the all-boys school next door. We'd disrupt their soccer games, then pedal hard as we climbed the high hill to the water tower. If you dumped your bike and climbed the tower, you could see the whole city and look for fires.

Our house was surrounded by woods where we spent hours exploring, picking wild blueberries, playing cowboys and Indians, and dodging behind trees and glacial boulders. Deeper into the woods was a granite ledge filled with passageways and cracks for hide-and-seek that we called the Seven Caves and a swamp that would flood over and freeze in the winter—we cleared the snow and we could skate there. There was also an occasional stolen car dumped in the woods or a forest fire started by the neighborhood juvenile delinquents in the backwoods surrounding our house. The firemen always used our driveway as a staging area and it usually seemed to start in the late afternoons and caused a certain excitement as they battled the fire.

At our house, there was a big broad lawn in the back and always enough kids to make teams and play games—Red Light, Capture the Flag, Kick the Can, Mother May I, Steal the Bacon, and kickball. In the branches of a large oak, my father had hung a thick rope perfect for shimmying. The rope burned my legs and hands, but the view from the top was worth it. Early on, our family also acquired a menagerie of animals. In addition to Winsor and Phillip, our two German shepherds, we had a collie named Miss Julie and a sheepdog-looking mutt named Rusty. When Winsor died we buried her ashes by the pool house. Rusty disappeared and we all thought he had been kidnapped by one of the neighborhood kids, and we looked for him every-where we went. Carter had a mouse and there were turtles brought home from various fairs. Several gerbils also joined the family. Dickie built a trop-ical fish tank and had two parrots named Nat (Hawthorne) and Jack (Green-leaf Whittier) that Dad had brought home after the opening of the indoor health club at Charles River Park. Jack had a bit part as the parrot in An-drew's school performance of *Treasure Island*, but stole the show when he flew out to a chandelier hung over the audience and spouted profanities throughout the remainder of the play. One of the parrots that lived in Carter's room would mimic Barbara when she yelled up to the third floor, "Carter get *up*!" Whatever else, our house was always filled with life, no matter how messy.

At the back of the house, a large brick and stone terrace loomed high above the backyard and the bulb garden, and a steep and winding stone staircase led the way to the swimming pool designed in the shape of a whale. I have a picture of ten of us (missing my youngest sister Elizabeth, who wasn't born yet), arm in arm, crowded onto the diving board of our pool. I am nestled between Andrew and Carter, hanging gleefully from their shoulders, sporting a yellow nylon bathing suit printed with a large turtle. We look like happy kids in this picture, and sometimes we were.

All of us learned to swim. My father was concerned that with so many kids, one of us might drown. For the sake of safety, we had to learn fast. His solution was to catapult us into the pool until frantic and terrified, limb over limb, we flailed for survival over to the edge of the pool. A few more times and we would be capable swimmers. I always thought this tactic was my father's invention, until Sydell Masterman told me that it was my mother's idea. She had started off with Martha, Amy, Judy, and Jim—pitching them into the pool as toddlers. I wonder if, when she watched her children thrash so helplessly and with so much fear, she might have been playing out a scene from her childhood—but this time giving it a happier ending and ensuring that no one she loved would ever drown again.

Despite our rough entry, the pool was our sanctuary. Removing heavy trashcans full of winter's rotting leaves, repainting, and filling the pool became an annual springtime ritual. Once the air temperature reached 72 degrees, we would spend hours around the water, jumping off the diving board and eating popsicles on the deck. When we tired of swimming, we biked to the candy shop to buy rolled red licorice and little cotton bags of Gold Rush gum.

While we played and biked and swam, my father would sometimes prepare cookouts on the terrace, slathering barbeque sauce with a long brush that seemed to magically extend his arm. He would flip hamburgers and serve baked beans and hotdogs. While he worked the grill, he wore sunglasses and listened to rock music. He had installed big speakers on the back terrace, and sometimes he'd blast Santana, Otis Redding, or The Doors so loudly that the pastor from St. Theresa Church at the bottom of the hill would call the house to complain. He enjoyed watching us play and chase the dogs, our legs and arms tanned and brown, all of us racing through the grass, climbing ropes and trees, gliding through the cool water like fish in our bright polyester bathing suits, letting our play soothe us and, I think, reassure him as well. He would sometimes play with us, too, letting me ride on his smooth back in the pool, although he was more likely to read by the poolside and do laps.

It was all too much for Barbara. We were loud and as far as she was concerned, we were out of control. Still, she threw herself into trying to be the suitable wife and competent mother. She felt that she loved my father much more than he loved her. My father agreed to hire additional help, so our new handyman, Dodi, moved into Bee's old second-floor room and took on some of the driving. He was later joined by his wife, Recia, who took over all the ironing while Dodi took care of the grounds and the house. Eventually Recia gave birth to two little girls during their stay with us, and we welcomed them into our brood as well. Dad was not always around. Sometimes the demands of Charles River Park took him away from us. When he needed to be late at work or traveling out of town, Barbara seemed especially impatient with us. At the slightest provocation, she would banish us to our rooms—often not for an hour or two but for a weekend; we came out only for meals. My brother Andrew thinks that with so many siblings and parents at war, we were basically raising ourselves. Although he had been the second smartest kid in his first-grade class, in the second grade Andrew earned straight C's. He tells me that once on a visit to Connecticut he stepped on a rusty nail and stuffed Kleenex in his sneaker to stop the bleeding. That night back home, his foot swollen, he knew that he needed someone to help him but wouldn't look to Barbara, for fear of punishment. He ended up in the emergency room when it was no longer something he could cover up.

Sledding in knee-deep snow one winter when I was in grade school, my brother Jerry and I catapulted recklessly down the hill, leaning into the curves, and collapsing in giggles. We pulled ourselves up, stomped the snow down, and giddily planned a faster run, negotiating who would sit in front and steer the sled. On the last run, the sled's metal runner ripped my pants and broke the skin on my thigh. I was bleeding into the snow, red on white. We trudged through the deep powder to a friendly neighbor's house. The mother arrived at the door with a warm laugh and a blonde bun twisted high on her head. She cleaned me up and put a large Band-Aid on my leg and served us hot chocolate in porcelain cups, and we lost track of time. When we eventually made our way home, Barbara was furious that we had detoured for comfort. I started to cry for Mama. "Stop it," my stepmother sighed, exasperated. "It's not my fault your mother killed herself."

Barbara and Dad fought bitterly as if in a tug of war, sometimes in silence, sometimes in small disagreements that would explode. Once my father brought home food from the Branding Iron, a restaurant that was going out of business, a bounty of frozen steaks and scallops, big cans of licorice, and huge containers of ice cream and caramel sauce—too much for Barbara, who now had to figure out the complex geometry of storing food and avoiding spoilage. It was just like my father, unable to resist a bargain and wanting to play bountiful Santa to the kids. In contrast to my father with his expensive tastes, Barbara was the epitome of frugality—she would often divide a single small Sara Lee coffee cake into eleven pieces and serve it to us kids. That night, she didn't get out of the way fast enough, and my father, piqued by her stony reaction to his treat, poured the caramel sauce over her head. We laughed, but of course we were horrified inside.

There were other rifts developing—grief and guilt, compounded by the challenges of attending to so many children. They had not predicted how difficult it would be to have so many kids. One of the challenges Barbara and my father faced was the logistics of transportation to school, to dance classes, to friends' houses, to birthday parties, to doctors' and dentists' appointments, to clothing and grocery stores. Some of these were quickly solved. The piano teacher came to our house and gave multiple lessons in a row. Visits to other people's homes were strictly limited. Shopping expeditions were consolidated. Shoes, for example, were purchased once a year in a single all-family trip to a discount shoe store. We would wear clothes too large or too small. And some of us would hitchhike around town while others of us discovered the taxi service: I delighted in the instant transportation to lessons and friends' houses. One day, when I was 10, my father summoned me to his office. Sitting in his waiting room, awkwardly tapping my feet against the floor, I was petrified, wondering what could have war-

ranted my being singled out for such scrutiny. He told me that he had received a $500 bill from the Red Taxi Company. He suggested perhaps I use
more restraint. But he was quick to forgive.

The truth is that our family was simply too large to manage. Whenever
we could, we escaped Barbara's watchful eye and retreated into a world of
children—where brothers, sisters, and fantasies were in charge, not a stepmother. I'm not entirely clear which of my brothers and sisters was the
leader of the pack. None of us was strong enough to take on the role of general, but then no one wanted to be bossed around either. Eventually, we all
drafted a Declaration of Independence together and agreed to follow the
rules, creating a family council with Martha in charge. Of course, it didn't
last long, but I like to think that it was our way of trying to negotiate a peace
that we were invested in keeping. Dorothy Newell tells me that my brothers and sisters could be mean to other kids. Jim once pushed her daughter
into the pool. "Everybody knew, but no one did anything." Our pediatrician
often asked suspicious questions—"Is everything all right at home?" Since
we didn't know any differently, we'd always just tell him everything was
fine.

Our family was driven by the concept that there are winners and losers,
and winners take all; after all, my mother lost a custody battle, her life. If
we ever left our belongings around the house, we would have to buy them
back at the occasional family auction. My father reigned supreme at the
head of the table, doling out bright tinfoil-covered Easter eggs or candy
from Halloween that we turned in, doling out approval for correctly responding to questions about the capitals of states, president's names, a host
of facts. Political races were closely watched at the time, with the bulk of the
kids supporting McGovern, and Jimmy alone supporting Nixon. At times
our competitions were tough too. In our games, we were merciless with an
edge of cruelty. We'd call each other dunce-o, fatso, retard, faggot. All the
boys were teased with girls' names: Jimmy was Ginny, Jerry was Geraldine,
Carter was Katrina, and Andrew was Andrea. There were no girls' names
for a Dickie, so he was just called Dorothy. Sometimes the cruelty became

physical. The smallest would be tickled until they cried "uncle" or started to cry. In this world, you couldn't always trust your siblings. Sometimes they bullied you. We scratched and hit each other. At times we'd be protected by a brother from a brother, only to be bullied by the protector minutes later. If we hurt each other, we seldom said sorry.

∞

Shades of gray. I am lost in thought about Sunil and my family, wondering how to give grief words. My faith is in the magic of this cure: It is not always what we do but how we listen to each other. We may not avoid disaster but whether we are undone may be decided by how we tolerate the uncertainty and make meaning by degrees. After eating dinner and reading a bedtime story, I found that Cory was crying while he drifted off to sleep. Nine years old, like I was when I used to spend hours sitting on the branch of the maple tree in back of our house thinking about what time meant, he had come to that startling realization that we all die. He calculated with the precision that comes naturally to him that if he lived to be 93, he had already lived one-tenth of his life, and that made life seem all too short. Some people, I told him, think that it is a privilege to die because it allows an entrance into heaven and closeness to God. He asked innocently, "If it's all so much better then why *wouldn't* people kill themselves?" I can understand now that Barbara and Dad might have avoided talking about my mother's absence because they did not know what to say and there was nothing they could do to change what had happened. The significance of our mortality, that we are on this earth for a relatively short time, has no easy answers. I cannot protect Cory from the inevitable disappointments that we confront as we all grow up. I have to restrain my impulse to extract a promise from him that he will never kill himself. I tell him that love lasts longer than death. I want love to be enough.

Chapter Twelve

Welcome home again, old neighbor.
Why, where have you been these
twenty long years?

—WASHINGTON IRVING,
"*Rip van Winkle*"

One summer Zoe sat in a kitchen chair dangling a skinny leg over the arm-rest, trying to persuade me to give her permission. At 13, she was exquisitely aware of even the slightest changes in her body. "*Everyone* in my class is doing it," she told me, pointing. I was hesitant. I did *not* want her to shave her legs.

Then off she went. After fifteen minutes in the upstairs bathroom, she hovered around me to see if I noticed how brazen she's been. She confessed finally, hardly able to contain her satisfaction at her newly acquired smooth legs. "I did it *anyway*. I found a razor upstairs."

I withdrew, nursing my hurt, at the same time knowing that I was being melodramatic. Although she did not appear to care about what I thought, deep down I believed that she wanted my approval. I don't want her to feel it's okay to ignore my authority. What's more, she knows that she's robbed me of the ritual I would have made of it, and she *should* feel guilty. (It's true that I would have drawn it out, making it into some sort of ceremonial rite of passage, wanting to go pick out a razor and shaving cream with her.) She'll push me to allow her to expand the boundaries; despite all my reluctance, she'll propel me forward. She's moving toward that liberating moment when, if she doesn't like what her mother says, she can defy her. Wait until she pierces her lip or stays out all night, I say to myself—I should be thankful for these mini self-assertions. I want her to trust me enough to at least *discuss* decisions with me. Zoe is on the cusp of change. Although she wants to gallop toward maturity, she longs for approval, and I suspect that Colin and I are formidable to negotiate with.

Zoe and I will need to learn to change with each other in subtle shifts. Earlier in the day, she collapsed like a baby on the lawn, exhausted from competing with Cory. For almost an hour they played basketball in the driveway one-on-one, Zoe moving quickly, but not accurately, and Cory, patient and slower, consistently challenging her ability to get the ball past him, forcing her to shoot from farther away. She finally quit in disgust, so frustrated. Yesterday she was disappointed that she was not yet heavy enough, all of eighty pounds, to drive the electric lawn mower. She reluctantly ceded that responsibility to Cory, and so her display of strength under the basketball hoop was particularly insulting.

Her enthusiasm for growth is palpable. Zoe is telling me that she wants me to trust her choices. I need to step aside so she can grow. It is hard for me to picture how we'll still remain close as she moves away. Today she surprised both of us: Defiance and shaving were easier than she thought. Am I falling into the parental trap of feeling dismissed when I can't control her decisions?

I hope that she will be strong in believing in herself, asserting that her voice be heard, but I want to matter. I want to inoculate her against that unavoidable, disorienting self-consciousness and keep her from the foolish pursuit of an elusive ideal beauty. She's so vibrant now, and I don't want to see her making alterations to please some vague but powerful other. I wonder if other mothers might have been delighted at her initiative. But she is stuck with me.

My mother wrote sentimentally in her diary about how girls' bodies change during puberty and warned that, without proper advice, girls can be less than enchanted with the changes. She seemed to glorify this transformation as opening the possibility for intimacy and creation. She was dead by the time her daughters reached this threshold.

> The whole process is so full of wonder, of amazement, of magic, and of the possibilities of disappointment, of chagrin, of degradation or disgust. Will the child be charmed and amused by the changes in her body and in her temperament, or will she be frightened and repelled? Another part of motherhood is the preparation of her child for reality, and there is no more gross and yet obscure reality than woman herself. So few of us were prepared appropriately by our own mothers; will it ever be possible for us to wade through the morass of Freudianism and black magic to the white magic that is our own essential reality, our purity, our beauty, our eternity, our salvation? Can the little girl with the budding breasts, so awkward, so useless, realize that here is her limitation in womanhood? As the warm juices of the maturity of the flesh begin to transform her childish angles and her infant physiology into the mysteries of Vesta [virgin Roman goddess of fire, hearth, and home] what will be her reaction, and how can it be directed into a realization of the enrichment and the dangers she is about to encounter?

I did not have a chance to experience these rites of passage with my mother, and so when my children reach a milestone, I probably embarrass them with my enthusiasm to celebrate that we are together. For all practical purposes, Barbara Scott (Sears) Rappaport was the mother I had during my teenage years since my mother had died and so had Bee. She was the one who corrected my homework and taxied me to doctor's appointments and chaperoned school field trips and sanctioned me to see a therapist. About the time I got my period, she had a hysterectomy and her marriage with my father was breaking up. Emerging sexuality was somewhat threatening for Barbara; eroticism was something to be renounced. Yet I allied myself with her and put up a fierce fight to stay with her when she was moving out of our home with my stepbrother Andrew and my two half-sisters, Elizabeth and Debbie. In her meek way, Barbara encouraged me to speak up for what I needed when I was growing up, and so twenty-five years later I turn to her for help. As things heated up with my father and he disagreed vehemently with how I understood my mother, he urged me to talk to Barbara. When I took him up on the suggestion and chose to pursue this, he became more elusive and told me that she was an unreliable reporter, but I was curious to hear what Barbara had to say.

These days, Barbara lives alone in a fifth-floor condominium on Beacon Hill—a stark contrast from her years at the sprawling Quail Street home with children underfoot and a very public, highly controversial husband engaged in a high-stakes, multimillion-dollar redevelopment project transforming Boston's downtown, or her more modest home that we moved to after the divorce from my father. The "doughy" and "despicable" young woman depicted in my mother's novel is today a dignified older woman. I went to hear her story. I had never asked her about my mother or how it came about that she married my father, and I'm hoping she will share her memories with me.

It's been a while since I've seen her, and as soon as I arrive, she asks if I want some tea and puts the water in the microwave. I settle awkwardly into the sofa and notice that her bookcases are stuffed with scrapbooks from our childhoods. Photos of all of us fill every square inch of extra wall space in the den.

She knows I want to ask about things we have never discussed before. She smiles. "Do you know that saying 'It's hard to be nostalgic when you can't remember the details'? I'm not sure how helpful I can be." We sit together on the loveseat as we talk.

A large painting dominates her small and slightly cluttered living room. It's a painting by Mary Rogers, a student of Hans Hoffman, and it used to hang on the wall above the staircase landing at Quail Street years ago where we would wait before going Easter egg hunting. "I worked the design colors of my living room around the blue color of the stream and the silhouette of trees," she says. "Your father and I bought the painting together."

I know things about Barbara that you know from years of living with someone—that she has a keen sense of smell, that she would do a hundred sit-ups a day to tighten her belly after five babies, that she liked to file her nails while warming up next to the radiator in the bathroom. She has a quiet steadiness I had not appreciated when I was younger. She gazes out at the skyline and then glances at me, surprised by my newfound interest in who she is and who she was.

Barbara tells me that her father, Mortimer Scott, was a municipal bond broker with an irregular schedule that required that he often be gone at night to attend town meetings. The vicissitudes of daily life created havoc and threw the children into strange roles. Barbara's mother sometimes had to borrow money from the neighbors to buy food for her family. Early on, her parents stopped speaking to each other and spoke only through their children. Barbara tells me that as a child she believed that the cause of their rift had something to do with the movie *Bambi* because in the movie the skunk, named Flower, says: "If you can't say something nice, don't say anything at all." According to family stories, her mother said that to her father and from then on they didn't talk directly to each other until all the children were out of the house. I want to tell her it must have been something more than that, but the logic of childhood is difficult to dislodge. Barbara is contemplative. "When I went back to my fiftieth high school reunion, people told me that the reason they never came to my house was that they were afraid of my father. He intimidated them; he was a loud, gruff man. I was grounded most of my childhood. I would have to take the dog out in the middle of the night and one day this very strong dog, he was a mean dog, my father made him a mean dog, he was *too* strong on the lead and he got away.

My father had me put the dog on the lead and take the dog out twenty times that day. You can imagine how confused the dog was, he didn't know what was going on," she says in a pitying, somewhat rueful way.

Her father was born with two clubfeet, a congenital deformity that causes the feet to point downward and curl inward. Without early and constant treatment, people with clubfeet are doomed to crippling pain—and good treatment was hard to find. The job of rubbing his feet after he had played eighteen holes of golf fell to Barbara, the oldest daughter of the four Scott children. Barbara tells me that growing up, it was her responsibility to massage her father's feet at least twice a week. She says with some disgust, "I had to learn a special technique and do it just right, or he would kick me."

"He didn't treat Ginny that way," she says indignantly, referring to one of her two younger sisters. "Ginny used to talk back to him. But I wasn't like that. I don't know why I was chosen for that assignment." Even as Barbara tells me this I can see she is both incredulous that Ginny could be so bold and resigned that she somehow always seemed to get the raw end of the deal. "I don't get along with Ginny," she admits. I ask quietly, "Did he hit you?"

She waves me off. "Sure, we were spanked, put in a corner, sent down to the basement a lot. Once he came in drunk and broke my violin. I never took lessons again. He never gave love. He was always looking for ways to goad me; he'd put some horrible-smelling cheese under my nose while I was sleeping or paint my eyeglasses with nail polish." Suddenly I understand why Barbara used to tell us growing up that "discipline is the hardest love to give," or fall back on her mantra, "Do it because I said so."

"I liked school," she tells me quickly. "We even moved so I could go to a better school. I would take five or six subjects and get A's except in trigonometry. The teachers knew that my father was making me get A's—he demanded perfection. Once I got a B in biology and he made me quit all my outside activities except school. My mother was passive and never stood up to him," she says exasperated.

When Barbara was in high school, she got a part-time job as a nurse's aide at Bellevue Place, a well-known mental hospital. She recalls that "Mary Todd Lincoln had stayed there, and when I was working there, there was also a woman who had been a famous opera singer, and a princess from Lichtenstein, and also someone who had been in Roosevelt's cabinet." She fed patients who could not or would not eat by themselves, and changed bedpans, diapers, and sheets. On another floor, patients received shock treatment, and Barbara tells me she didn't like how they were after the treatment, so tired and zombie-like. But she says the patients appreciated her and she did not mind the craziness. Her parents would have been horrified if they had known what went on in that place, so she never told them. Besides, she needed the money, and she enjoyed talking with the patients, most of whom were women who had been sent away by relatives who wanted to hide them from the world. "You know," she tells me, "I wanted to be a psychiatrist, too." I tell her she would have been a good psychiatrist because she is a good listener.

"My father made me pay rent when I turned 16," she adds. "But I was the only one of the four children who had to pay; I don't know why he played favorites." She says this with a bewilderment that I often see in patients who have been abused and can't understand why they were singled out by their parents.

"You were almost primed to make good choices in men," I remark, shaking my head.

She laughs. "You said it, not me."

Her father's insistence on good grades paid off, and Barbara managed to gain admission to Radcliffe. When I ask her what it was like for her to go off to college, she throws out her hands theatrically, something uncharacteristic for her. "Freedom," she beams. "I was in heaven." She pauses, savoring the moment. "I met Dick Sears within a week of arriving and fell in love with him. He was snobby, but nice to me. What else does a 19-year-old anxious to get rid of her father do? I went with him for two years and then I got pregnant and we got married. It was 1956. Predictable." Then she tells me, "He was addicted to bridge."

Barbara glances up at me with her sharp hazel eyes. "Dick was very bright, just like your father. Once when he was sleeping, I found some testing materials and reports tucked away in a drawer—the papers said he had a 161 IQ. The same IQ as your father's." I wanted to tell her that these guys have nothing on her, and that being smart isn't the only thing that matters in life.

She tells me that one day her building janitor got up the nerve to share his observation of her life with her. "I must have been 24. I will never forget what he said to me: 'You two don't talk to each other,' he said, and he was right. Dick and I didn't really talk to each other. If he hadn't said that to me, I wouldn't have realized I was unhappy."

She says that Dick put her down in front of other people, that he made fun of the way she spoke, and demanded that she not tell people who knew Dick that she didn't go to private school. In 1961, Dick offered financial help so that she could finish Radcliffe and suddenly she found herself back in college. "It was madness. I was always trying to find babysitters and I had a 5-year-old, a 4-year-old, and a 2-year-old. Poor baby Andrew would try to get my attention and my books would be filled with scribbles. I finally found a Swedish au pair. Dick paid at the beginning, but not after we separated. My last semester was such a struggle."

It was while she was a student that she and Dick started to socialize with my parents. Now I have the opportunity to explore the unusual connections among the four of them through Barbara's story. I have already heard Dick's side and my father's side and that of some of my parents' friends. I feel I am on a Rashomon type of journey,[1] hearing from each witness substantially different but equally plausible accounts, each person revealing a little more detail about my mother. Barbara recalls that Dick met my mother when he was doing work on her School Committee campaign. She remembers that one day my father came up to their apartment: "*Your father*," she starts, which is how she always starts when she is going to say something critical of him, "got on the phone immediately. I remember he was negotiating some deal. He was making a phone call to close the deal. That was his way of demonstrating that he was such an important, busy man," she says, still sounding irked.

I ask her what she thought of my mother at first. "She intimidated me. Here she was—very articulate, outspoken, so different. She was quite *large* and she would *say* things"—sometimes Barbara can be deceptively prudish—"things that I would *never* say." She goes on to give me details about my parents' sex life, how they would fight like cats and dogs and then neck in the garage. She is more graphic than I am comfortable hearing.

She has finished her tea, but holds onto the cup. "One day we went to the Cape, and we all were eating in a booth, and your father just kept picking at your mother. She threw down her clam roll and stormed out. I asked him if he was going to go out and comfort her, and your father laughed and said, 'I don't need to look for her, she'll come back.'" She looks at me with a piercing gaze as if for emphasis. "I know now that your father would bait your mother and get her going. I only came to appreciate that later."

I go on to ask Barbara about the whole spouse-swapping business. She doesn't flinch. She seems to remember that there was a well-known couple from the North Shore area of Massachusetts—a couple straight out of an Updike story—who were rumored to have hosted swapping parties. "Everyone was talking about it." According to her, spouse-swapping was definitely in the air, not unfamiliar in their kind of social circle, and the idea carried with it an aura of sophistication, though she's not sure she knew anyone else personally who was actually doing it. She says she can't remember how it all played out between the four of them. "I don't know who did what first. Your mother and Dick had a strong emotional relationship, but I really don't think that they consummated it until after your father and I did." While she may not recall or be willing to recount the details of how the four of them came together, she confirms Dick's version that they saw a psychiatrist afterward. "I remember that the doctor was furious at your parents," she says, underplaying her own role.

Does it matter who betrayed whom first? In wanting to understand my mother's story, I veer between being a detective in search of facts and being a realist. I'm grateful for Barbara's willingness to talk about this with me, but I'm also frustrated because I don't know how to process all that she says. The details of who did what first lose their relevance in the crush of the ensuing fallout. And with the facts locked in the fading memories of these survivors, with all the overlays of their mutual deceptions, it is hard to know if lies have calcified now into truths. I must accept what I cannot know, however close I get.

Barbara reveals that, at the time, she had already been thinking of leaving Dick: "I remember my mother-in-law sensing something and inviting me to lunch and wanting to know what I was going to do, but I didn't know what I was going to do. I was scared to death. I had no money and had to borrow from Dick's stepfather to buy food. All Dick did was play bridge or campaign with your mother. He made sure I paid the Social Register bill, even when there was little food in the house. I don't know what he thought I was supposed to do. Your father would sometimes visit me and bring ice cream for the kids, when what I really needed was a bag of groceries."

Barbara believes that my mother never took her seriously and never even saw her as a threat. "Your mother was so dismissive of me. She did not understand that one of my charms to your father was that I was a student at Radcliffe, having gone back after several years, and that had a certain intellectual appeal." Saddened, she goes on: "At the time I thought your mother was the bad guy. Your mother was a very powerful and outspoken person, and she did not seem to fear your father at all. One day she was beating him into the ground with her insults, and the next day he would offer to take her around the world. How could she behave that way toward him? I didn't understand why he put up with it." She shakes her head. "And I was never like that. I was so in love with your father, I was so drawn to him—he was brilliant and physically attractive. Back then, I wouldn't have called him controlling, but he was the head man in every situation. He was definitely in charge of things." Though she's talking about things that happened almost fifty years ago, she's still bothered that my father never acknowledged how much he meant to her.

When I ask Barbara why she thinks my mother left, she answers that my father probably insisted on it. "Your mother and Dick were saying that they were in love with each other, and your father was livid." Once my mother was gone, my father and Barbara began to date more often. "We would go out for dinner and then he would drop me off back at my apartment. I loved him. But I knew he was more concerned with punishing your mother." She knew my mother despised her and that it made her furious to know that Barbara and my father were dating. She tells me that the judge thought that she and Dick shouldn't be allowed in the presence of the six of us. "But your dad thought that was wrong. He would defy the judge's orders and bring—individually—Martha, Amy, Judy, and sometimes Jim to visit me. I remember Martha always said she was bored visiting me and wanted to go to your mother's house nearby." She looks at me sympathetically. "I understand you all didn't know me well. But your dad made a concerted effort to let you get to know me. He did what he thought was right."

"We got married on May 18, 1963, in my mother's and father's house in St. Charles, Illinois. I wore this greenish dress—I still have it somewhere—and I was so excited, so happy to be with him. Your father's sister Sandy and her husband Morty were there. Then, right before the ceremony your father pulled me into one of the bedrooms and gave me some papers to sign. He said, 'Just sign it,' and put the pen in my hand. I had no idea what it was, but I signed it anyway. Later on, I found out that it was a prenuptial agreement. In law school, I realized that his actions could be seen as coercion." She laughs a little and shakes her head at my father's daring. "That agreement said that in case he died I would receive only a certain amount. He was afraid that I wouldn't give the money to you children." She looks at me as if to tell me it was an unreasonable fear. "I didn't marry him for his money," she explains. "But he felt so possessive about *his* money. Every decision and interaction had to be considered with the money in mind. I wanted to prove to him that the money didn't matter to me—I loved him."

"We got married in the living room by a justice of the peace. Later that day, Jerry sent out a press release about our wedding. He wanted everyone to know he had a stable household so he wouldn't be at any disadvantage in the custody hearings." I think about this, and I note that in marrying Alex Stanley, my mother seemed to want the same thing.

"Once we were married, I was hoping your mother and father would stop their fighting. Your father was fairly certain he was going to win permanent custody, but then Judge Keville overturned the appeal. Your father was devastated. He was *furious*. He started yelling at me that he wouldn't be at Quail Street much. Here we were, married only two months, and he was planning to take an apartment in town so that he could spend as much time with the six of you as possible." There is something touching to me that he was so determined to stay close to us. In utter frustration, Barbara says, she started screaming at him. "And that's when I really understood it. He only married me to create the appearance of a stable family. It wasn't that he wanted to be with me—that's how obsessed he was, that's how much he wanted to win. I realized that, for him, our marriage was not serious. He was too involved in competing with your mother, and he was just obsessed with winning, with beating her."

She stops and says, "I remember your mother coming to the house to visit. She wouldn't want to be in the house when I was there, so she would sit outside and read to you in the backyard. It was so sad.

"When your mother took the overdose, one of her neighbors who knew us called and said that she had seen her taken out of her house on a gurney. She died a few days later. I thought to myself, rest in peace. When your father told you children, your sister Amy was the only one who wanted to go to the funeral." With my mother out of the picture, Barbara tells me, she imagined she had a second chance; if she could prove herself as a wife, as a mother, my father might just come to love her.

I can tell that Barbara is exhausted, yet I decide to show her now how my mother depicted her in the novel, as slightly catty: I am pushing the limit, not sure when we will talk like this again and it might be an underhanded tactic of pushing her away as there is no love lost in how she talks about my mother; we have a tenuous closeness. She reads my mother's words:

> In her hyperactive secret life, Margaret had decided that her defeat lay with the failure of her four Hs: her hair, much too stringy and always seeming to need a shampoo to liven the mousy color; her hips so wide as to necessitate the home sewing of all her clothes; her hickeys, which made her otherwise Dresden doll face ugly; her head, which somehow refused to perform the gyrations she asked of it. . . . Yet, she was in every sense a good woman, and her belief in the proper virtues was as strong as it was unreasoning and therefore vulnerable. . . . She was sharply critical, no less of herself than of her surroundings, and beneath a smooth, sweetly accommodating surface lay a serpent of unfulfilled desire.

Barbara laughs after reading this, and says that she certainly didn't have hickeys, and then, with her editor's eye, points out the extraneous adjectives and says that the writing is sloppy. She shoots me a mysterious look, then gets up and finds a letter in her desk—a letter she wrote to her father and mother more than four decades ago but never sent:

> *The difficulties this time started with meeting the Rappaports and with Dick and Nancy's attraction for each other. She is an extremely intelligent person with many civic achievements and an excellent reputation behind her. That she would withdraw from her published campaign for "personal reasons" and start divorce proceedings, giving up her six children to her husband and mother's custody, indicates her fanatic devotion and, incidentally, her extreme selfishness. She is 32 and fairly horsey, large, and has quite grey hair. The incongruousness of their situation and the resulting public and friends' responses only make them more stubborn in their isolated stubbornness. As for me, I am perfectly willing to lose myself of Dick; somewhere along the line I got tired of being hurt by his*

inconsiderateness, etc. and made myself stop loving him as a form of protection,
so now that this happened, I, perhaps, have suffered least.

She looks at me kindly. "I don't think now that your mother was selfish."

I am rattled by my astonishment—how familiar and yet unfamiliar Barbara is to me now. I have heard enough for today, and I offer a hasty thanks and scurry down five flights of stairs. I pull the parking tickets off my car and sit behind the wheel, staring vacantly. Barbara has been kind and gracious. She's made me tea and helped me understand more about my past. She has been open with her memories and feelings, and she has not judged me or pushed me away. And never once did she mention the fact that we had not seen each other in such a very long time. Was she protecting me from my own guilt because I had not talked to her in such an intimate way since I graduated from high school? She has seen my brothers and sisters occasionally, exchanges instant messages with Martha, and goes to some of my nieces' and nephews' events at school.

We have, in my family, a long history of banishment and self-exile, and in that respect I am no different. But I sit here now burning with shame, shame that I have not seen her for so long, and that "so long" is not a week or two weeks or even a couple of months, which is a long enough time for a stepdaughter and a stepmother to go without talking, and not even a couple of years. The fact is that until this meeting, Barbara and I had not spoken in decades.

When I was 18, I banished Barbara from my life *forever*. Since that time, I have ignored her timid yet persistent overtures, standing on the other side of the room at graduations and extended family events I could not avoid. There was never a major blow-out, no "precipitating event" that I could point to as the turning point. I just looked at her one day, made a judgment about the kind of mother I thought she was, and that was it. I realize now that she really did try to take care of me as best she could. But the rage inside her was always puzzling to me and sometimes frightening. At times, I could understand her sense of herself as victim. Both of us were dealt an unfair hand.

She was right to feel under-appreciated by my father—and by her eleven kids. But, when I was a teenager I could not excuse what I saw as her ineptness as a mother. I can only hope that if my kids are dissatisfied with me they will give me a chance to reconcile.

I was frustrated by her inconsistent ability to empathize. She did have a coldness about her. She was impatient with me when I said I missed my mother or complained that Barbara was stingy. I understand now that we needed more than what she could give.

I did not share with her my college escapades, my marathons, or my various adventures. I did not talk to her about Colin or my children. I did not invite her to attend my wedding or to hold my babies. There were no Christmases or summers with Barbara, no birthday celebrations. I left her out. It did not seem to matter to Barbara that I had exiled her when I met with her, or at least she did not confront me. She told me recently that she thought I wanted my children to appreciate my mother and that having this "extraneous grandmother would only confuse them." Martha's, Jerry's, and Amy's children call her "Grandma Barbara" and I am remorseful as I think about it now, not sure what lesson I am teaching my children.

But the more I mother my own three children, the less I feel the need to judge Barbara, and the more I understand that ours is a family of shifting alliances. I see now what she was up against, how hard she tried to manage us, and how heartbroken she was to have had her hopes for a life with my father not turn out as she wanted. She holds on to her green wedding dress and the painting, but she never really had a chance with him.

As she had feared, my father married her partly out of revenge, then stayed with her out of sadness and expedience. She deserved better. I'm not sure I would have done as well as she ultimately did. Give me nine distraught children at age 26 and I doubt I could have held it together for nine days, much less nine years. Now, when I catch Cory mocking me behind my back or Zoe complaining about my own ridiculous rules, I find myself reacting angrily to what I think is an unfair sharpness in their tone. I wince when Lila is critical of me as a mother. When she hears me talking to a friend's new baby, she rolls her eyes and says sarcastically, "God, I'm glad I can't remember when you talked to *me* that way"; her meanness cuts me in a way that I know from having been on the other side. What goes around comes around, I say to myself.

I'm disappointed that I can be so stubborn, and I am ashamed that it has taken me so many years to be less self-righteous about Barbara. I don't want to be unkind. Now she's older—we're both older—and her hands are gnarled with visible veins. She makes *do*, she says—the twenty-year-old dishwasher in her kitchen works "*just fine*." She's justly proud and independent and doesn't need my help, but it is not lost on me how alone she is. The modesty of her circumstances in comparison to those of my father, in comparison to Debbie's and Dick's, in comparison to my own, even, makes me gloomy. It doesn't feel right, somehow, but my place in her life is unclear. She has had two very rich ex-husbands, I tell myself, and five biological children of her own. I don't know how to move forward with Barbara or where we will go or how invested I am in rekindling a relationship after such a long separation. But for now, it's enough that we're talking, and that we're once again aware of each other.

It's summer, a few weeks later, and I'm in Italy with my family, celebrating Colin's and my twentieth anniversary. Here is the place where we went on our honeymoon; it is hard to believe that we have returned now with Lila 15, Cory 13, and Zoe 11 years old. I wake up temporarily disoriented. We are on vacation in a hill town in the southern part of Tuscany, a town built on a limestone ridge and protected by solemn grey sixteenth-century walls. I lie awake in this old hotel listening to my heartbeat, Colin's breath, a fountain's trickling sound in the courtyard. The churches are studded with Etruscan reliefs—hieroglyphs that stubbornly resist yielding their meanings, no matter how many scholars pore over their elegant shapes. It's five in the morning. My children are lost to sleep. Outside, the bells of the travertine church mark the hour.

As the early light slips through the outstretched pink dawn, birds scratch out their unfamiliar songs. The capacity to mourn, the capacity for solace, is found in the strength of loving and having my family close to me. I feel depleted, and I need to put aside the search to understand my mother and the confusion that comes from soliciting multiple perspectives of my mother's life and suicide. I need to revel in being alive in small moments of intimacy; it is so reassuring being together with my family. Moments: curled up next to my broad-shouldered, warm-blooded son, stroking his hair while we watch the World Cup on television, taking a walk with Lila where she tells me in a rush of animation about her possible future, enamored with the fancy sound of the words *pediatric oncologist*. My kids have the apparent security of living with a protective mother, while I have an insatiable longing for my mother that is coupled to an anxiety that I will somehow unpredictably lose my children. I have always hoped that they will come to see my search to understand my mother as a testament to enduring love, an inexplicable reminder to them that we are linked beyond death.

In the pale light, I set out for a run. By the time I return, Lila is up and eager to explore with me. We meander through a small graveyard. At each grave, there are carefully placed candles, flowers, and small black and white photographs in silver frames. The worn marble gravestones are cool and mossy. Lila bends down to read some of the notes attached to the dried bouquets, but neither of us can read much Italian. In some graves, families are buried together, reunited after decades apart. We study the remnants of a lived life and touch the dates carved deep in marble, the fading photos. We guess at their meanings and the lives behind them as if we are two archeologists on a dig. Sometimes, we can knit together a story. There was a man, he was a soldier, he died fighting the fascists. Other times there is no clue that illuminates the buried truths. He left behind a widow and one son. Did she get over her loss? She died before she was 35. But what happened to the boy?

Chapter Thirteen

They are the we of me.

—CARSON McCULLERS,
"The Member of the Wedding"

I come into the clinic from the pouring rain (I never have umbrellas when I need them—I am missing the weather gene that programs me to dress appropriately), and Laura is sitting in the waiting room holding a cup of warm coffee.

Over the six years I have been her doctor, starting when she was 14 years old, she has transformed her hairstyle many times. Sometimes it is short and dyed bright orange or flamboyant purple. Other times she has a perm. On this rainy day she looks subdued, early for our appointment, wearing large painter pants and a loose T-shirt. Her hair is long and pulled back. She makes steady eye contact. She looks more composed than I expected as she had called earlier and left a message saying that she had "duked it out with my boyfriend because he was ignoring me: it ended in a screaming match and I want to start drinking again so bad."

She sits lethargically in the chair and starts our session by telling me in a drained voice that her uncle killed himself at her age and that she is thinking of doing something like this but is holding herself back. Suddenly I am on alert, watching her closely as I try to pull her away from this drenching despair. She tells me heavily, "All I want to do is use, so badly." She has maintained sobriety and been drug-free for five years, except for one small slip recently when she smoked marijuana. When she was 12 years old, she experimented with a potpourri of drugs, numbing herself after being raped. She would drown out the sorrow as her schizophrenic mother struggled to provide for her, often in a stupor from her medications. Laura describes listlessly how sometimes in the middle of the night her mother would wake up terrified that her house was inhabited by demons that were in her mind and then frantically drag Laura and her sisters, half awake, into the street to protect them. Laura shows me a report from her high school saying that her "motivation and work completion appear to be inconsistent" and that she "lacks self-esteem" and is "easily distractible." It suggested "continuing counseling to address out of school concerns." There is probably not any more antiseptic way of describing Laura's desire, as she puts it, to "escape from my mother's womb and wash off the disease."

And now she sits here, feeling so miserable. She tells me it is not fair, and she is right. She goes on to denigrate herself. "I am a waste of blood," she says with contempt. She is disgusted because she just lost her job because she could not get out of bed and arrive on time. She shrugs and tells me that it wasn't the ideal job for her anyway but my heart sinks because I know that, as she stumbles into the abyss, the day-to-day structure of a job and the expectation to perform would have helped her keep some semblance of momentum. I have been in this same place with her before, praying as she leaves that she will come back alive. I want her to slow down from making any final decision to drink or to hurt herself. I tell her this belief that she would be better off dead is a sign of her depression, as if she has a high fever. She needs to be patient with herself as she finds a way to bear her pain.

She laments that she wishes someone cared for her; she is alone but she knows that she doesn't let people see how much she is struggling, how much she just wants it all to end. Dread—this is what I feel when I'm listening to her. I cannot force-feed her medication. I have to provide her quiet and steady consultation to make informed decisions. She has been through multiple "failed" medication trials where she has not had relief from her debilitating paralysis. I need to convince her that I will stand by her even if she chooses not to try yet another medication trial. I understand her reluctance to experience more disappointment. We weathered the results of a rare side effect to an antidepressant she took, getting much worse rather than better. The medication triggered a psychotic reaction. She was at the movies and she was convinced that someone, perhaps the devil, was following her. She managed to crawl to her car and then drove all night, too frightened to look behind her in the back seat. She was convinced that if she stopped, the imaginary stranger would get her. At dawn she collapsed, exhausted. She has never said that I betrayed her by giving her a medication that triggered the paranoia that her mother struggled with all her life. Thankfully the psychosis stopped when she stopped the antidepressant, but the fiasco increased her aversion to being dependent on needing a medication to function or survive her anguish. A year ago, when she had a manic episode of ten days of sleepless directionless but fervent activity, such as going to Walgreen's and buying plastic toys and wrapping them all night, or cutting up all her family photographs, she agreed to take lithium to stabilize her mood. When she took lithium she was able to return to school and complete some college courses, but she hated the weight gain. She is a big-boned girl, but on lithium she felt a layer of fat bulging out of her clothes. That the lithium dulled or turned off sexual satisfaction was an added indignity.

We sit now in this waiting game as the darkness descends on her. I have to monitor my desire to keep her alive, as I witness her despair while also respecting her strength; she has endured more than is fair or tolerable. I am not sure whether she will push her fear of medicine to the side and risk trying a medication with the hope of some relief. I don't want to pressure her to take one tiny pill, to try yet another mood stabilizer. I want her to know that I can be courageous with her, listen to her aching turmoil and not leave her. I tell her that if she uses drugs right now she will probably die. We would need to take immediate steps to hospitalize her to buy time if she went through with it. I ask her to be gentle to herself, to try to stop the endless litany of recriminations. She says fiercely, "I can't." But sometimes after we wallow in the abyss, she is able to suspend the self-flagellation. I ask her what she can do to take care of herself; she replies numbly as if even by responding she has to summon energy that she does not have. Her answers in a monotone voice share a well-rehearsed response but reveal that she is not convinced that she can overcome the inertia, "Call my sponsor, go to a meeting, take a walk, have a party." She looks at me slyly to see if I am listening; she has a grin that is contagious. I laugh, "Maybe having a party is not the best idea right now." I remind her encouragingly that we have been through this cycle before and come out on the other side, that there is a light at the end of the tunnel. Perhaps I am a glorified cheerleader, recognizing that she is tired but not tired enough. I do not have a crystal ball, but in my assessment she is not in imminent danger, not at the point where I need to commit her to a hospital to keep her safe. I don't want to minimize what she has endured. Each time Laura arrives at my office and nestles into the armchair, we are gathering momentum, allowing her time to gain strength and build a determination to hold onto hope's solace.

I still struggle with the harbored feelings from my childhood that I might help if I could see her daily, or if I was a better doctor or if I did something differently. If Laura takes a lethal overdose or drives into a tree I will be devastated, and I do what I can to safeguard her. But I wonder if surviving my mother's suicide brings with it a certain knowledge that there are limits to keeping people alive if they are determined to kill themselves. I want to do the best that I can to show Laura that I care and will make good clinical decisions, using my acumen to help her stay in the game. I still struggle with the guilt feelings from my childhood that somehow there is someone to blame when suicide happens rather than understanding it as a tragedy, a permanent answer to a temporary setback.

In the fall of 1970, I was enrolled in fifth grade at the Winsor School, an all-girls school across the street from Children's Hospital and Beth Israel Hospital. I took the bus with my sister Judy, who was five years older than I and in the tenth grade. We would stop at a donut shop and gorge on honey-glazed donuts, arriving at school giddy with grease and sugar.

Amy was also at Winsor, though on a senior's schedule, and both sisters advised me on who was who and how to get around, which teachers I could count on as allies, and the teachers I should avoid. Martha had also gone to Winsor, though by the time I entered, Barbara and Dad had already dropped her off at college. All of my older sisters were strong students or athletes. Martha had been swim team captain and president of the student council; Judy was a member of a school singing group; and Amy was a fierce debater. I wasn't sure at first whether I would be able to carry on in their footsteps.

In the beginning, Winsor's dimly lit corridors and brick façades did not seem welcoming to me. The schoolwork was much more rigorous than I was used to, and the teachers expected much more from me. I struggled at first to find my place. I squirmed at my desk, trying to keep up with math and Latin. I could be mischievous and even provocative—at Christmas I gave one of my teachers a small evergreen tree decorated with cigarettes because I knew she smoked and that she was embarrassed by her habit. The same year, I was caught drawing a cartoon of a teacher—naked—in a hymnal. And in French I whispered to my classmates and made fun of my teachers.

My homeroom teacher was stern and annoyed at my constant inter-ruptions. I found her rules tedious and so resisted them as best I could—determined that Winsor would not define me. Maybe my behavior was an effort to be noticed by someone—anyone—who might pay attention to the fact that I was one pissed-off, frightened kid. I cut the line in gym class and insisted on being first. And I started to steal things.

My friend Alice reminds me that I stole from her, even though we were best friends. I stole her coveted piece of turquoise mineral quartz, a sou-venir from a field trip to a Harvard museum. She says she felt sad for me at the time. "You used to come to my house and latch on to my mother," she remembers. Her mother was a social worker, a little overweight with red cheeks, cropped hair, and a decisive Yankee reserve that was comforting to me. They lived south of Boston, near the beach in Cohasset, in a rambling, warm house. I relished sleepovers at their house. We would drink hot chocolate on the beach. We would count stars and search the sky for the northern lights. Sometimes at night, I'd tell Alice my secrets, hoping she'd confide my tales to her mother. They saw me as a "needy kid," Alice confides now. She remembers hearing that my stepmother told other families in my school that my mother committed suicide because of me although she couldn't tell me who said it or why I was the only one who caused her suicide.

When I think about my "sticky fingers," the observation of revered British psychoanalyst D. W. Winnicott—that when an adolescent steals, she is looking for something that she has a right to, that she is making a claim on her mother and father because she feels deprived of their love—seems a plausible explanation for my impulse to steal.[1] I stole a tray of desserts before a team celebration. I stole rock candy and Sugar Babies on the way home. I stole pencils and colored Flair pens. I did Christmas shopping at the Harvard Square Co-op—coming out with a well-packed duffle bag of records, paperbacks, a scarf, and socks, all unpaid for. I stole copies of National Geographic and Scientific American from the Winsor library—and I was caught. My penance was to hold a bake sale in order to raise the money I needed to replace the magazines. On another occasion, I was caught stealing a magnifying glass. The victim, standing behind the teacher's skirt, stared at me. I flatly denied any theft and insisted I was being framed. My teachers called Barbara in to help get me in line, and she was mortified by what I had done. I, however, enjoyed that my crimes had caught my stepmother's attention. I was a rather obvious thief. More often than not, my teachers reprimanded me while upholding the belief that they could expect more from me.

In the spring of 1971, Amy graduated and went off to college. When fall came, I slipped quietly into my seat in the sixth grade, into my books, yet the only vocabulary word that I can remember learning that year was obnoxious, which my teacher scrawled on the board one day. It had a sophisticated sound to me at the time. Perhaps in an effort to give me more attention, Barbara had volunteered to be class parent, and she came along on every field trip. I tried to ignore her, but at the same time, I felt sorry for her—she took so much heat from my father—and I was touched that she wanted to be involved in my life. She seemed to enjoy reading my maudlin poetry, and both she and Dad came to school plays and watched me play Caliban in *The Tempest*. Both of them rooted for me when I recited a vitriolic Anne Sexton poem in front of the whole school, and Barbara even hung a copy of the poem in her study. But these moments of togetherness were few and far between—in reality, the tension in our family was getting worse.

By the time I was in seventh grade, my sisters' shepherding and my teachers' high expectations galvanized me and I was finally hitting my stride. Winsor had become more comfortable and even a nurturing place for me to be. The simple school rules now gave me a sense of security and much-needed boundaries. The routine of orderly activities created a steady rhythm to the day. School was a refuge from the deteriorating situation at home—from brothers who were angry and struggling with adolescence and intimacy; from my father, who, when he was home, which was now less often, yelled at and berated Barbara with frightening intensity; and from Barbara herself, who, in turn, ranted at us.

One morning, from the window in Ms. Dugan's seventh-grade math class I watched the snow fall, and I decided there was no reason to go home. At lunch I stowed away extra food in my book bag, let my good friend Alice in on my escape plan, and swore her to secrecy. Then I went off with my secret to history, gym, and art, and at the end of the day, instead of heading home on the subway, I snuck quickly into the quiet auditorium and hid myself in the thick velvet curtains in the wings of the stage. The quiet of the big room was broken only by the hiss of radiators and the rustling of squirrels scampering on the windowsills seeking shelter from the snow. In the deepening twilight, lying on my parka, I looked up into the rafters, to the grid of heavy lights above me, securely clamped in place. Yes, bad things could happen—they did happen. Even to me. But right then, I felt safe, close enough to an old radiator for warmth, not minding the musty velvet or the hard stage floor. Here, there was a peaceful quiet. I was the one and only person here, instead of only one of many children. I thought that Barbara had her hands full as it was, with Judy, Jim, Dickie, Carter, Andrew, Debbie, and Elizabeth—they needed her. I would not be missed. I could even live at school, I thought. Just go to classes in the day and stow away in the empty auditorium at night. I could go home and switch clothes if I needed to or borrow from my friends. If I stayed at school and promised to go to classes, I thought, Barbara and Dad might even accommodate this arrangement. I ate my extra cafeteria lunch, now cold and dry. For a moment, I missed my bed, but I could see the streetlights from the backstage window, and snow floating in their glow reminded me that there was a storm outside. I stretched out and closed my eyes. As I drifted toward sleep, I remembered suddenly that it was Dickie's birthday. I had not given him his present. I felt guilty—What if my disappearance ruined his party? I imagined Barbara's annoyance at me for not showing up, the cake, the special dinner she would be making. I guessed at what Dickie requested for his special dinner, probably German-chocolate cake with coconut frosting. But any pang of guilt I had been feeling was overcome as I drifted off to sleep.

The next morning I was startled awake by Barbara's and Dad's frantic calls on the other side of the auditorium. Disconsolate, they urged the headmistress to keep looking. I sat up and, for a moment, considered a possible escape. But it felt good to hear the panic in their voices, and I savored it. After a moment or two, I stepped out onto the stage from behind the curtain. My parents and the headmistress both looked at me, speechless, as I sheepishly came down the stage steps toward them. Then Barbara finally took a breath and the headmistress withdrew. When we got home, Barbara explained that they had called Alice's mother and had wheedled out of Alice where I was. Barbara said that until then she had thought I might have been abducted on the subway on the way back from school. When we got home, my father asked me what the hell I thought I was doing. He had a slightly more psychological understanding—he was exasperated by my "attention seeking." But neither of them understood that what I needed was an escape from the tension. Their fights unnerved me. What I knew about this sort of conflict was that it ended with someone you loved dying.

Soon after my disappearing act, Alice's mother took pity on me and suggested to my parents that I visit a therapist at Children's Hospital. She was fond of me and was probably worried about my influence on Alice as well. She said that maybe all this trouble I was getting into was just a distraction from figuring out what was going on inside and that I deserved to have some help. The school was still concerned and Barbara was quick to make arrangements for me to get counseling.

I went to see Dr. Walter, a man with a kind, patient presence, often with a bemused smile on his Jimmy Stewart–like face. His voice was muted, calming, and rarely changed in tone or intensity, and he chose his words precisely. It was a relief to talk openly with someone who would listen to my dread and memories. He never looked at me askance. Soon I was seeing him twice a week and continued to make the trek to his office for four years. Dressed in my aqua gym suit, I would bolt from school in the break between classes and sports and head to his office. I curled up in his black leather chair to get comfortable, shifting back and forth nervously. I stared out his fifth-floor window, mesmerized by the black clouds pouring from the hospital furnace and the thick puffs of steam spewing from smokestacks. My patient Laura may never know that I too felt helpless as a teenager; I had nervously guarded my hurt, slow to trust. It was only in the sanctuary of Dr. Walter's office that I began to feel safe enough to find the words for my sorrow and confusion.

Dr. Walter and I talked about a recurring dream that left me forlorn. In this terrifying dream, I am the one who discovers that my mother is dead. Heavy floral drapes dim the light. A large television, prominent at the foot of my parent's king-size bed, is turned off. There is stillness as I open the bathroom door. I see the fuzzy machine with the long silver pole that buffs my father's shoes. Multicolored cologne bottles line the windowsill, breaking light into colored pieces. In the reflection of the medicine cabinet, the door left ajar, there is a half-bottle of pills spilled open on the shelf, capsules red and grey, ten or twenty. Outside, a blackbird shrieks and I hear its shuddering wings. I see my mother on the bed. It is hard to tell if she is breathing, but I don't tell anyone, and I don't try to wake her.

I was afraid that my therapist would see my dream as evidence that my mother's death was my fault. If only I had recognized that my mother was unconscious, I might have gotten help to revive her. I agonized that my ignorance inadvertently killed her. Gently, Dr. Walter reassured me that nothing I did or thought had caused my mother's suicide. It was a relief to reveal my secret and then to be exonerated from my guilt. Dr. Walter helped me to understand intellectually that 4-year-old children often feel omnipotent and rely on "magical thinking" to make sense of the world around them. They see themselves as the reference point for all events, and this is a set-up for self-blame. By clinging to the idea that I could have saved my mother, I protected myself from a terrifying sense of helplessness.

Dr. Walter's unconditional acceptance restored my confidence. I had never before shared my pervasive sadness. It was too painful for my father to listen to us talk about our longing for our mother. Somehow I never felt permission to talk to my brothers and sisters, honoring a code of silence that is puzzling to me even now unless it speaks to the unspeakable confusion of the loss. Dr. Walter not only relieved my self-blame, he also acknowledged that it was natural for me to search for causes of my mother's suicide, no matter how faulty my logic. He helped me to see that my mother's suicide was tragic, unfair, and probably unexplainable. He sat quietly with me as I cried. He listened more than anyone had ever listened to me before about what mattered most to me. This got me back on track.

At the end of my seventh-grade year, my sister Judy graduated. As she stepped onto the stage in her white dress to receive her diploma, I was bereft. Next fall, she would go to college, and I wouldn't have anyone to ride the bus with me and gorge on donuts with.

That summer, Amy came home, and I was overjoyed to see her. The antagonism between my father and Barbara was like a brushfire gathering strength—and Amy gravitated to the heat.

Amy strived to make things better. She prepared sticky butterscotch brownies. She'd pass them around and entice us to eat them. But Amy never ate the brownies herself. Over the summer, she took a job scooping ice cream and making sundaes at a Brigham's restaurant. While she worked, she never ate—nothing except for a few spoonfuls of coffee ice cream at the end of a long shift. At first she lost weight slowly, but then steadily and dramatically. It terrified me to see her delicate hands grow scrawny where her veins had become more prominent. She was disappearing before my eyes. By the end of the summer, my five-foot-three-inch sister was down to eighty-five pounds. She tells me now that "I was not in the mood to accept any help; after all, I was anorexic. I was wasting away because I was trying to assert control over a system that I had no ability to control. I felt as if we were going back over the same old same old and the fighting between Barbara and Dad was a repeat of what had occurred to Mama. What was that important to fight over: was Dad going to win at all costs? I couldn't leave you all because I was terrified what would happen." Rather than have Barbara die, she was willing to sacrifice herself. One night, she looked hard at Dad and Barbara and implored them to stop the fighting. "What are you waiting for? For one of us to kill ourselves?"

Amy recovered, she tells me with a resigned laugh, when she realized "that there is only so much you can do. Plus I got a big boyfriend who would walk me home and he kept Dad in check, even though he was so gentle and would never have hurt anyone." Soon after, Barbara left Quail Street. My father had agreed to some concessions to close the deal—at one point trading a parking space downtown for the ingredients of a beef stew recipe. When I ask Barbara at our last meeting why it took so long, she hedges. "Do you know it took me years just to get a lawyer to represent me with your father?" Sharing does not come easily when my family divorces. Barbara says she doesn't want me to feel guilty, but much of the delay in their separation and divorce was about who would have custody of me, as the older kids had moved out and Jerry was decisive and wanted to stay with Dad. "I wanted to have you," she tells me. "I felt I couldn't leave you alone. I loved you and thought of you as one of my children." As soon as the details were finalized, she took part of her settlement and bought a gambrel-roofed house in a middle-class neighborhood just two miles from Quail Street.

Unwilling to battle anymore, my father agreed to leave the questions of custody to the court. A court-appointed guardian ad litem was called in to consult about what should happen with me. Martha, Amy, and Judy were in college. Jim and Dickie were just starting college, too, so it didn't matter much to them. Carter had left his private school and moved to Vermont, where he was attending a local school. It was decided that Andrew, Debbie, and Elizabeth would go with Barbara. Jerry chose to stay with Dad. When the advisor to the court asked me whom I wanted to live with, this time I was ready. I chose to live with Barbara because I could not afford to lose another mother and braced myself for Dad to retaliate. I needed to stand up to him in a way that he could not fail to notice. Jerry has always wondered at my choice to live with Barbara, "an unusual choice," he says, "since most kids stay with their DNA." But I didn't feel safe with Dad at that point, and it was very important for me to feel as if I could stand up to my father. I thought it might have even earned me my father's grudging respect. Unlike Barbara, I was not intimidated, and I wasn't afraid to challenge his authority. Both my father and I believe strongly that we are right and justified in our righteousness, and I was not easily persuaded at the time that my father thought it was better for me to stay with him; rather, I was almost certain that he wanted to retaliate against Barbara.

Jerry remembers that as Barbara packed up the house, he sat there stupefied while some of the furniture was moved over to her new home. My father quickly refurnished the house with leftover furniture from model units at Charles River Park. Jerry would live with Dad—just the two of them—in the seventeen-room house, now equipped with chrome ball lamps, a Naugahyde sofa, modern club chairs, and a glass coffee table. On the first night it suddenly dawned on Jerry that it would be just Dad and him in all these rooms, and he sat down and cried, missing the rest of us.

I initially felt triumphant living with Barbara. I thought I could even be alone, as long as I had Dr. Walter to listen to me. All I needed to know was that I could stand up to my father. In the beginning, I refused to talk to him.

I made it clear, through my 14-year-old infuriating defiance, that I was determined to have my space. My father felt shut out and frustrated. He didn't like me seeing Dr. Walter—he wanted to know what was going on, and when I refused to talk about my sessions, he refused to pay for my therapy. But I was not to be outdone. Dr. Walter dropped his rate so that I could pay for the therapy myself and Barbara encouraged me to keep it going. I started babysitting three or four times a week to earn enough money to pay the bills. Dad was stung by our estrangement and didn't understand why Dr. Walter wouldn't referee our standoff. At the time, I was too threatened to sit and talk it out with my father. He had acquired mythic force—he seemed too powerful, too persuasive, and I feared ending up like Barbara or my mother, bullied into giving up everything that was important to me. Now, though, I think that Dad had a good point: Dr. Walter should have invited my father into our session. After all, at some point I would finish up with Dr. Walter, and then my father and I would still need to address my suspicions that he was all-powerful—What if I *had* confronted him with my unanswered questions earlier and challenged his control? What if we'd had someone to guide us and help us to make sense of our history and our feelings? We might have saved each other a lot of time.

Barbara's new house—my new home—was gray, with six bedrooms and none of Quail Street's swimming pool, expansive yard, or woods. In choosing to live with Barbara, I had also become the oldest child of this hybrid group. I looked after Debbie and Elizabeth, but not Andrew, who was just six months younger than me and had withdrawn into the stony silence of adolescence that I tried very hard not to retreat to. Almost immediately after leaving my father, Barbara enrolled in law school. "Most of my life," she says, "I was like a sheep—a wimpy, typical Libra. It wasn't until I started law school and started talking to professors did I realize that I wasn't stupid." She looks back in her date books she has kept to see if there is anything else she forgot to share with me. "All it says," she reports, "is 'divorce final.' And 'now I am alone.'"

Our new house had a small fenced-in backyard where I planted five rows of radishes and decided that with my new blended family, I wanted to be called Radish. Across the street lived a boy in ripped jeans named Brian who would hang out on his front step. If I stopped on the street, he'd talk to me and awkwardly tell me off-color jokes. One day I kissed him.

My little sisters had the two back rooms on the second floor across the hall from Barbara, and Andrew escaped to the attic. Barbara's room was filled with newspapers, and she often worked there, barricaded by piles of law books. Barbara tells me, "I remember when I was studying for law school and you wanted me watch you practice your dance in your leotard. I had too much to do, and you looked so sad." She trails off. I say I get it— I have three kids, and they need me in different ways and they don't always get the mama they want. The house on Park Street was more like a dormitory than a home. We were roommates really, not a family. But I thought it was good enough.

My room was tucked next to Barbara's at the top of the stairs. She decorated it with homemade red bandana curtains and a shag rug, and it had a special built-in shelf made for my glass-animal collection. Barbara assigned us little chores and gave us a modest allowance—every bit of which I saved for therapy. And when we missed our dogs, she got us a sleepy black cat, whom I named Ultrabrite. Gone were the frogs' legs and calves liver; Barbara rationed basics and cooked simple meals.

Barbara reveals to me that she knew how I labored to engage her as a mother. I experienced her as formidable, tempestuous, and preoccupied, and did not appreciate how difficult it was for her to extract herself from her predicament. She asks, "Do you remember when you made me such a nice dinner and placed a gavel at the end of the table on my first day of law school?" I do remember that I tried with her, but I don't remember ever feeling that I mattered much. I worried that she could not appreciate who I was because I was my mother's daughter, my father's daughter. I was not hers.

And though I might have wished it at the time, my father did not disappear. Two or three times a week, Dad would come by in his brown Ford station wagon and drive all the sisters—me, Debbie, and Betsy—to school. I refused to talk to him, producing only monosyllabic responses to his questions as I sat in the backseat in stubborn contempt. The radio blasted the news—troops firing, a hijacked Italian airliner. I would sit there, tense, and stare out the window and wonder what was for lunch that day.

Some nights, Debbie, Betsy, Jerry, Andrew, and I would have dinner with Dad at Quail Street. He'd cook dinner in the kitchen fireplace, slowly grilling steaks or chicken, and ask us about school, friends, the books we were reading. I knew he missed me, but I was indifferent. Dad often didn't come home from work until very late at night, but Jerry remembers that the two of them always ate breakfast together. Dad would prep him for the SATs and talk about the development business, summer internships, and Jerry's teachers at the Noble and Greenough School.

Soon enough, I realized my dad would refuse to give up on us. He would always answer a call, make an effort, take an interest. He understood that sometimes gentle and indirect work better than full-on confrontation. He let us take our time; he gave us room and even smoothed the way. I didn't totally exile him, and I wasn't ready to give up the possibility of having fun with him either.

Barbara reminds me of a trip I took with my father to St. Maarten when I was just 14. He snuck Jerry and me into the casinos to play blackjack and ordered up virgin coladas for us. We would watch, impressed, as Dad, in his lizard-print pants and fluorescent shirt, almost seemed to will the dice to perform. He bought me a fluorescent-orange halter top with a matching skirt—way too sexy for a girl my age but he knew how much I wanted it. I wore it every chance I could get.

Slowly things between us thawed. Comfort came in unpredictable ways, as did the knowledge that Dad wanted to be loved by me—and that he would fight for my love. He explains now that he never allowed his kids to define the relationship. He means that he will never let us make the final decision to retreat; he will continue to make overtures and create opportunities to open dialogue. If I didn't want him around, I would need to make active and repeated decisions to reject him. Throughout my teens, he stayed in the game. He made repeated efforts to engage me on subjects that were important to me. We talked about my classes, books, politics, and sports.

He liked that I had taken up running. One afternoon, we took off for a run on the Charles River Esplanade. We started out at a brisk pace and after a few moments I realized, as I listened to his labored breathing, that Dad was not going to be able to keep up with me. I would beat him, instead of the other way around. I slowed my pace slightly, and after a couple of easy miles, I called off the run earlier than I had planned. He smiled, grateful, I think, that I had not run him into the ground. He was proud of my growing speed and endurance—and of my restraint.

A few weeks later, he came out to watch my first road race. It thrilled him to know that I had intentionally positioned myself between the formidable marathoners Frank Shorter and Bill Rodgers. I told Dad that my plan was to try to beat them at the first quarter. Nobody cheered me on more enthusiastically than my father.

I suspect that one of the reasons Barbara might have been so angry with me was that, by this time, I'd figured out how to get along with my father. Andrew had already moved back to Dad's house, rejecting Barbara's "annoying supervision" and living with "too many girls." Sometimes after school, I would go to Quail Street instead of going home and would hang out with Jerry, Andrew, and my friends. Dad let us charge food at the grocery store, and I would pick up steaks and quarts of ice cream and take them back to his house where we would make extravagant dinners and stuff ourselves. We'd camp out in the big living room and play card games with our friends. Purposefully or not, my father gave us room to be ourselves. Sometimes late at night I would talk with his new girlfriend and she entreated me not to judge my father so harshly, as she told me his side of the saga.

One night while the others were in St. Martin, Andrew got drunk at a school party and passed out in the snow wearing only a thin shirt and a pair of pants. "He could have died," Barbara says. "He could have frozen to death." It alarms her to think about this even now. She thinks my father gave us too much freedom. Jerry acknowledges that ours was a notorious "party house" because often no adults were home to supervise.

Barbara admits now that she felt betrayed by my spending more time with my father. She thinks I was manipulated by what he could offer and by the freedom we had over there. I tell her that it wasn't that my integrity was for sale.

I could see that he was happy to be with me. When I told him that I wanted to be a doctor, Dad arranged an internship for me in a research lab at Mass General—assisting with heart transplants in animals and studying how the immune system mounts rejection. Whenever I called on him, he quickly responded. It was my father who comforted me after Owen Russell, a snotty-nosed jock, broke up with me on Valentine's Day. He knew we needed him, and in his own way, he was extraordinary. I think one of his biggest frustrations was that he could not be a mother too.

Time and distance—even two miles between houses—can be salves for bruised feelings. Somehow, my father and I found a way back to each other. When he is boxed in, he panics. But give him room to be a good man, give him space to be kind and generous, and more often than not my father will rise to the occasion. Familiarity breeds forgiveness; we are all woven together, inextricably linked—and I have chosen to let go of the anger, the recriminations, the self-doubt, and to make room for the momentum forward. Dad is at his best as a father when he can be proud of us, when he can step aside with dignity and give us center stage. His pleasure in our successes is genuine. He will take credit for positive outcomes, but what he does not want is to be blamed for our mistakes or my sense of betrayal.

When I work with children and teens in crisis, I can't make any promises and I can't magically protect them from misfortune. Laura will always need more than I can give her. It is not I who will "give" her sobriety. But all of us share a desire to be seen, to be loved for who we are—a love that can be cultivated by an inward gaze and caught in the gaze of another. I had a certain fragility that comes from my insatiable longing for a mother, a pursuit to resurrect her from the dead, a pursuit that I have not relinquished easily. I have come to appreciate over the years how vital it is for those of us who have lost loved ones to understand the meaning of the loss in ways that are tolerable and to forge the steadfast belief that it is possible to love deeply despite disappointment. Growing up I had a caring school, a therapist who listened, Barbara and Dad and my brothers and sisters, compensation for a yearning to be close to someone who was gone. I find joy in providing for my patients a sanctuary and take refuge in knowing that they are loveable and capable.

Lila used to stand in her crib when she was little, announcing, "I am waking up." And waking up she is as she approaches womanhood, separating from me with the confidence that she can return when she needs to fortify herself. Every year, our neighborhood marks spring by an abundance of lilacs blooming all variations of purples. I planted some lilacs at our house ten years ago in memory of my grandfather, but something about the acidity of our soil makes the flowers averse to producing much bounty. In the backyard of my childhood, the distinctive aroma of lilacs (my mother's favorite flower) intoxicated the spring awakening. Now starting around mid-May I surreptitiously, on my early morning runs, plan which lilac tree will provide me with an aromatic treat. If the tree is laden with blossoms, I descend. Or if the blossoms seem so high that no one else can reach them, I go after those. There is a thrill and a sense that I am taking what is rightfully mine as I snap the brittle branch. It is with this sense of entitlement and a recognition of the absurdity that a 49-year-old child psychiatrist is stealing lilacs that I realize logic is being defied. It is no surprise that I ended up working with wayward adolescents. What part of this story is rightfully mine? I have pursued my mother, cherished her, never quite predicting which early morning I will feel compelled to write this story of longing and abundance, wanting to be seen, to inhale the distinct invigorating aroma of lilacs, the temporary burst of flower, illicit but now mine with an obscure emotional force that drives my fable.

Chapter Fourteen

I could be bound in a nutshell
And count myself a king of infinite space
were it not that I have bad dreams.

—WILLIAM SHAKESPEARE, *Hamlet*

I often joke that I'm a doc on wheels because I don't have a designated office at the high-school health clinic. Sometimes my appointments are conducted in rooms outfitted with tables for pelvic exams and posters about the food pyramid and warnings about drunk driving. We make do with periodic interruptions over the intercom. I am always amazed that the teenagers I see in therapy are able to concentrate at all as we sort through fears and feelings and consider the pros and cons of different choices, building trust amid disruptions and medical-waste containers. But this is the way teenagers work best—in the interstices of life around them. Many parents know this intuitively—we know that when we least expect it, teenagers open up and say what is on their minds, such as when driving in the car, shopping at the mall, or watching some inane sitcom.

My patient Matthew was usually punctual for our appointments. Matthew sat alone in a corner of the waiting room with his head down and looked relieved when I called him in. He sauntered into my makeshift of-fice with an ease that makes people naturally gravitate to him. He has a chiseled jaw, bushy eyebrows, and auburn hair carefully groomed to one side. He flashed me a grin, offered a gently mocking comment about my luxurious surroundings, then deftly folded his 17-year-old six-foot-three-inch frame into the stiff chair, achieving a polished slouch, with none of the awkwardness that sometimes is seen with oversized teenagers. As I looked at him there, with his air of confidence masking his anxiety, I thought that out of all the kids in these crowded classrooms, he'd be the last student some people would suspect was struggling with sleepless nights. His teachers noted that he was capable of doing better work—polite school lingo for "lazy"—but they never saw his guarded, tortured state of mind.

Matthew and I were in a high-stakes negotiation; he reluctantly tolerated what he has sometimes felt to be an intrusive cross-examination as we tried to figure out what has gone terribly wrong for him. He was haunted by "Tap-per," as we came to refer to his auditory and visual hallucination.[1] He had felt increasingly paranoid, as if someone was following him. He had a delusion, an implausible belief, that Tapper made the branches scrape against his win-dow at night or mysteriously moved a trashcan on the street. The danger of psychosis, this type of abnormal thinking, is that it damages a person's abil-ity for self-reflection and includes a problem with "reality awareness."[2]

It's hard to explain psychosis to Matthew because the explanation is com-plex, and we know only so much. Psychosis is associated with abnormalities in the levels of certain neurotransmitters, chemical messengers in the brain. Medications such as antipsychotics can help by correcting the balance, but many drugs have troubling and sometimes severe side effects. It is impor-tant to figure out the right diagnosis, as patients can be psychotic because they are so depressed or bipolar or struggle with schizophrenic delusions and the diagnosis shapes the choice of medication. Treating mental illness in children and adolescents with medications is a relatively new phenom-enon and an evolving science and sometimes it is trial and error. There are still many unanswered questions about how a developing brain responds to these medications. With Matthew and his family, I try to be transparent about how we make sense of a confusing, bewildering time and then chart a prudent path.

Psychosis often strikes in adolescence and is typically acute.[3] It is one of the most serious signs that the brain is struggling to maintain order.[4] Untreated, a patient can become increasingly disorganized, aggressive, and unable to function. Many patients experience a pervasive sense of panic as they lose control; for others, depression and irritability make it difficult for them to see that they are not well. They become belligerent when the rest of the world will not cooperate with them or accommodate their needs. Most adolescents are already conflicted about being dependent. It feels counterintuitive to them to cede control and allow someone to help so that, paradoxically, they can become better and stronger. A teenager who has a broken leg will usually accept crutches, but a teenager with mental illness may feel a fierce pride and insist that he or she be allowed to manage this alone. It is even harder for such teens to accept help if they have experienced severe disappointments, abuse, or conflict with their parents. Rarely is a teenager in crisis willing to talk with me unless he or she is extremely scared. I know I will often be dismissed, insulted, or ignored. I accept Matthew's worry that I might not be able to help; he came to me because his family was alarmed that he seemed increasingly withdrawn and caustic. I initially thought that he was depressed and smoking too much marijuana, but over time as he revealed his hallucinations it became clear that he was struggling with emerging schizophrenia.

Sometimes I am limited by what I can do, but in any case Matthew needs to give me permission. There is an art of persuasion to show that I care while allowing him to save face and not seem patronizing toward him. Patients who have suffered the humiliation of losing control of their minds understandably want to make a choice about medications. Taking a pill is a daily insult, a reminder that something is wrong. I encourage an informed choice, but ultimately patients need to come to terms with their condition and choose the most appropriate way to maintain dignity and sense of self.

Matthew stared down at his topsiders and talked with me about the sailing team at his high school. He knew his skill at navigating the boat would be an asset to the crew, but he was reluctant to sign up. He felt pressured to stick with it and feared the school would shut the program down if there weren't enough participants. He knew that whatever he chose, it would require him to find a strength that he wasn't sure he had. He has struggled to separate from his old teammates, as some of them were the same buddies he smoked marijuana with before and after class the previous year.

It was in that haze of dope that Matthew first collided with Tapper. Although every teen who has smoked pot is aware that the high often comes with a dose of paranoia, most teenagers are unaware that on rare occasions this paranoia can become permanent. Researchers have discovered that marijuana can throw a switch that activates psychosis in vulnerable individuals—especially if there is a family history of mental illness.[5] This topic is not typically part of most health education classes, and my own warnings to my patients to stay away from drugs are often met with disbelief.

In Matthew's case, Tapper first signaled its presence after a house fire. Last summer, while on vacation with his family at their new second home on Cape Cod, Matthew left a scented candle burning in his bedroom to disguise the smell of smoke from his joint, then wandered off stoned to hang out with his friends at the beach. When he returned, a fire truck was outside his house.

Soon after the fire, Matthew was adamant that Tapper, an eerie force, had visited him during the night. He was asleep in the unfamiliar guest room when suddenly the lights turned on and off, and the bed shook and spun as if there were an earthquake—details I recognize from *The Exorcist*, images that evoke the darkest of supernatural forces. Completely "freaked out," Matthew called his best friend, Lars, looking for reassurance but only got his answering machine. Scared by the power of Tapper, he hung up and rushed out of the house. He spent the night wandering the streets, smoking one cigarette after another and looking over his shoulder, terrified that he was being followed. When I asked him why he didn't knock on his parents' bedroom door, he said resolutely that he wanted to try to manage this on his own. Unnerving, yes, this new presence; but he wanted to keep it a secret from his parents.

Since that night, Matthew tried to come to terms with Tapper's visits, and for about six months, he had been reluctant to tell others about Tapper. He paused at one point in mid-sentence, trying to stifle a yawn, but the insistent yawn overtook his face. Fearing the worst, I asked how he slept. Usually Tapper came at night, sometimes with a loud tap, sometimes by scratching against the window. It didn't matter whether Matthew slept in different rooms or different houses—Tapper followed. Last night, Matthew confessed, Tapper was knocking on his closet door with an irregular, unpredictable rhythm. When he opened the door, Tapper's shadow loomed menacingly. Matthew was adamant that this wasn't "his mind playing tricks," my euphemism for auditory, tactile, or visual hallucinations. He told me if I looked right then, I would see his muscles contracting, proof of Tapper's presence. Incredulous, I checked the palms of his hands, and indeed the small muscles of his hands were twitching slightly. I sighed. It was a delicate process: If I directly challenged the existence of Tapper, Matthew would withdraw and I would run the risk of alienating him. I needed to gently build an oasis where Matthew could make sense of this frightening presence or at least trust me enough to agree to take medication to get some relief from the torture. Matthew alternated between attributing his bodily changes to the presence of Tapper and dreading the isolation that came from his disturbing thoughts.

Matthew said he found comfort from reading the Bible—its words were a form of ablution. He worked hard at convincing me that he was not afraid, but there was an uneasiness; the words did not match his mood. Too soon, there was a voice over the loudspeaker, and we both startled reflexively:

"Dr. Rappaport, your next patient is here." Matthew tensed. If we could talk a few more minutes, he might be ready to manage his fear. With time, I hope to help him come to understand that he needs to consider that Tapper might be more than a spirit or a force of nature, that it could well be a real illness, and that if it's untreated, it will damage him. I looked at him. "See you next week, right?" He nodded and bolted out of the room.

Somehow, Matthew managed to graduate from high school despite the fact that he was distracted and often had trouble sleeping because of Tapper's presence. We had managed to contain the disruption of his mind enough for him to cross the stage and receive his diploma. It was a small, private victory that he celebrated by bounding down the aisle. But he was still haunted. In spite of my unambiguous recommendation, he refused to take an antipsychotic regularly—he did not like that it made him feel lethargic and "stupid." His parents agreed with me that, for Matthew, taking the meds was a process of negotiation. It was his decision, an informed choice. Matthew decided that he also wanted to "graduate" from meeting with me. Maybe he could manage Tapper on his own; never mind that his grandfather had schizophrenia and had lived as a recluse, Matthew wanted to strike out on his own. I left the door open in case his family needed help and I assisted with planning the transition.

After graduating, Matthew worked as a volunteer renovating a homeless shelter. But before long, Tapper stepped up its insistent demands for attention, and Matthew became increasingly agitated, especially with his mother. In a matter of weeks, his whole body shifted into a fight-or-flight mode—he was tense, easily startled, on guard with a pervasive outrage that Tapper was mocking him.

Matthew's unraveling accelerated and unlike before, despite his parents' pleas, he refused to come to talk to me about it. He became suspicious that I was intent on poisoning him and that he needed to stay far away from me. I suggested other doctors to his parents but he was unwilling to see anyone else either, bolting from the house at the time of the scheduled appointment. He destroyed his room, smashed his television, and became increasingly menacing. His family could not handle his tirades, despite their stalwart efforts to maintain normalcy. They clung to the hope that with the right religious guidance, Matthew would settle down. This outcome struck me as unlikely, especially when they called me urgently and told me how he had tried to grab the steering wheel during an argument with his mother. With his parents' reluctant agreement, I arranged to have Matthew committed to a hospital against his will. This planned hospitalization was necessary both because of the danger that he might hurt himself or someone else and because of his unwillingness to see a doctor regularly to help him stabilize. After just two days, Matthew's parents told me they wanted him released. Matthew insisted that keeping him in that "hell hole" would only make him hate us more. "Locking me up is humiliating," he bellowed, and he demanded that his parents find him his own apartment.

I met with his father, a handsome, intimidating man who, as a successful hedge fund manager, was used to relying on his intuition. He proposed temporarily renting an executive hotel suite for Matthew if he was "too stressed" to live at home. Seasoned by my father's contrary and protective nature, I was not afraid to negotiate with money and power—to cajole Matthew's father into understanding that a superficial rescue would not be enough. I acknowledged that he and his wife felt that the care at the hospital was inadequate and that it was frustrating to feel so helpless. It was hard for them—they believed in Matthew's potential. But they needed to suspend their hope while Matthew battled his inferno. I wanted them to see what I saw, that Matthew was ravaged by an infection of the mind that has nothing to do with their parenting. They needed to choose which fight they were willing to win; temporary release would not give them time to come up with a safe, viable plan.

Matthew's father appreciated the danger. His wife had retreated into numb silence and had left him to make the decisions. He tried hard to manage, aware of what a betrayal this hospitalization felt like to his son and wondering whether he would ever be forgiven. I told him that this was a concern for another day—we wanted Matthew to survive so that we could find a way for him to heal. But to see his son so sick and helpless was excruciating.

It is humiliating for most patients to surrender control. Psychiatric hospitals are usually a last resort, and I sympathized with Matthew's father's apprehension. Matthew's free-fall pandemonium left us all exhausted, breathless as we watched his illness dismantle any semblance of equilibrium. For now, the psychosis had shattered his ability to focus, to make any plans or decisions. He could not manage his thoughts. He could not stop his fear. He could not reason his way out of this nightmare.

In my work, there are times like this when I fumble, reaching for a light in the dark. I too am dismayed that it has gotten to this point, and heavy-hearted that I cannot make Matthew better. As a doctor I am an active witness, busy trying to figure out how to help, and there is a certain distance and experience that allow me to navigate with confidence. In emergencies like this, I am at my clinical best, calm and analytical, proceeding with cautious determination. In an ironic way my mother's suicide has given me endurance, an equanimity that allows me to do the best I can; it may not always be enough, but as long as someone is alive, we can all continue to hope he will find the relief and comfort he needs. Unlike Matthew's family, I am not linked forever to Matthew. It is different to feel helpless as a mother, daughter, or sister. Matthew's parents will become well seasoned in a courageous battle fortified by a faith that Matthew will rise again, battered by the storm of his illness but finding his way.

If one of my own children were to struggle with mental illness, my sister Debbie would be a sobering teacher. She has wrestled with her own demons for years with schizophrenia, persisting proudly and steadily despite her insecurities. She now lives alone in a small ranch house in Colorado, where she looks out onto a few horses grazing in a field of wildflowers. To keep busy and not get too isolated, Debbie volunteers at a food co-op, works at the Nature Conservancy, studies tai chi, and sings in a choral group. Her constant companion is Penny, a shaggy black dog she adopted from a shelter. At first Penny was skittish and chewed the furniture when she was left alone, but now each offers the other a secure base. Debbie is more alone than I could tolerate, but she never complains. It takes enormous effort to arrange order in her life and to keep up with the nuances of relationships, so she avoids family celebrations.

Debbie has rounded shoulders as if to brace herself against the inevitable disappointments of a difficult life. She is my half-sister, now 45 years old with a full head of graying chestnut hair. She has become heavy-set.

Debbie was born to my father and stepmother Barbara six months after my mother died. Was she destined to be a child of melancholy? Although I was protective of Debbie growing up as her big sister five years older than her, we have grown distant. We now meet usually for brief visits at a restaurant or a short hike once a year. We are both on guard, trying to steer clear of sensitive topics as she can become quickly annoyed with me. Sometimes I slip, curiosity and concern getting the better of me, and I ask her, feigning casual interest, about her medications and about how she is managing. She will respond with silence, scrunching her aquiline nose and grimacing, letting me know that I have crossed a boundary. As a doctor who prides herself on being able to make conversation when most people are stymied, I am awkward and frustrated at not being able to connect with Debbie. Even though she has banished me, I have not made a consistent effort. But Debbie is not my patient—she is my sister, and she is reluctant to give me permission to enter her world.

I don't always appreciate her penetrating insights, especially not at first. I'm not sure when she will launch an attack and criticize me. She gets irritated if I seem smug or complacent; she quips that I have successfully insulated myself with being a doctor and raising three kids, a fine package that keeps my insecurities at bay.

When I showed Debbie some of my early writing about her, she was honest. Her clarity was readily apparent when she told me that she was insulted by the way I described her paranoia and psychotic break. In my early drafts of this book, I tried to describe my view of her both through the eyes of a critical sister and as a clinically detached psychiatrist. She told me, "It is hard to look back on my painful days of feeling victimized. I feel it all over again when you remember me as I was and ignore who I have become."

What she says is true. She has had a different trajectory than either of us would have predicted, and before she was diagnosed and taking medication regularly I was frightened by her change in personality. I misconstrued Debbie's sarcasm as mean-spiritedness. I did not understand that she was miserable and frightened of changes that were beyond her control. She was victimized in ways that she only alludes to, restrained once in an emergency room, voluntarily hospitalized for six months, and subjected to the indignity of not being able to trust her own mind or body. Debbie has changed and grown and because we do not see each other often, it is hard to rebuild with shared new experiences. I'm often caught in the past, focused on big dramatic moments that happened years ago, longing for answers to my questions and only respecting from a distance that she has found a precarious balance.

Debbie sparkled when we were growing up together. She loved horses and had become a fearless rider by the time she was 13, cantering through fields on a big stallion, her thick hair flying behind her and sporting a Cheshire grin. In school and at home she was often center stage, acting in *Midsummer's Night Dream* as Puck, imitating radio commentators, singing with perfect pitch, and playing guitar. When I headed to college, she went to boarding school and was captain of her lacrosse team. There were no obvious indicators that she would start to have trouble until her first year in college. Even now, I know only the outlines of Debbie's loosening grasp on reality, her fixation on the changes in her body, her paranoia. I was not as generous or comforting to Debbie as I am now with my patients. As Debbie fell apart, all I felt was alarm. I wonder now if this is yet another parallel that I have with my mother, loving a sister who cannot be saved.

Debbie dropped out during her first year at Berkeley because she found it hard to get out of bed, let alone complete her term papers, and she moved back to Boston, where Barbara and Dad and Phyllis lived and also where I had just started medical school. She seldom left her apartment, did not sleep at night, and would sit in the dark and brood. One day after talking with her, my father called me, concerned that she was so troubled, and we strategized about what might help her. He asked whether Debbie might see my former therapist, Dr. Walter, whom I had not seen since high school. Looking back, I understand that this was the "prodrome," the foreshadowing before her schizophrenia manifested itself, but at the time we thought she would get better if she could find someone to talk to about Barbara and Dad's divorce and going off to boarding school.

I called Dr. Walter. He asked me if it was okay with me and I figured that as I had not seen him for six years since finishing high school, enough time had passed, and I did not have exclusive proprietary rights. Besides, he had helped me so much that maybe he could do the same for Debbie—and so I agreed. In hindsight, I wish both of us had realized that seeing my former therapist would place Debbie in a difficult position. Since she was struggling with boundaries, feeling unsafe and resentful that I was in love with Colin and moving forward, becoming a doctor while she was at an impasse, she might have been better off with her own therapist. It didn't help when Debbie told me that during a session with Dr. Walter she had smashed a hand-crafted pot that I had made for him. She needed to shatter the reminder of me, the suggestion that I was a favored patient and that she was competing with me for his attention.

At key transitions in my life, starting medical school, getting married, giving birth to Lila and Cory, I stopped to notice that Debbie was getting progressively sicker. In my wedding pictures, Debbie stands on the sidelines, a guest, not a bridesmaid. I did not ask for her participation, although my sister Judy read at the wedding and my niece was the flower girl, and given how close Debbie and I had been with each other growing up, it would have been natural for her to sing in my wedding. By that time, we had become distant and I did not feel as if I could predict how she would behave. In the pictures, she tries to look into the camera, but she's self-conscious. At the time, I saw her attitude toward me as willful and angry. I didn't recognize that it emanated from her unhappiness at being robbed of the things she wanted most and deserved—a quieter mind, the ability to make a plan and carry it out, to love without suspicion, to be at ease with other people.

She left my wedding and took a flight to California, where she was hospitalized after being found disoriented as she wandered around the airport. I was relieved that other people in my family took over. There were times early in my marriage when Colin and I would be sitting in our apartment kitchen—a flagrant red, or orange, or even purple, as we experimented with novel colors—and Debbie would call to tell me what she'd been up to. She would drop casual hints about driving around with her foot glued to the accelerator, racing dangerously on the highway, obsessing about colliding with a tree. I thought she was teasing me, knowing that my mother had killed herself, that this was her way of hurting me most. I felt she was pressuring me to take charge of her out-of-control life by telling me this but I was helpless and resentful of her self-destructive urge. I hated the sense of danger she brought into my life; I thought she was holding me hostage because I cared about her and I withdrew even more.

When my daughter Lila was born, Debbie showed up at the hospital. She held Lila, teetering from side to side as if she might drop her and teasing me about disappearing with my new baby. Her black humor did not sit well with me.

A few weeks later, Debbie had minor surgery to remove an ovarian cyst. After the operation, she told me that the surgery had "neutralized" her sexuality, that she was invaded by toxicity and would never be a mother herself. Somehow, in Debbie's mind I was connected to this turn of events because I had brought her to the hospital for the operation. I felt guilty for staying away from her, for keeping Lila away from her, but the truth was that Debbie was frightening me.

Two years later when I was about to deliver Cory, during my residency, my sister Judy, five years older than me, ten years older than Debbie, called me and urgently told me that Debbie was much worse than we all really knew. Debbie was 28 years old and living on her own at the time in western Massachusetts and Judy, who regularly had a weekly call with Debbie, had not heard from her for two weeks. Judy has a way of being decisive and mobilizing the troops, and she called Dad and Phyllis, who were in Paris on vacation. Dad then asked my oldest brother Jim if he could help out, because Dad was in Europe. Jim and Barbara went out together.

Jim found a private-detective firm and went out to western Massachusetts to look for Debbie. With the detectives' help he was able to find out which bank machines she used. He staked out one of them and posted the detectives at the other two machines. The detectives found her at a motel late at night. She had been living in her car (she had gotten increasingly disorganized off her medications) and would check in every once in a while at a motel for a shower. Jim suspected that once he found Debbie, she would need to be hospitalized because she might be psychotic. By that time my father was back, and he met Jim and was able to get a court order that justified to the state that she was a danger to herself and needed psychiatric care. After stabilizing, Debbie agreed to go to a hospital called Austen Riggs, a sanctuary in Stockbridge, Massachusetts, that provides long-term treatment. She stayed there for ten months and afterward stayed in a group home where she trained to become a teacher's assistant.

While Debbie was in the hospital, my father and Barbara attended therapy sessions together and were able to put their differences aside for the sake of Debbie, and Phyllis helped this progress. Dad offers readily how proud he is that Debbie accepted the help and seems relieved that she worked so diligently to get better.

I had only one strained visit. My father can be inordinately protective of us, and in a crisis he always makes time to offer the best he can. The dedicated parents of some of my patients are no different—if I told them that their child could be better if they took a toothpick and shoveled the snow off Mount Everest, they would ask me where the trail was. Debbie has persisted with a dignified strength, making several transitions, living with our sister for five years in Chicago and, for the last ten years, living on her own.

My dad says that he is grateful for how well she has "handled a lousy break." Both of us are humbled by the limitations of power but also by Debbie's stalwart courage.

One day when I returned from work, there was a message from Debbie. Out of habit, I hesitated at first to call her back, but I was happy when I finally got her on the phone and discovered that she was preparing to do a presentation at a state hospital where she co-leads a peer support group for patients with chronic mental illness. Her group encourages members to take an active role in designing their recovery process, to identify triggers that may cause a crisis, and to take responsibility and manage their psychiatric symptoms. She was amused that I was so impressed and quickly got to the reason for her call. She asked me if I would be her health care proxy, willing to make decisions if she can't make them for herself. I took it as a compliment that she trusted my judgment, even though I haven't always been available to her while pursuing my dream of becoming a doctor and raising a family. We don't spend much time together as we live such separate lives. I can only hope she knows how often I think of her but hesitate to call. No excuses. I got dealt a better hand.

That night at dinner, I told my family that Debbie wanted me to make health decisions for her if she couldn't make them for herself. Lila in a rare moment of vulnerability asked me if mental illness is "in our family. Or is it just that we have such a large family?"

"We do have depression and bipolar disorder in our family," I answered slowly, "the way some families have diabetes or cancer. It doesn't mean necessarily that you are destined to have it happen to you." I looked at her steadily. "And these are treatable illnesses; it is not fair to be derailed, but we would make sure to get you help if this ever happened." She has watched me invest so much with my patients and their families and she knows that I would want to be there for her. "But," I said, reassuring her yet not wanting to make false promises about the future, "I haven't seen any signs and I hope that it doesn't happen."

I watched the moonlight shadow on the white snow as we ate and my mind wandered, settled by the routine of the kids' day. In the case of Matthew and Debbie, it was clearly mental illness that derailed them—and their families mobilized. As for my mother, she got terribly depressed and she killed herself, but it is not clear to me whether she would have managed just fine had a different scenario unfolded. It is the argument that I go round and round on. Did she have an affair with Dick because she was unhappy and that was the beginning of the end? Or were the affair and her suicide manic, impulsive decisions? Were the loss of her sister and the alienation from her mother the roots of her demise? At the end my mother sounded as if she was stripped of everyone but Alex, who felt sympathetic to her plight. And she spiraled down.

I reminded Lila of something that happened right after the twin towers were destroyed, at a time when I was preoccupied. I had pulled up to the local gas station, and the man working the pumps greeted me warmly, as I was a regular customer. I rushed across the street to grab a newspaper and got back in my car and started to drive away. I noticed, curiously, that people were yelling at me and that a truck was honking at me. I realized belatedly that I was still attached to the gas pump. Shaken, I got out of the car. Understandably, this once amiable gas station attendant was furious. He made a motion toward his mouth as if to suggest that I was drunk. I apologized profusely. He looked at me disgusted. I paid up and left with no idea why I'd had that momentary, somewhat dangerous, lapse in judgment. But there was no fallout, just a reminder to pay more attention.

What would it be like to suddenly brace yourself for an unpredictable fall, never being able to rely on who you are from one day to the next? To live alone with no words to make sense of the edge of reason? To be so preoccupied with the business of survival that there is no time to dream? What the living do,[6] what we yearn for is the spring to return and the winter to pass and grow to cherish who we are. We choose to carry on as best we can, to see beyond the shadow.

Chapter Fifteen

Wait
Don't go too early
You're tired. But everyone's tired
But no one is tired enough

—GALWAY KINNELL, "Wait"

When I was a resident, a psychiatrist I knew killed herself, leaving me bereft. The gossip was that she was infatuated with another doctor, and that he rejected her affections. Humiliated, she barricaded herself in her apartment and downed too many pills. On a frigid winter morning, I boarded a train to New York for the memorial service. In an austere stone chapel filled with blue flowers, the doctor's mentor stood up to pay his respects and commended her for her conscientiousness. He noted with admiration that the day before she died, this diligent doctor had assessed ten new patients in the emergency room—an impressive feat. One by one, patients had filed into her office, closing the door behind them. She had asked the same diagnostic questions ten times, the equivalent of the physician taking a pulse, about sleeping at night, having trouble concentrating, hearing voices, mood changes, loss of appetite, plans to commit suicide. I wished that she had interrupted her "mental status examinations" long enough to get help for herself. I was saddened by her fragility despite her having tried to put up a good front. I was frightened: Now I had to relinquish the fantasy that if I learned this profession it would somehow protect me from the forlorn legacy of suicide. Even if you are proficient in this craft, it does not inoculate against the forcefulness of depression.

At the memorial, my medical colleagues speculated on her state of mind just before she died, offering armchair analyses of why she might have killed herself and wondering whether it was premeditated or a passion of the moment.[1] In the rush for an explanation and with the disturbing sense that things are not always what they appear, they had a morbid fascination and dread that she was able to function with apparent ease professionally while struggling with private anguish. And yet there was also a heaviness—as if we had failed her.

Over the next few days, I was irritable, haunted by disturbing dreams and a sense of foreboding anxiety. The psychiatrist's suicide evoked the loss of my mother. My therapist told me that when someone kills herself it is as if she puts her skeleton in your closet. I did not want this skeleton, and I resented the intrusion. I could not do this work if it felt futile, but in the aftermath of this doctor's death, I did not want to think with my patients about the urge to end it all.[2] I wished that I could bag groceries, do any other job that did not involve making sense of suffering and sharing the responsibility for keeping someone alive. But my therapist reassured me warmly, with the intimacy that comes from years of talking with each other, that it is normal to be shaken to the core when a colleague kills herself; it did not mean I was unstable or destined for a free fall. I have cultivated a determination and a skill to recover my balance when life has unexpected detours. I was depleted and needed to give myself some time to be with the people I love and who provide me solace. After a cross-country ski trip with Colin, awestruck by the pink sunset etched into the silhouette of the branches in the sky, painting valentine boxes in Cory's class and resuming the outward semblance of routines in my life, I felt less overwhelmed. My sadness would run its course not because I would avoid the flood of feelings but because I could replenish without drifting too far from my center.

I always find myself incredulous that when someone commits suicide—when my mother took the overdose, when a teenager hangs himself in the closet, or a man shoots himself—this person truly wants to die. When I was younger I often dreamt that my mother and I were careening down a hill in a car out of control and in the back seat I was valiantly trying to reach down for the emergency brake to avert disaster. For the tortured souls who are intent on suicide, there is no territory beyond the present. The "mind tumble" means that they are not thinking clearly, and their judgment is clouded as they reach for pills or jump from a bridge.[3] As I investigate my mother's suicide, with the stealth of someone who wants to break the code, the inexplicable mystery of why this was the moment that she lost her determination, I return to her diary. I wish that I could have shown her the sunset that I found so comforting or that she could see her grandchildren, anything to have her hold on to a fighting spirit, to find the invincible shield of self-preservation. To develop the wisdom that premature death will not bring the peace that she ached for. In her diary she is wrestling with her demons, trying to stay alive, to anchor herself in her love for us. Yet that was not enough to keep her grounded in survival.

In this passage she laments,

> God, what an ordeal. Bearing one's soul to a piece of paper is more devastating than conversing with a mesh screen or emoting on the analyst's couch. In my time I have submitted myself to the masochism of both these exquisite tortures. The limit must be the pride and self-respect of my descendants, my only loves. My Holy Ghost or my babies. This is my last testament and here I bequeath it to my Holy Ghost, to be given to my six darlings of my womb and as when he sees fit. Perhaps they'll never be strong enough to read my naked soul. Most children prefer a mother to a human being, so do most mothers. My great cross is the inability to lose me in my mother, whether the mother is me or the woman who carried me. Those of us who fight must die. We are all consumed one way or another.

I just chose to die from life rather than from the slow creeping death of boredom and rote and repetition and habit and conformity and vile hatred passed off as love. The flame of desire, desire for truth, for reality can burn up all the peace we're rationed. Oh God, where are you? I can tell you what I wanted before but what do I want now? I guess I'd settle for peace, but that's second best, it's really admitting defeat and after all the years, the searing, aching search how dare I settle for the peace of death that was always an escape for the weak. No, not peace, but life is what I wanted and want and I'll settle for no less even now, basket-case that I am. I can only eat life intravenously in my weakened condition but it's still better and richer.

I weep for her, wanting to hold her, give solace. I tell her in her fleshless state that "the baby of your womb" sees you as human and fallible and wishes that you could have held onto the search, the battle, the assertion that life is still better and richer than the "blessedness of drugged oblivion" and the "long black insomniac nights."[4] What could have kept her alive in her "weakened condition," and did others know how much she was struggling to hold on? And what does she mean by "chose to die from life" while also asserting that "life is what I wanted"? My family seems sometimes a bit exasperated by my dogged effort to understand my mother's suicide, as if reasons and "what ifs" are not instructive. But understanding my mother's suicide matters to me—as a doctor I spend my life trying to avert disaster, to offer a safe retreat to find strength to stay alive. It is always a calculated gamble but there is an intensity that comes when I am debating with teenagers why we need to find another way than tying a telephone cord around their neck or drinking Drano. I actually feel better when someone is talking to me, figuring out how to ease his pain. Some of what I have learned about suicide, depression, and substance abuse in general has helped to define, yet has also complicated, the mystery of why my mother killed herself, and it guides my assessment of how to help my patients not take the lethal next step.

Most people who are diagnosed with depression don't kill themselves or ever make a suicide attempt, even though a depressive's risk for suicide is twenty times higher than that of the general population.[5] Over half of the people who complete suicide are not depressed, according to interviews with their family and friends.[6] It is not an easy task to discern what makes some individuals struggling with mood swings or depression or over-whelming stresses commit suicide but not others. And even more baffling is why some people who seem deceptively *happy* kill themselves. In such cases the deception seems almost willful rather than a guarded shameful secret. According to one of the leading experts on the causes of suicide, suicidal behavior requires an underlying predisposition, a propensity for impulsiveness, without which the probability for suicide is small, no matter how bad things get.[7] As numerous studies show, impulsiveness and its cousins, aggression and explosiveness, are more closely linked to suicide than is the severity of the depression or psychosis.[8] In other words, it is not the hopelessness that gets you—what suicide needs, ironically, is an adrenalin rush, a reckless abandonment of the survival instinct.

Impulsivity is action without reflection, a broken circuit that prevents knowledge or wisdom from being able to guide—or even *slow down*—actions. When a man presses the gas pedal and accelerates into a tree, or a psychiatrist—or a mother—downs a bottle of pills, these are not carefully considered responses to extreme stress, trauma, or loss; rather, these are trigger reactions.

Impulse drives our animal selves; it is a way of responding to the environment that is more instinctual than deliberate. Neurologist John C. Mazziota observes that most people don't realize "that the [human] brain is really an inhibition machine"[9] and that we expend considerable mental energy corralling and managing our urges. All of us have impulsive moments and can give in to satisfying them. We buy things on a whim—the displays surrounding checkout counters are designed to appeal to our impulsive natures—and we often accelerate through a yellow light. Or we say something mean that later, upon reflection, embarrasses us. Acting without much thinking can sometimes transform us into heroines—we step out into traffic to protect a child, or we break up a fight. Acting on instinct can make life exciting, but it may also put us at risk—we may take drugs or have sex with strangers. Impulsivity is not so much about speed; the human mind is very capable of making highly informed split-second decisions (think of race car drivers and surgeons). But this type of proficiency demands a cool head and a laser-beam focus on the task at hand. A person hijacked by emotions, devastated by the present reality, with no hope for the future, becomes impulsivity's plaything.

When fueled by anger, impulsivity can be especially destructive. A mother has an affair with her campaign manager and leaves her six children. A mother takes an overdose when she cannot reconcile with her husband. A husband hits his wife. A mother loses a court battle and takes an overdose.

Cognitive behavioral therapy, one of the more popular and effective forms of psychotherapy practiced in the United States today, can help patients learn to manage their impulses and it has been shown to ease depression and suicidal thoughts by teaching reflective skills that allow patients to think through why they feel so hopeless and to challenge the idea that their impasse is permanent.[10] Patients are taught to allow time to examine their emotions so as not to "catastrophize" their situations or think in extremes. My mother's therapist was not a cognitive behavioral therapist; as with most such practitioners in the early 1960s, the form of treatment he provided was psychoanalytic, focusing on the present echo of the unresolved past. I try to imagine my mother's sessions with her doctor and what would have happened if he had helped her recognize her extreme responses and learn to pause. In particular, if he had helped her to understand that the setbacks she faced in her custody battle were not necessarily the end of the world and that the children would grow and make their own choices, she might have weathered the immediate crisis and tipped the vital balance from death to life.

She saw her doctor for two years and in her small blue datebooks embossed with 1962 and 1963 I stare at his name. "Dr. Adler," her psychiatrist. In her now familiar handwriting, she marked appointments at 11:20 Tuesday and Thursday each week starting in September 1962 after her first suicide attempt. She did not see Dr. Adler in the month of August 1963 but was scheduled to resume her sessions after September 13, 1963. I saw that she'd noted 11:20 in the September 14th slot, but by that time she had taken her lethal overdose. Datebook of death interspersed with nursery school meetings, dinner dates, picking up birthday cakes. If my mother had learned how to slow down her decision-making process and to manage her feelings about her competition with my father, her grief at her diminished role in our lives, and her frustration with the court procedures, she might have stopped her lethal sense of defeat.

I tried to locate Dr. Adler, but after forty-five years he is dead. I wanted to ask him whether he was worried that she would overdose when he took his summer vacation. Did he know how desolate she felt? Did he see her as impulsive? Did she talk about what family and friends described as "flare-ups" and "flashes" of a sudden "Irish temper"? Many of the big decisions in her life—the college she chose, the man she married, her affair with Dick Sears—seem rash, in retrospect, because her choices were unusual and unexpected: a southern coeducational university instead of a more predictable northeastern school; an intelligent Jewish lawyer from New York instead of someone from a Boston political family; and, for her affair, a younger married man with three young boys instead of a single man.

The more I learn about her, the more I recognize a fiery reactivity in her behavior—a sharp and aggressive wit, a short fuse, irritability. But how did Dr. Adler see it? Would the outcome of her life have been different if they had developed a course of action, a way to put one foot in front of the other and walk with a little more confidence toward a happier resolution? One step, and then another—she might have found her way. I will never know, but narrative is the alchemy of psychiatry and I keep trying to follow in her wake, moving in and out of my grief buoyed by the voyage of exploring her dark reality as a way of helping myself to understand her and learning to overcome my trauma of losing her and then retreating to the shore when I need to rest.

Even though at times medication can be life-saving for a depressed patient, each time I write a new prescription I do so with apprehension, balancing the risks. Finding the right medication for each patient can be a matter of trial and error, a combination of clinical experience and a carefully tested algorithm. When I present my recommendation to a patient, I give him or her the same advice I would give to someone in my family in the same circumstances. Some medications help dampen impulsivity; others can make it worse. If I overlook a patient's mood swings or do not elicit an accurate family history, antidepressants can dangerously activate a patient, like pouring gasoline on impulsivity's fire. But if the impulsivity is caused by underlying irritability and depression, an antidepressant like Prozac can increase serotonin and provide relief and restore the pause that allows for self-control.

I would have encouraged my mother to take lithium in a heartbeat. In *Darkness Visible*, his memoir of madness, William Styron starkly describes feeling his "life slipping away with accelerated speed" and cautions against the disappointment that can come with an expectation of a quick fix.[11] If the desperation is accompanied by rapid mood swings, plummeting depression followed by unbounded energy, a mood stabilizer such as lithium can be life-saving. After starting lithium, one of my patients confided to me that without the drug, he would have made a fatal leap from his high-rise apartment. The therapeutic benefits of lithium in suicidal patients, particularly those with a bipolar disorder, are indeed compelling.[12]

But for my mother Dr. Adler prescribed barbiturates, powerful sedative hypnotics, even though other options such as lithium were available. It would have been common practice to help my mother sleep, but barbiturates probably made her worse. I find one of the prescriptions in her trunk, packed by Alex after she died. And when I order her death certificate from Boston City Hall, the "certified copy of record of death" has an air of finality and formality with its embossed seal and typed capital letters "detailing" the cause of death: "barbiturate poisoning suicide ingestion of massive amount of barbiturate autopsy." Grim. The medications that we prescribe can be destructive if not used properly. The sleeping pills that killed my mother were from a class of barbiturates called the barbitals, which were prescribed from the 1940s to the 1960s to patients who had trouble sleeping or who were anxious. In those years, most family doctors would have been somewhat cavalier in prescribing such powerful sedative-hypnotics. But beginning in the early 1950s, some doctors expressed serious concerns about these medications. Patients found them to be increasingly less effective with continued use. At the same time, they discovered that they could no longer sleep without them. This was a deadly combination of effects: As individuals took more pills intended as a therapeutic dose to relax or sleep, they would simultaneously inch closer to a lethal dose. Both then and now, prescribing a person a bottle of barbiturates (like Phenobarbital) is dangerous because of the risk of both addiction and tolerance.

I worry that when my mother took barbiturates, given the combination of depression and dependence on drugs (a lethal combination present in many suicides), they allowed the "cessation of effort, the absence of will to continue"—an insidious habit when combined with impulsive despair. When I look at her novel for a clue as to whether my mother was addicted to the sleeping pills, it is disquieting how familiar she seems as she described the welcome release that comes when her main character downs pills to shake off the sleepless nights:

> She felt the tingling in her toes, then in her fingers, with relief.
> Soon it would not matter anymore, and she would sleep again.

Perhaps in this night of release, alone in bed, waiting for the blessedness of drugged oblivion, she would be able to find what the day of action had withheld. . . . She burningly contemplated her bottle of sleeping pills. Almost once a month the fear of becoming an addict overcame her and for a night or two she slept fitfully between direful and strenuous dreams in an effort to convince herself that she would still sleep naturally and that she might continue the pills but she didn't really need them.[13]

In 1970, with the passage of the U.S. Drug Abuse Regulation and Control Act, the barbitals became recognized as drugs with a "high potential for abuse," drugs that could lead to "severe psychological or physical dependence." Today, these medications are rarely prescribed except in very specific situations—as anesthetics before surgery, for example, or as powerful anticonvulsants. These prudent restrictions are too late for my mother. I won't hesitate to prescribe medication if it may save someone's life, but I am appropriately wary of its possible harm.

It is never pretty when someone overdoses, whether on aspirin or antidepressants. I have had patients say that having their stomach pumped out is enough of a deterrent to not take an overdose again. A year before my mother died, Marilyn Monroe committed one of the century's most famous and sensationalized suicides with an overdose of pills. The lurid details—her naked body sprawled on the floor, the champagne-colored satin lining of her casket—occupied the papers for months afterward and resulted in a temporary 12 percent increase in the U.S. suicide rate.[14] Monroe's suicide would certainly have made an impression on my mother. It is not so far-fetched to think that the publicity surrounding Monroe's death opened that door a little wider for my mother.[15] But the newspapers did not capture the gruesome way the body collides to a halt. As I review how barbiturates do their damage, I realize that there is probably no clean way to go. Yet "drugged oblivion" is no companion to my mother's asphyxiation.

Barbiturates depress the central nervous system by blocking the uptake of gamma-aminobutyric acid (GABA), an inhibitory neurotransmitter. When you take an overdose of barbiturates, you experience dizziness, confusion, and delirium as GABA floods your brain. Even at low doses, you grow drowsy and numb. Your eyes, your hands, your entire body become unbearable weights. The drug poisons the hypothalamus, your brain's command center, so that your core temperature drops, slowing the body even more. Then the part of the brain that regulates respiration, the medulla, grows unresponsive. You begin gasping and breathing shallowly. Your heart may not contract in an organized way or as forcefully as before. It sputters. Without adequate oxygen and a steady pulse, your body goes into shock. You lose consciousness.

Barbiturates also slow your stomach and intestines. You vomit a little. The protective reflex that usually keeps you from choking fails. You vomit again. The corrosive acids of your stomach, your own vomit, your spit—you breathe it all in. Your lungs burn and leak plasma. Eventually, you drown.

When my mother arrived at the Massachusetts General Hospital emergency room, one of the doctors assigned to her care was Dr. Arnold Weinberg. He was the one who pronounced her dead.

In one of the many newspaper accounts of my mother's death, Dr. Arnold Weinberg is described as "a staff physician who had been caring for the former wife of Atty. Rappaport who noted that she was admitted for treatment of a massive dose of barbiturates."[16] He was the last person, as far as I know, to see my mother alive.

My assistant at the hospital urged me to call him. But I was wary. I left a vague message with his answering service, asking if he really was the doctor who treated my mother. I half hoped that he would not call me back, as I couldn't bear to hear the stark facts.

But Dr. Weinberg returned my call within hours.[17] "I don't remember specifics so much," he said. "But I will tell you anything that I know," he added gently. I asked tentatively how he could remember the event at all, after treating and handling so many people over the years.

"When a fundamentally healthy young woman commits suicide, even if you have no personal involvement, you don't forget it.... Always a tragedy when someone decides to take her own life."

We talked doctor to doctor. "There was no pupillary reflex... significant change to nervous system... acute respiratory distress... pneumonia... hypoxic damage... spontaneous abortion... depth of coma... irreversible coma... *coma*... vegetative state... quality of life." These are the kinds of words doctors use when a body shuts downs, when life stalls. "There was little we could do to reverse the damage," he said. "It was pretty much a foregone conclusion."

It took some time for me to absorb what he was saying. She was in a coma. For a while. For five days. I was flooded with feelings. I imagine my father visiting at her bedside, his shoulders hunched. Did he feel free to say what he wanted? To apologize? Or was he furious at her for leaving us all behind? If she had been in a vegetative state and incapacitated for many years, we would all have a different story to tell, and I wonder if my father would have been relieved that she was not trapped in this condition. A fragment of herself. Was there a certain grace associated with letting her go?

Dr. Weinberg's voice pulled me back into the present. "I was brought in to consult about the pneumonia—I was the senior resident specializing in infectious disease at the time. The bottom line is that even if we could have treated her pneumonia and oxygenated her well, there was no indication that there would ever be any cognitive recovery." He told me, "I can say with great assurance [that] there was no turning back the hypoxic damage, no cognitive recovery." That is a comfort to me. I feel a hint of closure.

Even though I have always known clinically that my mother was in a coma for five days before she died, it sounded so final and somber coming from a doctor's analysis. I am known to be an active sleeper in my family, occasionally letting out a blood-curdling scream in the middle of the night, and Colin will tease me that the neighbors could think that I was being attacked. It is more the remnant of a night terror that my mother slipped away and could not find her way back to us.[18] What if she didn't want to leave, if she just had the "cessation of effort, the absence of will to continue"? The answers died with her.

$$\infty$$

My mother's friend Peggy Melgard welcomed seeing me even though it was not so often that we meet at a restaurant for lunch. She was visiting from Florida. She wanted to know what my brothers and sisters were doing and told me proudly that her grandson was having a confirmation. Then I eased into my question of how she learned about my mother's suicide and she revealed something that makes things even more complicated. "Your mother firmly believed that each time that she went to court, she'd get you back. She was always planning. Once she showed me the basement of her Marlborough Street house because she planned to raise the ceiling and build—" Peggy paused dramatically, "—a basketball court for you kids. . . . You know, your mother called me the day before you children were scheduled to return—she was terrified that your father was too politically connected and that the judge would side with your father. She was afraid the case would go against her, not on its merits, but for political reasons. I told her impatiently, 'Don't be ridiculous, that will never happen.' The last time, it was such a build-up, and it looked like she was going to win."

Peggy glanced out the window as if she was back in time, dazed from getting the shocking news. "The next day, I got the call from Alex. . . . I was vacuuming," she added, remembering a detail that would otherwise be forgotten save for the fact that the mind creates strange connections when important events occur.

"Alex called me from the hospital and said that your mother had taken an overdose. His voice, I don't know—I will never forget it. He was horrified. He never saw it coming. He said they were playing chess together after that morning in court, then she just excused herself from the chess table to go upstairs and when she came back she told him that she had taken a bottle of pills. When the court reversed the decision, she thought it was a losing battle. I think she felt trapped and hopeless, and thought that by taking the pills she would make the judge see that she needed to get her kids back. Alex panicked. He didn't call an ambulance because he wanted to protect your mother. He was worried that if an ambulance was called the press would find out about it and that it would impact her ability to gain custody. So he brought her to the hospital. He just could not believe what she had done. By the time they got to Mass. General, she was unconscious." Peggy went on, crestfallen, "It's all so sad. They lost the baby first."

I had not known that my mother was pregnant when she killed herself. When I asked my sister Amy she glossed over it, saying that she had heard that Mama was pregnant but she was pregnant all the time. Peggy revealed to me that my mother was about four months along, long enough to have felt the baby's kicking in her womb, to have seen her body changing shape in her mirror, to have imagined with Alex the baby they would soon have together. She must have gotten pregnant around the time my father married Barbara.

I wonder how real her baby was to her and if this little baby had become a person to her yet. She must have sat on the sofa next to Alex and placed his hand on her abdomen and let him feel the baby's kicks. Did they have names picked out, both boys' and girls'? Did she share with Alex the birth stories she had about the six of us and playfully let him know what he was in for? Would I have shared a room with her new baby? What kind of mother kills herself—and kills her baby? It is rare. And despite my mother's pain and anguish it seemed brutal. I want to condemn her.

I remember how uncomfortable I was when, while pregnant with Lila, I had to admit into a state hospital a suicidal patient from the criminal system who had killed her baby. I had no empathy for her. When I was writing the medical orders to assign someone to watch her "one to one" because she often mutilated herself, she asked me whether she could have pens to write in her journals. I told her that she couldn't because she might use them to hurt herself. But actually I was retaliating, angry that she would kill a young child regardless of her reason or nonreason, and I wanted to take something away from her.

After my mother's death, Alex and my mother's childhood friend Margaret Murphy went to see their priest. As Margaret explained to me, the priest laid out the conditions under which my mother's soul could be saved and her body buried in consecrated ground. The priest interrogated Margaret as to whether my mother intended to kill herself, whether she had repented before her death and was she given the last rites, the anointing of the sick, the sacrament of penance, the viaticum? Catholics regard suicide as a mortal sin and this must have weighed on my mother if she was contemplating it. According to the Catholic catechism, "We are stewards, not owners of the life God has entrusted to us. It is not ours to dispose of. . . . Suicide contradicts the natural inclination of the human being to preserve and perpetuate life."[19] St. Thomas Aquinas made the most vigorous and enduring argument that suicide is murder—this is still part of the church's reasoning against assisted suicide today. The person who kills herself goes against God and the commandment *Thou shalt not kill*, and unless she repents and seeks forgiveness (which is hard to do in cases of suicide, for obvious reasons), her soul is lost. For my mother to be saved, her death needed to be explained, and that duty fell to Alex Stanley, who was also a Catholic and appreciated the urgency of the situation.

Alex was troubled by the sin of lying and when the priest asked if she had been lucid enough to repent, Alex said that she was not conscious. But Margaret kicked him under the table and didn't mind stretching the truth. Together, they showed the priest letters my mother had written—surely these suggested that she did not want to die. Eventually, as Margaret remembers, they convinced the reluctant priest, and arrangements were made for my mother to be buried in the blessed grounds of St. Joseph Cemetery in West Roxbury.

Behind the scenes, Margaret also tried to orchestrate a restrained public announcement. At the time, she worked in Governor Endicott Peabody's press office and her boyfriend was a reporter at the *Boston Herald-American*. She managed to keep my mother's pregnancy out of the papers.[20]

The wake was held at the new Marlborough Street house, and friends and politicians came to pay their respects. There was an open casket, and my mother was dressed in her lavender gown, the dress she had worn the day she married Alex. Around her neck was a silver cross, a wedding gift, I imagine, from Alex. Peggy said that rather than focusing on what my mother had done, Alex repeatedly tried to convince my father to allow the six of us to attend the funeral. She described this effort as Alex's "crusade at the moment." Only my father, Edith Vahey, and Bee came to the wake. My father thought that he was protecting us from viewing our mother's dead body. Peggy told me that she remembers that as she was sitting dazed, she watched out of the corner of her eye as Alex, distraught, used an inhaler. Then she heard him shout when my father entered the room that my father was a murderer.

My father did not attend her funeral. He did not think it was a good idea for us to go, but Bee begged him on behalf of 9-year-old Amy. Amy tells me that she threatened to walk by herself if she had to, and he reluctantly agreed that Bee and Amy could go. I asked Martha if she remembered the funeral, and she doesn't remember anything. Margaret says that even without all of us there, the funeral at St. Cecilia in the Back Bay was "enormous," with old friends and even local politicians paying their respects. Elaine remembers the church being solemn and crowded, the overwhelming scent of incense, the celebrants in formal dress walking toward the altar sprinkling holy water, and Alex, alone and ashen.[21]

After my mother's funeral, Alex disappeared quickly from our lives. I remember he took the rest of the kids out to bowl after my mother died, but

I stayed in bed with a stomachache and did not see him again. He never had any children of his own, though he was eventually a stepfather to his fourth wife's child and a doting uncle to his sister's children. Last year, after chasing some leads to find where his niece Barbara lived, I spoke to her for the first time. She was stunned when I told her about my mother's suicide and that she had been pregnant at the time. A few days after our conversation, she called me back after trying to process all this. "I am reeling from the events forty-four years ago. I have a whole new empathy with my uncle and feel so sad at his profound loss.... I also feel a sense of loss for his unborn child—both as his child and as my little cousin and not having you and your siblings as my step-cousins. And I feel a deep sadness and frustration that no one—neither a new husband nor an unborn child—could lead your mother out of her profound despair."[22]

∞

I go down to dinner exhausted by the sheer energy I have expended, and I am distracted as I think about my phone calls with Barbara and Dr. Weinstein. Lila is bubbly about her newly acquired freedom with her driver's license. The chatter is comforting, but later on as I lie down next to Zoe and start to read her a story—"Gossip Girl" or something equally erudite—my tears start to come and I can't read without my voice breaking. She looks at me inquisitively and I tell her quietly, "I don't want to burden you." She says with a steady concerned gaze, "I want to know."

"I talked to the doctor who cared for my mother when she was in a coma." She says, surprised, "She was in a coma?" The question hangs in the silence. I cry. I say with a laugh, trying to make light, "It is silly for me to cry. It was a long time ago and yet sometimes it feels like it happened just a few days ago, judging from the way I feel tonight."

"You can choose to cry," she says. I mumble, "Sometimes I am too sensitive." A quick hug. Lights out.

Chapter Sixteen

You have begot me, bred me, loved me: I
return those duties back as are right fit,
Obey you, love you, and most honour you.

—SHAKESPEARE, *King Lear*

When we dropped off Lila at college and drove away from her newfound home, I found myself wondering how far is too far away. I was apprehensive, as I did not have the luxury of these kinds of natural transitions with my mother. But Lila was ready to leave home and we have found a way to stay close, in a way I had always hoped we might find.

When I left for college, my father had remarried and, wanting a fresh start, he donated our Quail Street home to Roxbury Latin School, an all-boys school whose grounds bordered our house. For a brief time, the school used the building to house faculty, but decades of dynamiting at the nearby quarries destabilized the old house. Dry rot further weakened its shaky joints, and the house grew increasingly unsound. Unable to rescue the old Quail Street estate, the Roxbury Latin School (RLS) demolished it. As the school's alumni magazine reported, "Demolished is definitely an appropriate description, as repeated tramplings beneath the bulldozers' treads reduced most of the house to splinters not more than a foot long. The three-story building was no match for the bulldozer which tore through the walls as if they were paper, chewing up the wood and spitting out the more valuable lead and copper pipes and the rather stringy copper wires."[1] Accompanying the article are pictures of the house in its death throes, a voracious bulldozer, then mountains of sticks and rubble.

My son, Cory, is a junior at RLS. I am surprised that he chose to attend this school, as it involves a forty-five minute commute. He was attracted to its predictable routines and rigorous academics. Four of my brothers had attended RLS and I had not anticipated following a family tradition, but I come back often now, driving down the solitary road, not to return home but to revisit the athletic fields for family sports day and parents' back-to-school nights. With its expansive skyline, the spot where our house once stood—the home where we were a family once upon a time—has been leveled for an athletic field. I can see the leathery green leaves of the rhododendrons and the big rock where I would soak up the warmth of the sunshine, and I often ask myself how we carry our sense of home from one stage to the next. What do I want my children to carry with them from our time together?

After many years of never socializing by ourselves, I decided to meet with my brother Jerry at a coffee shop to finally talk with him about what Mama meant to us. We both have promised to "watch each other's back," and I often look to him for reassurance if there is a family feud. Phyllis and Dad are upset with me that I have been distant and guarded with them, and I have not shared with them the reason—that I have been so preoccupied with what happened to my mother. My brother seems uneasy being with me sometimes, and often it is tough to know what he is thinking, but he agrees quickly to meet with me after I drop off Cory at a game.

Standing at the café counter, Jerry seems so tall, taller than Dad, but not nearly as imposing. He orders a triple iced nonfat caffé macchiato with an extra shot of espresso on the side, and an extra glass of ice—unlike me, Jerry is precise about what he wants and he is indulgent. He instructs me, always the older brother, that this is the sure way to get the maximum jolt of caffeine. I ask for a cappuccino quickly, and we find a table in the back. We both stir sugar into our coffees and I pull out a small blue six-ring binder that belonged to our mother. We have not looked together at anything that belonged to her. This is her daily recordings of her presence in the afternoons during tense visitations at our home after she had left and moved into the apartment with Dick Sears when I was 2 years old and Jerry was 4. I read selected pieces: "Nancy had stepped on a lighted cigarette butt 6/10, been taken to the doctor, and I had not been told. I bathed and dressed and cut nails of Jimmy, Jerry and Nancy and shampooed Jerry. . . . I lay down to nap with Jerry until 3:00 before I left, gave both Jerry and Nancy their baths and talked further of weekend arrangements with children. . . . Jerry and Nancy had to be sent home from school in a taxi."

I lean closer to Jerry. "I like the idea of us riding in a taxi, two young passengers, our legs barely reaching the floor. I am glad that we were inseparable and that we kept each other company during the musical-chairs marriages, fights, court battles, Mama's death. She made agonizing choices and she must have been beside herself with worry about what happened to us when she wasn't there to protect us." I stop, entertaining the different possibilities. "Maybe she was sick, depressed, angry, whatever; maybe she was bipolar, self-destructive, and impulsive." But then I interrupt my analysis impatiently. "Never mind what it *was*—she didn't get the right treatment and Dad was understandably too clouded to see that. Maybe there was nothing anyone could do. Maybe she was a tragedy waiting to happen. Sometimes it's hard not to feel she betrayed us, hard not to want to blame someone." I ask him, exasperated, "Do you think I'm asking too much to ever make sense of what happened?"

I am so relieved that I can share this with my brother. Jerry understands exactly the sorrow I have about our mother's suicide, even though we have never spoken directly or dared to approach the topic of her death. But as we talk it was as if we had. He flushed red the way he does when he feels something strongly. "It makes me furious," he says, "that our mother couldn't wait. All she had to do was wait. Wait another month or so. Dad had lost every appeal and she would have won the custody court case in the end. He was just doing what he does—intellectualize, compete, refuse to lose: he is a tenacious fighter. When she killed herself, she let him think that this was the way to deal with conflict, and as her children we had to pay the price." He pauses and his face crumples with angst. "Didn't she know that she would leave all these shattered children wondering if it was their fault? Didn't she know the shame we would feel, that it was such a selfish move on her part?"

I say, almost as if we are conspiring together, building a case that she was selfish, that she killed herself just days before Martha's twelfth birthday and I ask him if he knew that she was four months pregnant when she died.

Jerry seems defeated. He leans over the table on his elbows as if the table would rise to receive him, and cups his hands around his eyes for privacy. He is now, quite literally, crying a puddle of tears. Grief inhabits his body and he fights back against a visceral shudder. I look at him—I know our father could be hard on him, his namesake. Jerry takes a breath, and, to save us from being too maudlin, he smiles and blubbers with his self-deprecating humor, "So, how come we're still standing?" I reach over and hold onto his wrists. "Imagine how much stronger we'd be if we hadn't lost her," he says, pulling himself together.

He recognizes one of his neighbors walking into the shop and he bellows a loud hello, back to being his gregarious self. They talk about the changing market and the next Patriots game. He introduces me, and with a quick hug he says that he needs to get moving. We make plans for meeting up soon around my father's birthday.

∞

It has taken us years to get here, but I am sitting with Dad in the cavernous dining room of a Cambridge seafood restaurant. The big communal tables are covered with red-checked tablecloths, and the waiter brings us two large glasses of diet soda as we wait for our meals. After he discovered that I was writing this book, Dad and I were at a standoff; he felt that I needed to get past the business of our mother. He had let me know that I was not welcome at family functions, exiled from the farm in Vermont and from the house in Nantucket. At various times, both his calls and mine went unanswered by the other, though he still managed a warm relationship with my husband and a grandfatherly exuberance and affection with my children.

But somehow, while I wrote and my father smoldered, our mutual distrust dissipated. Compelled to pull together as a family, to support each other through health issues, to celebrate birthdays and weddings, graduations and funerals, we have found our way back—enough so, at least, to be sitting here over lunch for reconciliation. He has finally accepted that I will tell this story.

Even before our salads come, he tells me that he was furious that I made him out to be the villain. I want to tell him that he is, more accurately, one of its heroes. He was the one who persevered, the one who was our parent long after Mama had killed herself. My father remained strong. He raised us and helped to shape the people we are now. I tell him he is an extraordinary father.

"Look, you're dealing with someone who is used to having unpleasant truths and falsehoods published about him. I am well aware how nasty things get when they are wrapped up in yesterday's packages." His jaw tightens. I don't dare flinch—it's rare for Dad to reveal his vulnerabilities, even if his tone borders on disapproval. I don't want to push back at him yet and am surprised that I'm able to remain quiet while he speaks.

"The picture you painted of me had no charm or style," he says with sadness. "And there was no acknowledgment of what Phyllis has done for you." Phyllis told me that I had "cloaked myself in hurt" and pulled away from Dad. "The relationship that we had with you and your kids and Colin was sidelined. To have my image caught in that place—to be portrayed as a bully, ruthless, violent—that was devastating. You were closed. You had done your research, and my truth had no relevance or validity." He looks wounded.

"What was upsetting," he goes on, "was that I thought we had so much love and respect in the lives we shared over time, yet you dismissed all that. In order for you to find your mother, I became irrelevant. It became all-important for you to visualize history through her eyes or how you imagined she would see it, and you closed me off."

I wanted to tell my father that he was wrong: He was never my intended focus. I wanted to write about my mother and in that process to learn and think about who she was—my mother was the missing parent, not him. But at this moment, he can't understand. He'll take it as further proof of his point that as far as I'm concerned he's "beside the point"—collateral damage. So I say nothing for now. I wait. One day, I hope he will understand. To miss one parent—to mourn and ache from loss—is not the same thing as blaming the other.

"I don't have it all perfectly analyzed, but it was discouraging to see the position you seemed to be taking." He pokes at his salad and considers a slice of red onion before taking a bite. "I didn't think your portrayal was fair or, for that matter, accurate. You know, memories are never the whole truth." "Facts I honestly had repeated all my life turned out to be incorrect. The street I thought I was born on? That was not the street at all, according to the census." He looks at me frustrated that I don't understand the possible unintended consequences. "What you say in your book will be indelibly etched in the record—and you have all the wrong dates." I assure him that I've done additional research to get the facts right. I've done the best I can.

Our meals arrive and we eat quietly for a few moments, chatting about my kids. Then he glances at me. "My goal, you know, was never to destroy your mother or negate her except when it became essential to defend myself."

I tell him that I have a better appreciation for how difficult my mother must have been, how her impulsivity must have made it impossible for him to feel secure with her. I let him know that I know it can be frightening and enraging just to keep up a relationship with someone who threatens and even attempts suicide as easily as she seemed to do.[2] My mother's actions had repercussions for all of us, though I do not always know if he is comfortable admitting that.

I tell him too that I now understand more about impulsivity and that it has informed my practice. I am better at listening to people's deepest feelings when I understand my own. He seems relieved, and even willing to believe that maybe I'm not out to damage him after all as I intrude on his privacy. He has assumed that I would publicly blame him for my mother's suicide. He shoots me an appreciative look.

I ask Dad whether he went to the hospital after my mother had taken the overdose. He responds, "Yes, I went because I had been married to her for ten years. I had very ambivalent feelings; she was under for a long time before she got to the hospital. I saw her as inanimate, in a comatose state. Brain dead. But it was a way of your mother giving peace to you kids too. It was a sad time when it was ended."

This is hard for me to hear but I still have one more question I want to ask him. I ask if he said anything to her when he saw her at the hospital. He looks away for a second and then says slowly, "I didn't remember until you asked, but I told her that I would take care of you kids."

I reply quietly, with tears, "And you did."

I ask how he did it. "How did you survive?"

"There was no time to grieve or wonder about it all. I had a houseful of children to take care of. It may surprise you, supporting a family of nine, plus Edith, Barbara, and Bee—that was a challenge."

He says he has no regrets, but his life did not turn out as he had imagined. "After your mother died, I did change some life patterns, luckily for the better. I might have continued as a national developer, but with all you kids, I couldn't afford the time.[3] Earlier in life, I had thought about a political career, but that, too, wasn't possible given my responsibilities. I had my law practice, and I was busy building the first sections of Charles River Park. And then to keep myself busy, I went back to school—there's a certain security I get from being in school." As he says this, I reflect on how the Kennedy School of Government must have served as an anchor for him, a way to rebuild his confidence after the divorce and my mother's death, and I appreciate why he is one of its most enthusiastic benefactors today. He is not the first person who has thrived on being the bright student or wanted to return to the safety of the classroom when real life got tough.

He looks down, a little defeated by all the memories I'm extracting, the what-ifs and second thoughts. "I thought about a political career—that was something your mother and I always shared. The failure of our marriage may have been due in part to our political involvements." It is awkward for me to watch him still struggling to explain his failure with my mother—it was a long time ago and he has been married now for more than thirty years to Phyllis. I want to tell him again that it's difficult to have a marriage with someone as unpredictable as my mother seems to have been. But my father overestimates what he can do or fix, sometimes, and my attempts to soothe his guilt would feel like a rebuke.

He is wistful when he talks about their political days, as if recalling the first months of their love in the wake of the mayoral victory. "Any ambitions I had in a political arena were not realistic after the divorce and all the West End controversy." He glances up at me quickly. "And besides, with six then nine then eleven kids, what time would I have for politics?"

I ask him where he found the strength to go on. He brushes me off, and then says, "I got a lot of support from your grandfather. I have a lot of my father's values and strengths. My dad focused on family and providing leadership. We could have fights, my father and I, but ultimately we were close." He is quiet for a moment. "Despite all the fights, I loved your mother and respected her. There were occasions, even after our divorce—." He trails off. Does he sometimes imagine that he might have reconciled with her, raised the whole brood together, run for office?

He sounds resigned. "It doesn't matter why she killed herself—what I was left with was the reality that I was the only parent. Even if I could not make sense of her death, I had to make sure the kids turned out as well as possible. I had no choice—I didn't have time to feel sorry for myself—there were too many people dependent on me." I look down so it won't seem that I am challenging him. I don't want him to stop.

"I know I've told you before that I regard my marriage to your mother as my first big failure. I couldn't stay married to her, and my parents stayed married fifty years. Before your mother, I didn't believe in divorce. And it was a mistake that I didn't try harder to reconcile with her. But after we split up, I had to take control of my life. Your mother's death made me more responsible to raise you kids. If I were a saint or someone different, maybe I could have forgiven your mother's relationship with Dick Sears and the fact that she abandoned six kids."

As my brother Jim has described my father's perspective, "Here they were, a power couple for whom anything was possible—she had a man who prides himself on loyalty, living a storybook life, a great house, great kids, a great future—and what does she do? Dump him for some 23-year-old loser with three kids!" Jim's loyalty to Dad is fierce. But in hindsight, and from a more clinical perspective, Dad might have seen my mother's actions as an indication that she needed help.

As if reading my mind, Dad says, "I don't think I could have ever really forgiven her and reconciled. She made her choice and it wasn't me. If you agree to live with each other, to have a family together, then that's what you do. Your mother would not live with that agreement. And I could not accept the change in our agreement and not fight. That's not me."

Familiar with my criticism about his backing my mother into a corner, his ruthless tactics, and his need for power and control when he follows this line of argument, my father adds, "I wasn't a martyr and I certainly didn't feel like a martyr. You have to understand that we were divorced for more than two years before her final suicide. It was *over*. We had both re-married and we were getting on with things. Barbara was an attractive woman and I did love her at the time. Every therapist I ever had says I married her as a reaction to your mother's affair; every therapist said I never got out of the first relationship before I was on to the second. But Barbara did more than just meet a need. I loved her, and I thought she was beautiful as well as brilliant. She made me feel good about who I was—she made me feel strong and capable and lovable. After your mother left, I was vulnerable." He looks at me, wanting to make sure I get the point. "My relationship with Barbara was *not* about getting even."

He says with pride that he and Barbara did their best to create a stable environment for all of us. "I don't think we did too badly, but I know it wasn't perfect. After all, eleven kids is beyond the skill of mankind. In hindsight, I know now that there were limits as to what I could do to try to save all eleven." He seems to be thinking of Dickie and Carter, and Debbie. "I had all the responsibility and time with the kids, the continuing connections—yes, we had problems, lots of ups and downs. Maybe I failed, but at least I didn't die with her."

"You know," he says, his tone changing, his eyes narrowing slightly, "Barbara is a bright woman, but she is not a good witness. You shouldn't believe everything she tells you."

The waiter comes to clear our plates and refill our water glasses, and for a while we just sit here in the dining room. The lunch rush has come and gone in the time we have been here. Normally, during such a pause in our conversation, I might gather up my counterexamples and slowly lay them out like cards on the table. Having observed while he played his hand, I might challenge his accounts, his rationalizations, what I think of as his excuses. But today, for a change, I am here to listen.

"You know I like kids—and I love my grandkids." His voice is full of genuine warmth. "It wasn't only responsibility that I felt. Being a parent was something I really wanted. And I knew that if I were going to be divorced, I did not want to lose out on that experience. So I also wanted custody. Lots of dads want custody—they just don't always get it. And I was determined to be in your lives." I reach across the table and give his hand a warm affectionate squeeze.

"I did not want you moving to that other house. I wanted you to stay at Quail Street with us. I wanted you to have continuity."

He wants me to say something, so I talk about how in the aftermath of 9/11, in my role as crisis counselor in the local schools, we had to think hard about whether to hold school the next day. In a crisis, it's important to protect the routines that give young people a sense of security. But sometimes in a crisis you also need to be reflective.

I ask him how he got past being so infuriated with me about the book. He tells me that he saw me as frightened. This hangs in the air—it feels a bit like a challenge. "Why did you think I was frightened?" I ask him quietly.

"Probably because you came to believe your portrait of me. You were afraid to antagonize me, afraid you would be attacked. You were the defender of the victim; you needed to resurrect this woman to create a sense of self and I was in your way."

I say nothing, hold my tongue, sip my water. He goes on. "We passed through this because we have a deep relationship. I see how many parents have problems with their children. But I have never let the child define the relationship. The parent needs to keep the doors open.

"I know that you will never write a perfect book," he says, "and I'm happy that you have had some insights, but I'm worried. There is a price to pay for going public."

I ask him why he changed his mind—why he opened the door again, even though he knew I would not back down. "Yes, there was a breach of trust," he tells me. "But I am not going to live in fear of what you have to say. Whatever happens, it doesn't take away from how proud I am of you. And to the extent I played a part in who you have become, I feel great."

We pay the check and get ready to leave. Then he looks at me. "I'm not responsible for your mother's death. I can imagine now doing some things differently, but I know at my core I did not cause her death." In the parking lot, he hugs me and I get in the car. I look at him through the side window, the wind blowing his silver hair about, his hazel eyes brilliant and sharp. I watch as he settles heavily into the car. "I love you," he says from the other side of the car window. I know what he's saying, but I can't hear him through the glass.

I head back to work to see patients, then get in the car to pick up Zoe from piano lessons. On the way home I tell her I had lunch with Dad, and she is curious about what we talked about. She likes it when I'm getting along with my father and she always seems to notice how we're behaving toward each other. I stall, but I want her to know that if you hang in there, you can get to the other side, that life is made up of gentle loops, not neat lines and destinations. That love lasts longer than death.

"He talked about how he loved Mama and me," I say, and then I tell her how once, when I was 16 and full of bravado, I invited my father to go on a hike with me in the Green Mountains. We headed up a steep path, winding through spruce and spindly birches and ferns. I had chosen an easy trail but one that nonetheless held a few challenges and privately wondered if Dad would be able to keep up with me. We followed a rocky path through dense forest and brush, talking occasionally but mostly enjoying the thrill of rising higher into the mountains. Near the top, as the trees became stunted and the trail grew even rockier, it was easy to see how far we had come, and I led Dad out from the shade into the dappled sunlight toward a granite ledge. One false move and you could plummet off the mountain. But if you walked out on that ledge, which cantilevered out from the side of the mountain, the prize was a view of a silvery river winding its way through a valley. I led the way but then couldn't hear him behind me. I turned to look at him and discovered he would not follow me off the trail onto the ledge. Dad looked ashen and was uncharacteristically hesitant. I warned him to be careful and kept going. But I could hear him breathing hard behind me, and when I looked back, he would not move. With all the cockiness I could muster, I reached out my hand and encouraged him to step out with me.

Knowledge helps, I want Zoe to know, and I want my father to know too, even if we don't reach conclusions or tie up loose ends. The accumulation of details may never add up completely, but they do provide scaffolding for understanding and work-lights for the darkness. My father shares what he can, his pride, his respect, his love, and even his anger. He can tease me about my accomplishments, state his pride, and also take his share of the credit. We have found our way back to a place of mutual respect and love. It is not perfect, but it is meaningful to us both.

❦

It is August and in these last weeks of summer before the demands of September infiltrate our calendars, Phyllis and Dad's kids have organized a party to celebrate his eightieth birthday in Vermont, not in Boston, so that we might enjoy the vibrancy of August in full green. The party is limited to "just family," but family in our case is seventy-five people.

In the argot of wealth managers and consultants, G1 is Dad. My siblings and I are G2. Lila, Cory, and Zoe are G3, and G3 has grown to almost twenty, plus spouses. For the first time, G4 is here, too, the first two great-grand-children—toddlers in overalls, both the children of gay couples, reflecting a new age. My father and Phyllis know that love and family are more important than anything else and are worth preserving. *Today, we celebrate.* As Dad likes to say, much better than the alternative.

When we pull up to the farm after our long drive, Lila, Cory, and Zoe bound out of the car and are ready to join the soccer game with the cousins. Dad is giving a tour of the barn to display the calves. Each birth is like a lottery ticket. He knows the pedigree and lineage but he always has the angst of whether the calf may reach her potential, whether the new heifer will be the next great one or if the calf may fall and break a leg. During the day, we've been confused by the quick shifts of weather—one moment clouds overtaking the sky, then a blinding sun, then sultry heat streaked with cold and rain. When night comes, it comes in thick with fog.

The birthday dinner takes place the following night at Riverrun, a rambling family restaurant more accustomed to preparing piles of pancakes and grilled catfish than the lobster and steamed corn and clams that have been arranged for our party. Sue, the farm manager, has ordered up fifty claw crackers and passes them out as we scramble to find seats. The youngest generation gravitates together and is soon engaged in animated catching up. Lizzie is talking about a college tour; Miguel, barely 25, is figuring out what he wants to do, maybe take a trip to Hawaii; and 6-year-old Saul is holding court about his last days at camp. More than one of us could create

some scene-stealing drama if provoked, but today we are all on our best behavior. G1 is becoming an octogenarian, with staying power and prestige
deserving of respect.

Dad and Phyllis are pleased, beaming with pride. They circulate among
tables, stopping to chat with each of us. Dad stands, large in stature, but
stooped forward, as he squeezes his way from crew to crew, hands in his
pockets, his herd is grazing and he moves with stamina from one table to
the next. He pulls up a chair—when he talks to you, you are the only person in the world. He drills down with a legal attentiveness to detail. Where
are you going? When? What else? He wants to know. He wants to know it
all.

He nestles in next to my sister Amy who has flown in from California to
be here. He says to her gratefully as they pop open steamed clams, "I'm glad
you made the trip." He is not impatient that it is taking a long time for the
lobsters to be served. He knows it is no small feat for this tiny kitchen to boil
seventy-five live lobsters at once. It is a good thing we cannot hear them in
the kitchen. When the lobsters are ready, they come in steaming, piled high
on big trays. Their meat is sweet and succulent, and the corn young and
tender. We are right now together.

The G3 folks give the toasts tonight so as not to be completely inundated
with toasts, and they have a lot to say. They acknowledge Dad's guidance and
interest—they make jokes about how he always wants to know about the latest band. My father looks satisfied. He nods with approval. Families have
their stories and their own ways of passing them from one generation to
the next, and sometimes these stories have more meaning than truth.

The party breaks up and I walk into the night. The Big Dipper is hovering on the horizon and there are the crickets making a high-pitched rhap-
sody. I wander down to the river; the water laps against the bridge and my
mind wanders. What do I carry with me now that I am back in the fold of
our family? Tonight our mother is not with us. She might have liked hearing her grandchildren bantering together.

I want to put her to rest on this summer night. Even now I sometimes
feel at a family party that she is the missing guest, hoping foolishly that she

will make a surprise appearance, come sweeping in as if she had never left. I am never sure, though, whether she would come in stooped and showing her age or as if she'd just walked out of a photograph with her pearls and penetrating gaze. But with all the exploration I have done over eighteen years, she has not vanished the way that she did when we were growing up. I still love her and tonight as I watch the breaking of the water on the rounded stones, I am somehow profoundly aware that when I die a part of me will remain with my children the way that we carry in our bones the same minerals that compose a star.

I have grown to love my mother in a way that is different from when I longed for her as I wrote my composition "Trial in Love" as a little girl or hung from the jungle gym thinking about jumping to join her or ran away from home believing no one would notice I was missing. She was magical then, the mother who could make me better, and I blamed my father for keeping her from me. And with each round of reworking the story has gotten more complicated and nuanced; nothing that happened was fair.

In a sense I have tried to resurrect my mother, to know her as her youngest daughter, feeling the responsibility that comes with carrying her name and with receiving her "last testament," as if she had unfinished business that she needed us to figure out. I have pursued any lead that might give me a remote sense of who she was and to unravel the mystery of her death. I have tried to decipher her manuscript as a hieroglyphic of what she wanted to be as a writer, and I have struggled to make sense of the story. I don't think I will ever understand what it was like for my parents so far in the past to be caught in a passionate battle, and why they decided to do what they did—my mother deciding to kill herself and Dad giving up on her and letting her go and making it about winning. But I have begun to see how poisonous it can become when children are used as weapons in such a battle.

The river seems to catch the light of the moon, and I watch lost in thought. When I was in labor with Lila, eighteen years ago with a full moon, as my body contracted, the mystery of how my body could create another was overwhelming. I had fallen to my knees sobbing. Giving birth felt like I was hovering between the boundary of living and dying. And I had yearned for my mother to show me the way, to give me what I did not have, the quiet confidence that comes from being held when you are scared. Told that everything will be all right.

Losing our mother when we were so young cannot be sugarcoated. We needed her. I will always want my mother, but raising my own family and having the steady presence of Colin next to me make it less urgent most of the time. I still sometimes get swept away by the "looking disease"—what I have come to call those moments when I search for a favorite shirt or a certain book with such determination, feeling that I must find the object to avert potential disaster. My kids are always slightly amused by my warning to be careful. I am always preparing for the change of my good fortune, preparing myself in ways that are not the most logical.

But I am fortified for now. I cannot avoid the fact that there may be times when I am tested. Plummeted into a darkness. Ravaged by sorrow. Yet I have cultivated an endurance of will and stubborn refusal to succumb to the current of despair. Fighting back. Reaching for help from my family when all I want to do is retreat. And knowing that we are not alone makes it possible to move on from the sorrow.

NOTES

CHAPTER ONE

1. "If there is one word that aptly describes Justice Arthur Whittemore the man, it is 'kind.' . . . His well-deserved reputation for fair dealing and clarity of thought was such that he was often employed to mediate matters where other counsel had proved unable to do so, and was often able to effect a wise settlement of a dispute by the application of his ability to convince others, including his own clients, to do the fair thing" (Supreme Judicial Court of Massachusetts, "Memorial: Arthur Easterbrook Whittemore," 1971; available online at http://www.massreports.com/memorials/358ma850.htm).

2. Jerome Rappaport, personal interview, February 3, 2009.

3. Jim McLaughlin and Ed O'Connor, "Society Wife a Suicide," *Record American,* September 17, 1963, pp. 1, 3.

4. *Go Ask Alice* (Englewood Cliffs, N.J.: Prentice-Hall, 1971).

5. A prior suicide attempt is the strongest predictor of a self-inflicted death, and more than a quarter of patients who have made a previous attempt at suicide will eventually kill themselves.

6. McLaughlin and O'Connor, "Society Wife a Suicide."

7. Leston L. Havens, "The Anatomy of a Suicide," *New England Journal of Medicine* 272 (1965): 401.

CHAPTER TWO

1. David A. Brent et al., "Suicidal Behavior Runs in Families: A Controlled Family Study of Adolescent Suicide Victims," *Archives of General Psychiatry* 53, no. 12 (1996): 1145–1152; David A. Brent et al., "Familial Risk Factors for Adolescent Suicide: A Case-Control Study," *Acta Psychiatrica Scandinavica* 89, no. 1 (1994): 52–58.

2. David A. Brent et al., "Familial Pathways to Early-Onset Suicide Attempts: Risk for Suicidal Behavior in Offspring of Mood-Disordered Suicide Attempters," *Archives of General Psychiatry* 59, no. 9 (2002): 801–807.

3. Margaret Gatz et al., "Importance of Shared Genes and Shared Environments for Symptoms of Depression in Older Adults," *Journal of Abnormal Psychology* 101, no. 4 (1992): 701–708; Madelyn S. Gould et al., "Psychosocial Risk Factors of Child and Adolescent Completed Suicide," *Archives of General Psychiatry* 53, no. 12 (1996): 1155–1162.

4. Jerome Rappaport, personal interview, February 3, 2009.

5. Douglas M. Teti, Donna M. Gelfand, and Daniel S. Messinger, "Maternal Depression and the Quality of Early Attachment: An Examination of Infants, Preschoolers, and Their Mothers," *Developmental Psychology* 31 (1995): 364–376.

6. Susan B. Campbell, Jeffrey F. Cohn, and Teri Meyers, "Depression in First-Time Mothers: Mother-Infant Interaction and Depression Chronicity," *Developmental Psychology* 31 (1995): 349–357.

7. Emily Macy, "Busier the Better Is Volunteer Credo," *Boston Evening American*, October 3, 1958.

8. Elaine Tyler May, *Homeward Bound: American Families in the Cold War Era* (New York: Basic Books, 1988), pp. 49–80.

9. Ibid.

10. Robert Coughlan, "Changing Roles in Modern Marriage," *Life*, December 1956, pp. 108, 117.

11. Curt Norris, "Who Killed Mabel Page?" *Yankee Magazine*, July 1976, p. 78.

12. Historians are critical of the fact that James did not encourage Vanzetti to speak at the trial, and that after the trial he formed a law firm with the prosecutor—a move that even today raises questions about the vigor of his defense. See Bruce Watson, *Sacco and Vanzetti: The Men, the Murders, and the Judgment of Mankind* (New York: Penguin, 2007).

13. K. S. Bartlett, "He Delivers the Goods When the Chips Are Down," *Boston Sunday Globe*, March 6, 1949, p. A-9.

14. "Body of Millis Child Discovered in Swimming Pool," *Milford Daily News*, January 28, 1936, p. 1.

15. Tenacre School, "Report Card for Nancy Vahey," 1936.

16. S. S. Rubin, "The Wounded Family: Bereaved Parents and the Impact of Adult Child Loss," in *Continuing Bonds: A New Understanding of Grief*, edited by D. Klass, P. Silverman, and S. Nickman (Philadelphia: Taylor & Francis, 1996).

17. Jerome Rappaport, personal interview, February 3, 2009.

18. Ed English, personal interview, October 15, 2004.

19. David C. Treadway, *Dead Reckoning: A Therapist Confronts His Own Grief* (New York: Basic Books, 1996).

20. David C. Treadway, *Before It's Too Late: Working with Substance Abuse in the Family* (New York: W. W. Norton, 1989), p. 12.

21. Ibid.

22. Carmen van der Zwaluw et al., "Parental Problem Drinking, Parenting, and Adolescent Alcohol Use," *Journal of Behavioral Medicine* 31, no. 3 (2008): 189–200.

23. Nancy Hogan and Lydia DeSantis, "Basic Constructs of a Theory of Adolescent Sibling Bereavement," *Continuing Bonds: New Understanding of Grief*, edited by Dennis Klass, Phyllis R. Silverman, and Steven L. Nickman (Philadelphia: Taylor & Francis, 1996).

CHAPTER THREE

1. Jerome Rappaport, personal interview, February 3, 2009.

2. Peggy Lamere Melgard, "To the Rappaport Children," 2000.

3. Samuel Beckett, *Nohow On: Company, Ill Seen Ill Said, Worstward Ho: Three Novels* (New York: Grove Press, 1995).

4. Paul John Eakin, *How Our Lives Become Stories: Making Selves* (Ithaca, NY: Cornell University Press, 1999); James Olney, *Memory and Narrative: The Weave of Life-Writing* (Chicago: University of Chicago Press, 1998).

5. Nancy Vahey, "The End of Freedom" (unpublished novel), 1962.

6. Ibid.

7. Ibid.

8. Nancy Vahey, private journal.

CHAPTER FOUR

1. James Vahey, "Letter to Nancy Vahey," March 11, 1949.

2. Jerome Rappaport, personal interview, February 2007; T. E. Murphy, "Youth Wins Against Misrule," *Redbook*, March 1952, pp. 61–63.

3. C. J. Doyle and Larry Overlan, "The Look of Boston, Thanks to Curley," *Boston Globe*, November 15, 2008, p. A11.

4. Jerome Rappaport, personal interview, February 2007; Murphy, "Youth Wins Against Misrule"; Thomas H. O'Connor, *Building a New Boston: Politics and Urban Renewal, 1950–1970* (Boston: Northeastern University Press, 1993).

5. O'Connor, *Building a New Boston*.

6. Wilton Vaugh, "Death of Vahey Is Mourned," *Boston Post*, November 4, 1949, p. 18.

7. Nancy Vahey, "The End of Freedom" (unpublished novel), 1962.

8. O'Connor, *Building a New Boston*.

9. Miller Associates, "Scientific Selection for Management Leadership—Report of Psychological Testing of Nancy Vahey," 1950.

10. O'Connor, *Building a New Boston*.

11. Ibid.

12. Vaugh, "Death of Vahey Is Mourned," p. 18.

13. Nancy Vahey, "The End of Freedom" (unpublished novel), 1962.

14. Ruth Duskin Feldman, *Whatever Happened to the Quiz Kids? The Perils and Profits of Growing Up Gifted* (Chicago: Chicago Review Press, 1982).

15. Joyce Carol Oates, *On Boxing* (Garden City, NY: Dolphin/Doubleday, 1987).

16. Sandra Sommer, personal interview, December 2004.

17. Nancy Vahey, "Letter to Jerome Rappaport," July 10, 1950.

18. Sydell Masterman, personal interview, November 2006.

19. "Nancy Vahey Becomes Bride of Atty. Rappaport," *Boston Globe*, February 25, 1951, p. 37.

20. Ed Masterman, personal interview, November 22, 2006.

21. Ibid.

22. Hal Clancy, "A Young Crusader Cleans Up Boston," *Coronet*, July 1953, pp. 137–141.

23. Ibid., p. 137.

24. Ed Masterman, personal interview, November 22, 2006.

25. Jerome Rappaport, personal interview, February 3, 2009.

26. O'Connor, *Building a New Boston*.

27. Sydell Masterman, personal interview, November 2006.

CHAPTER FIVE

1. The psychiatrist Peter Kramer writes, "The art of psychotherapy often feels more like ballroom dancing or, to be honest, like the art of prize-fighting, or of the bullring, than literary composition." See Peter Kramer, *Moments of Engagement: Intimate Psychotherapy in a Technological Age* (New York: Norton, 1989), p. 211.

2. Jerome Rappaport, personal interview, February 3, 2009.

3. Biloine W. Young and Nancy Ankeny, *Minnesota Women in Politics: Stories of the Journey* (St. Cloud, MN: North Star Press of St. Cloud, 2000), p. 252.

4. Jerome Rappaport, personal interview, February 3, 2009.

5. Nancy Rappaport, "Franny's Trial with Love," 1967.

CHAPTER SIX

1. One such book is Herbert Gans's *The Urban Villages: Group and Class in the Life of Italian-Americans* (New York: Free Press of Glencoe, 1962).

2. Marian Christy, "Controversy Is Rappaport's Middle Name," *Boston Globe*, April 11, 1990, pp. 41, 46.

3. Milan Kundera, *The Book of Laughter and Forgetting* (New York: A. A. Knopf, 1980), p. 3.

4. Nancy Vahey, "The End of Freedom" (unpublished novel), 1962.

5. Sydell Masterman, personal interview, November 2006.

6. Peggy Melgard, personal interview, May 2004.

7. Anne Lamott, *Bird by Bird: Some Instructions on Writing and Life* (New York: Anchor Books, 1995), p. 18.

CHAPTER SEVEN

1. Wendell Berry, "A Homecoming," in *The Country of Marriage* (New York: Harcourt Brace Jovanovich, 1973), p. 33.

2. Nancy Vahey, "The End of Freedom" (unpublished novel), 1962.

3. Ibid.

4. Augustus Y. Napier and Carl Whitaker, *The Family Crucible* (New York: Harper & Row, 1978), p. 159.

5. Ibid.

6. Frank S. Pittman, *Private Lies: Infidelity and the Betrayal of Intimacy* (New York: Norton, 1989).

7. Frank S. Pittman and Tina Pittman Wagners, "Teaching Fidelity," *Journal of Clinical Psychology* 61 (2005): 1407–1419; Frank S. Pittman, "Beyond Betrayal: Life After Infidelity," *Psychology Today*, May/June 1993, pp. 33–82.

8. In the National Health and Social Life Survey of 1993, only 21 percent of men and 11 percent of women reported having affairs. See Edward O. Laumann, *The Social Organization of Sexuality: Sexual Practices in the United States* (Chicago: University of Chicago Press, 1994).

9. Pittman and Wagners, "Teaching Fidelity," p. 1412.

10. Richard L. Burt, "Citizens' School Group Official Quits in Huff," *Boston Globe*, June 29, 1961, pp. 1, 3.

11. Barbara Sears told me that the doctor the four of them saw that weekend was Lester Grinspoon, a Harvard-trained psychiatrist and an expert on schizophrenia. Adultery was not his specialty, but at least he was a minor celebrity, which would have appealed to my parents. Six years later, Grinspoon became notorious for promoting the psychiatric use of marijuana.

12. Like many laypeople, Dick doesn't make a distinction between psychoanalysis, psychotherapy, and psychiatry, although these words refer to different approaches to treatment. *Psychoanalysis* is a special kind of talk therapy, premised on the idea that just below the surface of our awareness we struggle with the unresolved conflicts of our past and that these conflicts shape who we are in the pres-

ent. By uncovering old conflicts and addressing them consciously, a patient can begin to heal. Psychoanalysts receive special training in techniques of capturing and analyzing memories, but most analysts are not medical doctors. *Psychotherapy* is really an all-encompassing term used in describing the treatment of patients with mood, behavior, or thought disorders. In the United States, psychotherapy can be cognitive behavioral in its approach, focusing on understanding why we behave the way we do and helping patients make changes, break patterns, and build needed skills and perspectives. Some psychotherapists take a psychodynamic approach to treatment instead of a cognitive behavioral one—this means their methods are more akin to those of psychoanalysis. Psychiatrists like me practice both psychotherapy and medicine. To the work of psychotherapy, *psychiatry* adds the dimension of the biological self and may include treating patients with medication when a psychiatric illness is diagnosed. These distinctions are important. In my opinion, a psychotic individual or anyone who is in an extreme or dangerous emotional state ought to be immediately treated by a psychiatrist. My mother apparently saw an analyst and not a psychiatrist. Her outcome might have been different if she had gotten appropriate treatment.

CHAPTER EIGHT

1. John Mordechai Gottman, *The Marriage Clinic: A Scientifically Based Marital Therapy* (New York: W. W. Norton, 1999).

2. Judith S. Wallerstein and Shauna B. Corbin, "The Child and the Vicissitudes of Divorce," in *The Scientific Basis of Child Custody Decisions*, edited by R. M. Galatzer-Levy and L. Kraus (New York: Wiley, 1999).

3. Ibid.

4. "Wife Wasted Cash," *Record American*, June 14, 1962.

5. Jerome Rappaport, personal interview, February 9, 2009.

6. Ibid.

7. As a member of the Boston School Committee, Louise Day Hicks garnered national attention for opposing the desegregation of Boston's public schools. For many, Hicks personified intolerance and contributed to the prevailing view that Boston was a racist city. In 1976 she became the first woman president of the Boston City Council.

8. Jerome Rappaport, personal interview, February 9, 2009.

9. It was politically prestigious at the time to have license plates whose digits were four or fewer in number: The Brahmins usually had the three-digit plates; the politicians, four.

10. Mike Alexander (brother-in-law to Jack Holtz, the lawyer for my father in the custody case), personal interview, May 2005.

11. James Gilligan, *Violence: Reflections on a National Epidemic* (New York: Vintage Books, 1997), pp. 11, 110.

12. Anna Freud, *Psychoanalysis for Teachers and Parents: Introductory Lectures* (New York: Norton, 1935), pp. 65–66.

13. Betsy McAlister Groves, *Children Who See Too Much: Lessons from the Child Witness to Violence Project* (Boston: Beacon Press, 2002).

14. Ava L. Siegler, "Home Is Where the Hurt Is: Developmental Consequences of Domestic Conflict and Violence on Children and Adolescents," in *A Handbook of Divorce and Custody: Forensic, Developmental, and Clinical Perspectives*, edited by Linda Gunsberg and Paul Hymowitz (Florence, KY: The Analytic Press, 2004), pp. 61–81.

15. Ed Corsetti, "Tells Story in Custody Battle, Pills Felled Mother of 6," *Record American*, June 7, 1962, pp. 3, 8.

CHAPTER NINE

1. "MD Calls Mrs. Rappaport Fit to Tend Six Children," *Record American*, June 14, 1962, p. 3.

2. "Wife Wasted Cash," *Record American*, June 14, 1962, p. 4.

3. "Practice Parameters for Child Custody Evaluation," *Journal of the American Academy of Child & Adolescent Psychiatry* 36, no. 10 (1997): 57–68.

4. Probate court custody document, June 19, 1962.

CHAPTER TEN

1. E. Mavis Hetherington and Margaret Stanley-Hagan, "The Adjustment of Children with Divorced Parents: A Risk and Resiliency Perspective," *Journal of Child Psychology and Psychiatry* 40, no. 1 (1999): 129–140.

2. M. D. Bramlett and W. D. Mosher, *Vital Health Statistics: Cohabitation, Marriage, Divorce, and Remarriage in the United States* (Vol. 23), Department of Health and Human Services, National Center for Health Statistics, 2002; Paul R. Amato, "Children of Divorce in the 1990s: An Update of the Amato and Keith (1991) Meta-Analysis," *Journal of Family Psychology* 15, no. 3 (2001): 355–370; "The Divorcing Kind," *Time*, October 8, 2007.

3. Judith S. Wallerstein, Julia Lewis, and Sandra Blakeslee, *The Unexpected Legacy of Divorce: A 25-Year Landmark Study* (New York: Hyperion, 2000).

4. E. Mavis Hetherington and John Kelly, *For Better or For Worse: Divorce Reconsidered* (New York: W. W. Norton, 2002).

5. Diana Siskind, "Psychotherapy with Children and Parents During Divorce," in *A Handbook of Divorce and Custody: Forensic, Developmental, and Clinical Perspectives*,

edited by Linda Gunsberg and Paul Hymowitz (Hillsdale, NJ: The Analytic Press, 2005).

6. Ibid., p. 332.

7. Ibid.

8. Janet R. Johnston, "Clinical Work with Parents in Entrenched Custody Disputes," in *A Handbook of Divorce and Custody: Forensic, Developmental, and Clinical Perspectives*, edited by Linda Gunsberg and Paul Hymowitz (Hillsdale, NJ: The Analytic Press, 2005), p. 343.

9. Constance R. Ahrons, *The Good Divorce: Keeping Your Family Together When Your Marriage Comes Apart* (New York: HarperCollins, 1994).

10. Johnston, "Clinical Work with Parents in Entrenched Custody Disputes," p. 344.

11. Ibid.

12. My mother had her first marriage annulled so she could marry in the Catholic Church.

13. It's not clear that my mother ever fully embraced her ten years in the Jewish faith. There were no baptisms, christenings, bar mitzvahs, confirmations, or communions. But during her marriage to my father, my mother continued to attend Catholic masses, celebrate Christmas, and speak to her parish priest whenever she felt the need. After my mother died, Barbara took us to a Unitarian church, where we participated in church bazaars and plays. The only Jewish education we had growing up came from my father, who warned us about anti-Semitism, instilled in us a deep respect for education and charity, and regularly fed us lox and bagels. Since marrying Phyllis my father has rediscovered his faith.

14. In the 1960s, Massachusetts probate court proceedings were generally not recorded.

CHAPTER ELEVEN

1. Pauline Boss, *Ambiguous Loss: Learning to Live with Unresolved Grief* (Cambridge, MA: Harvard University Press, 1999).

2. Rainer Maria Rilke and Franz Xaver Kappus, *Letters to a Young Poet* (New York: Norton, 1954).

3. Martin E. P. Seligman, *Learned Optimism* (New York: A. A. Knopf, 1991).

4. William A. Dickson, "Letter to Mr. Jackson J. Holtz," Boston, August 10, 1963.

5. Jerome Rappaport, personal interview, February 10, 2009.

CHAPTER TWELVE

1. The Rashomon effect, named for Akira Kurosawa's 1950 film, refers to the subjectivity of perception when recalling an event. Multiple observers can have quite different, but equally possible, recollections of the same event.

CHAPTER THIRTEEN

1. Donald W. Winnicott et al., *Deprivation and Delinquency* (London: Tavistock Publications, 1984), p. 121.

CHAPTER FOURTEEN

1. Hallucinations are false perceptions involving any of the senses.

2. Timothy E. Wilens, *Straight Talk About Psychiatric Medications for Kids* (New York: Guilford Press, 1999), p. 181.

3. Ronald C. Kessler, "Age of Onset of Mental Disorders: A Review of Recent Literature," *Current Opinion in Psychiatry* 20, no. 4 (2007): 359–364.

4. A diagnosis can be complicated if a teenager is experimenting with drugs or if there are other contributing factors—family conflict, for example, or medical conditions. Family history offers clues if there is a delusional relative or a parent with severe depression. Often with children, the illness evolves—a patient who is severely depressed before age 12 has a 25 percent chance of having bipolar disorder with a manic episode in adolescence. See American Academy of Child and Adolescent Psychiatry, "Practice Parameter for the Assessment and Treatment of Children and Adolescents with Bipolar Disorder," *Journal of the American Academy of Child & Adolescent Psychiatry* 46, no. 1 (2007): 107–125.

5. Louisa Degenhardt and Wayne Hall, "Is Cannabis Use a Contributory Cause of Psychosis?" *Canadian Journal of Psychiatry* 51, no. 9 (2006): 566–574.

6. Marie Howe, *What the Living Do: Poems* (New York: W. W. Norton, 1998).

CHAPTER FIFTEEN

1. Physicians are as vulnerable to depression as the general population is, but they seek care at lower rates and die by suicide more frequently than nonphysicians. There is a particularly dramatic elevation in the incidence of suicide among female physicians (250 percent higher than that of other women). See Tracy Hampton, "Experts Address Risk of Physician Suicide," *Journal of the American Medical Association* 294, no. 10 (2005): 1189–1191.

2. Scott Anderson, "The Urge to End It All," *New York Times*, July 6, 2008.

3. Ibid.

4. Nancy Vahey, "The End of Freedom" (unpublished novel), 1962; Nancy Vahey, private journal.

5. American Psychiatric Association, "Practice Guidelines for the Assessment and Treatment of Patients with Suicidal Behaviors," *American Journal of Psychiatry* 160, no. 11 (Supplement, 2003); Kevin M. Malone et al., "Major Depression and the Risk of Attempted Suicide," *Journal of Affective Disorders* 34 (1995): 173–185.

6. Alexander McGirr et al., "An Examination of DSM-IV Depressive Symptoms and Risk for Suicide Completion in Major Depressive Disorder: A Psychological Autopsy Study," *Journal of Affective Disorders* 97, nos. 1–3 (2007): 203–209.

7. Ibid.

8. J. John Mann, David A. Brent, and Victoria Arango, "The Neurobiology and Genetics of Suicide and Attempted Suicide: A Focus on the Serotonergic System," *Neuropsychopharmacology* 24, no. 5 (2001): 467–477; J. John Mann et al., "Toward a Clinical Model of Suicidal Behavior in Psychiatric Patients," *American Journal of Psychiatry* 156, no. 2 (1999): 181–189.

9. Quoted in Barbara Strauch, *The Primal Teen: What the New Discoveries About the Teenage Brain Tell Us About Our Kids* (New York: Doubleday, 2003), p. 31.

10. G. Feldman, "Cognitive and Behavioral Therapies for Depression: Overview, New Directions, and Practical Recommendations for Dissemination," *Psychiatric Clinics of North America* 30, no. 1 (2007): 39–50; Martin E. P. Seligman, *Learned Optimism* (New York: A. A. Knopf, 1991).

11. William Styron, *Darkness Visible: A Memoir of Madness* (New York: Random House, 1990), p. 57.

12. In a rigorous analysis of thirty-one studies involving 85,229 patients, the overall risk of suicides and suicide attempts was found to be five times smaller among those receiving lithium. See Ross J. Baldessarini et al., "Decreased Risk of Suicides and Attempts During Long-Term Lithium Treatment: A Meta-Analytic Review," *Bipolar Disorders* 8 (2006): 625–639.

13. Nancy Vahey, "The End of Freedom" (unpublished novel), 1962.

14. David Phillips, "The Influence of Suggestion on Suicide: Substantive and Theoretical Implications of the Werther Effect," *American Sociological Review* 39 (1974): 340–354.

15. In January 1963, the poet Sylvia Plath also committed suicide. While my mother was at Boston University studying for her master's in English, she may have overlapped briefly with Plath, who, along with a young Anne Sexton (another poet who killed herself), was attending Robert Lowell's creative writing seminar at B.U.

16. Jim McLaughlin and Ed O'Connor, "Rappaport Custody Row Ends in Wife's Pill Death," *Record American*, September 17, 1963, pp. 3, 8.

17. Arnold Weinberg, personal interview, January 2007.

18. Richard H. Seiden, "Where Are They Now? A Follow-Up Study of Suicide Attempters from the Golden Gate Bridge," *Suicide & Life-Threatening Behavior* 8, no. 4 (1978): 203–216.

19. Catholic Church, *Catechism of the Catholic Church* (Vatican City/Washington, DC: Libreria Editrice Vaticana, distributed by United States Catholic Conference, 2000).

20. Margaret Murphy, personal interview, May 1990.

21. Peggy Melgard, personal interview, February 2007.

22. Barbara Whitehill, personal interview, February 28, 2007.

CHAPTER SIXTEEN

1. In addition to the description of the demolition, the student-written article contains an inaccurate account of the provenance of 60 Quail Street. See Allen Downey, "Faculty House Razed," *Roxbury Latin School Tripod*, September 10, 1984, pp. 1, 3.

2. A 2005 study found that men who had lost their partners to suicide or other causes of death were forty-six times more likely to commit suicide themselves. See Esben Agerbo, "Midlife Suicide Risk, Partner's Psychiatric Illness, Spouse and Child Bereavement by Suicide or Other Modes of Death: A Gender-Specific Study," *Journal of Epidemiology and Community Health* 59, no. 5 (2005): 407–412.

3. Jim tells me that when our mother died my father made a conscious business choice to limit his development projects to the Boston area. At the time of her death, he was involved with projects in San Antonio, New Haven, and Philadelphia. He couldn't spend a quarter to half of his time away, which is what it would have taken to get the buildings started. As a result, my father did not achieve his dream of becoming "America's Greatest Developer."

RESOURCES

FURTHER READING

Burns, David. *Feeling Good: The New Mood Therapy*. New York: William Morrow, 2002.

Cournos, Francine. *City of One: A Memoir*. New York: W. W. Norton, 1999.

Earley, Pete. *Crazy: A Father's Search Through America's Mental Health Madness*. New York: Berkley Books, 2006.

Fine, Carla. *No Time to Say Goodbye*. New York: Broadway Books, 1997.

Hull, John M. *Touching the Rock: An Experience of Blindness*. New York: Pantheon Books, 1990.

Jamison, Kay Redfield. *An Unquiet Mind*. New York: A. A. Knopf, 1995.

Lewis, C. S. *A Grief Observed*. New York: HarperSanFrancisco, 2006.

Saks, Elyn R. *The Center Cannot Hold*. New York: Hyperion, 2007.

Styron, William. *Darkness Visible: A Memoir of Madness*. New York: Vintage Books, 1992.

Trussoni, Danielle. *Falling Through the Earth: A Memoir*. New York: Henry Holt, 2006.

Wagner, Pamela Spiro, and Carolyn S. Spiro. *Divided Minds: Twin Sisters and Their Journey Through Schizophrenia*. New York: St. Martin's Press, 2005.

WEBSITES ON MENTAL ILLNESS

National Alliance on Mental Illness (NAMI)

http://www.nami.org

- NAMI is the largest grassroots organization for people with mental illness and their families. With local groups in many communities, it provides education, support, and advocacy and works to raise awareness of mental illness.

National Institute of Mental Health (NIMH)

http://www.nimh.nih.gov

- NIMH supports research on the mind, brain, and behavior in order to reduce the burden of mental illness and behavioral disorders. Its website provides information, statistics, and science news.

Depression and Bipolar Support Alliance (DBSA)

http://www.dbsalliance.org

- DBSA is a grassroots network of more than 1,000 patient-run support groups across the country focusing on bipolar disorder and depression.

American Academy of Child and Adolescent Psychiatry (AACAP)

http://aacap.org

- AACAP is an organization of child and adolescent psychiatrists and other interested doctors that distributes information to promote understanding of mental illnesses and reduce associated stigma. Its website has many resources for families.

American Psychological Association (APA)

http://www.apa.org

- The APA is a scientific and professional organization that represents psychology in the United States. Its website provides information on psychology topics, tools for finding a psychologist, and news about psychology.

WEBSITES ON SUICIDE PREVENTION

National Suicide Prevention Lifeline
1-800-273-TALK (8255)
http://www.suicidepreventionlifeline.org
- The National Suicide Prevention Lifeline provides 24-hour, toll-free, confidential help for those in crisis.

Stop a Suicide Today: Screening for Mental Health
http://www.stopasuicide.org
- This website, started by a Harvard psychiatrist, gives information about recognizing signs of suicidality and emphasizes the relationship between suicide and mental illness. It also provides statistics and resources.

American Foundation for Suicide Prevention (AFSP)
http://www.afsp.org
- Working to understand and prevent suicide through research and education, AFSP organizes Out of the Darkness Walks to support research, prevention, and awareness programs. Its website provides information for survivors, statistics, and resources.

The American Association of Suicidology
http://www.suicidology.org
- This website provides fact sheets for survivors and their support networks, a bibliography, personal stories, and links to support groups.